Food Security

To Kate, and for Jed

Food Security

BRYAN L. McDONALD

polity

First published in 2010 by Polity Press

Polity Press
65 Bridge Street
Cambridge CB2 1UR, UK

Polity Press
350 Main Street
Malden, MA 02148, USA

ISBN-13: 978-0-7456-4807-1
ISBN-13: 978-0-7456-4808-8(pb)

A catalogue record for this book is available from the British Library.

Typeset in 10.5 on 13 pt Minion
by Servis Filmsetting Ltd, Stockport, Cheshire
Printed and bound by the MPG Books Group

For further information on Polity, visit our website: www.politybooks.com

Contents

Acknowledgments

This book is the result of years of research and thus also the accumulation of numerous debts. I would like to thank Richard Matthew for encouraging me to study the intersection of environment, politics, and security. I also wish to express my gratitude to Joseph DiMento, Timothy W. Luke, and Daniel Stokols for their support of the dissertation this book is based upon. Comments and suggestions offered by a number of colleagues have improved my work; I am especially grateful to Geoffrey D. Dabelko, Helen Ingram, Cecelia Lynch, Kenneth R. Rutherford, and George Shambaugh. Research included in this book was presented at a number of conferences and I benefited from the thoughtful comments provided by discussants, including Kristine J. Kalanges, Marilyn McMorrow, Craig N. Murphy, J. P. Singh, and Matthew J. Hoffmann.

I am grateful to the Samueli Foundation and the Center for Unconventional Security Affairs at the University of California, Irvine for their generous support of this project. This book emerged out of a dissertation project that was supported by a number of grants, fellowships, and funding agencies. I am indebted to the following for their support: the Center for Unconventional Security Affairs; the National Science Foundation (Project #0624165); the UCI Newkirk Center for Science and Society; the University of California Institute on Global Conflict and Cooperation (IGCC); the University of California, Irvine Chancellor's Club Fund for Excellence; the School of Social Ecology Dean's Dissertation Fellowship; the Department of Planning, Policy and Design at the University of California, Irvine; the Justice Stephen K. Tamura Fellowship; the Drew, Chace, and Erin Warmington Chair in the Social Ecology of Peace and International Cooperation; and the UCI Center for Global Peace and Conflict Studies.

An earlier form of portions of chapter 6 were included in Bryan

McDonald, "Global Health and Human Security: Addressing Impacts from Globalization and Environmental Change," in Richard A. Matthew, Jon Barnett, Bryan McDonald and Karen L. O'Brien (eds), *Global Environmental Change and Human Security* (MIT Press, 2009). I am grateful to MIT Press for permission to include this material here. An early version of the argument presented in this book was explored in a chapter on "Environmental Ethics," by Richard A. Matthew, Bryan McDonald, and Heather Goldsworthy in Antonio Franceschet (ed.), *The Ethics of Global Governance* (Lynne Rienner Publishers, 2009). I am grateful to Lynne Rienner Publishers for granting me permission to include this material.

I would also like to acknowledge Kate Merkel-Hess and two anonymous reviewers who provided comments and suggestions that greatly improved the final volume. I would also like to thank my editor at Polity, Louise Knight, for her interest in and support for this project.

Abbreviations

BMI	Body Mass Index
BSE	Bovine Spongiform Encephalopathy
BTWC	Biological and Toxin Weapons Convention
CAFOs	Concentrated Animal Feeding Operations
CBD	Convention on Biological Diversity
CDC	Centers for Disease Control and Prevention
DEFRA	Department for Environment, Food and Rural Affairs
FAO	Food and Agriculture Organization of the United Nations
FFPI	FAO Food Price Index
GHG	Greenhouse Gas
GM	Genetic Modification
GMO	Genetically Modified Organism
IFOAM	International Federation of Organic Agriculture Movements
IPCC	Intergovernmental Panel on Climate Change
MDG	Millennium Development Goal
SARS	Severe Acute Respiratory Syndrome
UNDP	United Nations Development Program
UNEP	United Nations Environment Program
UNFPA	United Nations Population Fund
UNHCR	United Nations Refugee Agency
UNICEF	United Nations Children's Fund
USDA	United States Department of Agriculture
WCED	World Commission on Environment and Development
WFP	United Nations World Food Program
WFS	World Food Summit
WGBU	German Advisory Council on Global Change
WHO	World Health Organization
WMO	World Meteorological Organization
WTO	World Trade Organization

Introduction: Twenty-first Century Challenges to Food Security

Throughout time, human societies have struggled to ensure that all people have access to sufficient food to lead active and healthy lives. Despite great global effort in recent decades, events of the early twenty-first century clearly demonstrate that providing sufficient food to all people remains an urgent problem situated at the nexus of nature, society, and technology. In recent years, rising food prices have motivated unrest in many parts of the world and increased the number of people who do not receive proper nutrition to levels not seen in decades. Agricultural and food production activities have been recognized as key drivers of environmental and climate changes at the same time that studies have revealed that food production could face significant and widespread impacts from these changes in coming decades. National and international food safety incidents have raised awareness of the continued peril that food systems can transmit health threats among human populations. This book explores these threats and vulnerabilities in the emerging network of global food systems. Through analysis of three central challenges to food security – nutrition, global environmental change, and food safety – this book considers how globalization and global change are reshaping the food security landscape in ways that have significant impacts on human, national, and international security. Building on the growing scholarly and policy interest in the interconnections between food security and human security, this book asserts that a clearer understanding of these interconnections is critical to facing world food problems in the twenty-first century.

The aim of this book is to analyze the ways the global food system has been changed as a result of the development of a more interconnected world, and to consider both the chronic and sudden challenges these new connections raise. Globalization has given rise to a complex, transnational network of food systems that includes a range of activities and processes involved in the production (which entails a variety of methods including farming, fishing, hunting, raising livestock and gathering), harvesting, processing, transportation, and consumption of food. The network of global food systems that now connect almost all human populations brings new opportunities, from a greater variety of foods to development and economic growth. However, a full investigation of the global food system reveals that, alongside many benefits, increased interconnection has created a more complex landscape of world food problems by creating new risks and amplifying traditional sources of threats and vulnerabilities that impact food security.

Food security – the idea that all people at all times have access (including physical, social and economic access) to sufficient, safe, and nutritious food necessary to lead active and healthy lives (FAO 2009) – is critical to this book's exploration of the risks and opportunities posed by globalization and global environmental change. The notion of food security encompasses examinations of a variety of ecological, social, economic, and political factors to identify the choices and challenges that determine whether people have the food they need. These examinations are conducted at multiple levels of analysis, including individual, household or community, national, international, and global (see for example Sen 1982, 1999; Pottier 1999; Smil 2000, 2001; Alston, Taylor, and Pardey 2001; Devereux and Maxwell 2001; Webb and Weinberger 2001; Fogel 2004; Federico 2005; Brown 2009; Clapp and Fuchs 2009). By drawing on the deep body of scholarship on food security across fields as diverse as agricultural sciences, ecology, ethics, public health, and sociology, to name a few, this book posits that, without an understanding of the intersection of recent globalizing processes with the challenges and opportunities of food security, food networks cannot be used to their full potential to address pressing global problems. As events in the early twenty-first century have demonstrated, food security remains an important area of global concern. Lack of sufficient, safe, and nutritious food has significant impacts on the health, well-being, and livelihoods of people around the world.

In addition to altering many aspects of the global food system, globalization has resulted in considerable turbulence in world affairs and led to transformations in the global security landscape. In recent decades, changes in technology, interconnectedness, and mobility have amplified traditional national and international security challenges and given rise to new threats and vulnerabilities. Traditional security threats such as interstate war, nuclear proliferation, and peacekeeping operations remain vital elements in national and international security affairs. However, many contemporary security challenges – such as infectious disease, terrorism, and trafficking in drugs, people, or illegal goods – operate in different ways than traditional security challenges. These new security threats are transnational, crossing borders but generally not directly linked to foreign policies and state behaviors (Matthew and Shambaugh 1998). While transnational security threats have impacts on national and international security, these new threats are most often felt in people's daily lives through events such as ill health, attacks by terrorists or insurgent groups, and reduced livelihoods, well-being and life-choices due to environmental change or natural disasters. Human security addresses these day-to-day concerns, asserting that the achievement of human security includes protecting people by providing freedom from fear and want as well as empowering individuals and communities to take action on their own behalf (UNDP 1994; Commission on Human Security 2003). The enduring wisdom of core security lessons of the twentieth century, such as the ability of want and instability in one country to have global security impacts, has been underscored by recent global experiences with disease pandemics, attacks in the United States, Spain, United Kingdom and many other places linked or inspired by transnational terrorist networks, and natural disasters – such as devastating earthquakes in Haiti and Chile and the global disruption in air travel and transport prompted by the eruption of the Eyjafjallajökull volcano in Iceland – that have significant social and economic impacts.

The absence of food security, also described as "food insecurity," is a daily reality for billions of people around the world, making their lives and livelihoods less secure. This volume examines challenges to ensuring food security in the twenty-first century by considering the primary ways that food insecurity is felt in the daily lives of people and communities around the world. The first problem is the classical food security challenge of malnutrition which remains a significant and widespread form of food insecurity. Though often popularly conceptualized as hunger, malnutrition is actually a set of three distinctive problems (often referred to as the "triple burden of malnutrition"): energy deficiencies, nutrient deficiencies, and excessive net energy intake (Pinstrup-Andersen 2007). Large numbers of people in the world are chronically hungry, meaning they are undernourished because they don't receive enough energy to lead active lives (FAO 2009). While chronic hunger has been an issue of global concern for decades, recent events, including a global recession and rising food prices, have significantly increased the number of chronically hungry people. The Food and Agriculture Organization of the United Nations (FAO) estimates that in 2009 there were more than 1 billion chronically hungry people in the world, 85 million more than in 2008 and the highest number of energy deficient people since 1970. While the continued magnitude of chronic hunger is alarming, energy deficiency is not the only way malnutrition influences people's health and welfare. Deficiencies of key vitamins and nutrients (including vitamin A, iodine, iron, zinc, and folate) affect billions around the world and these deficiencies cause and contribute to a range of problems, such as increased maternal death rates, birth defects, blindness, and reduced resistance to diseases (Micronutrient Initiative 2009). Finally, more and more people in developed countries, and also increasingly in developing countries, are confronting problems related to consumption of energy-dense, nutrient-poor foods combined with reduced levels of physical activity which result in overweight, obesity, and chronic diseases such as type-2 diabetes, cardiovascular disease, and hypertension (WHO 2003). Around the  world, more than 1 billion adults are overweight and at least 300 million of them are obese; however, even more rapid and alarming increases in overweight and obesity are occurring among children (World Bank 2006; Pinstrup-Andersen 2007).

Concerns about food insecurity have motivated tremendous effort to increase global food supplies through infrastructure development and poverty reduction. These efforts are not new. Ensuring food security has been a prominent feature of global agreements since World War II, some of which set ambitious targets to address food insecurity. For example, the World Food Summit of 1996 sought to halve the number of undernourished by 2015, while the Millennium Development Goals (MDGs), set in 2000, aspired to reduce by half the proportion of people suffering from hunger. While these efforts have led to significant increases in food and agricultural system productivity, improvements in standards of living, and considerable gains in human health, well-being and security, they have not guaranteed universal food security. Given the magnitude and complexity of factors contributing to world food problems, food security thus remains a key challenge in the twenty-first century. It is not a problem that will be less complex in the future. Scholars and researchers from a variety of perspectives stress that contemporary food insecurity is driven by trends such as population growth and urbanization, rises in food prices, a global economic crisis and changing diets and food consumption patterns, and processes such as environmental and climate change (Smil 2000; Pinstrup-Andersen 2007; Brown 2009). Concern about the impacts and likely directions of these driving forces have led many analysts to conclude that the world faces a significant set of challenges in the coming years as impacts of climate change, population growth, water scarcity, and energy shortages will all contribute to and magnify the impacts of food insecurity (Beddington 2009).

If current trends continue as expected, the number of hungry will grow. Future discussions of how to address food shortages and other food crises will likely take the shape of earlier efforts – addressing the immediate, short-term needs of hungry people. Out of such necessity, food security discussions often focus on sudden and hurtful disruptions – issues such as wars, famines, and natural disasters – as these disruptions attract considerable attention from policymakers, the media, and international organizations. However, fully confronting contemporary world food problems, and particularly the most critical problems of the coming decades, such as malnutrition from nutrient deficiencies and excessive net energy intake and the impacts of global climate change, requires also addressing the chronic aspects of food insecurity. These issues, along with factors such as ill health and lack of clean water, also have major impacts in the lives of many people and, at an aggregate level, on societies and states. In order to bring these critical issues to the fore, this book focuses on the human security implications of world food problems. Like food security, the definition of "human security" emphasizes the provision for and freedom to lead a full life. According to the most influential formulation from the United Nations Development Program (UNDP), the concept of human security has two main aspects: "It means, first, safety from such chronic threats as hunger, disease and repression. And second, it means protection from sudden and harmful disruptions in the patterns of daily life" (UNDP 1994: 23). The guarantee of food security can thus be understood as a key component of human security. At the same time, adopting a human security perspective allows us to consider both chronic and sudden challenges to food security, while also encouraging us to move beyond consideration of issues that have impacts at the state level to consider security from a more comprehensive perspective that includes the economic, health, environmental, personal, community, and political dimensions of food security.

While the particular form of and specific causal factors of food insecurity varies from place to place and even from person to person, it is possible to identify patterns in food insecurity. Undertaking a comprehensive review of world food problems, this book identifies three primary sets of disruptors, or unexpected destabilizing factors, which present core challenges to food security in the twenty-first century. First is the necessity to develop policies and methods to address all three aspects of malnutrition: energy deficiencies, nutrient deficiencies, and excessive net energy intake. Second is the need to manage global environmental change to confront the environmental impacts of food and agricultural production as well as impacts that processes of environmental change, including localized environmental modifications as well as global climate change, are having and will likely have on food and agricultural production. Last is the requirement to make sure that food safety is optimized to keep crops, livestock, and food supplies free from infectious diseases and contaminants, and to protect food supplies from actors with nefarious intent who might intentionally wish to cause harm.

While each of these sets of issues – ensuring nutrition, managing global environmental change, and optimizing food safety – represents a pressing area for action, their complexity is enhanced even further by recognizing that these concerns are also complex and interactive and each challenge has synergistic feedback effects on the others. Efforts to reduce food prices by increasing food production could increase the environmental impacts of agricultural and food production systems. Efforts by the poor to gain access to needed food through hunting and fishing could amplify health and food safety dangers by exposing them to new diseases and increasing the environmental impact of informal strategies like poaching and overfishing. Efforts to manage environmental change and address climate change could cause significant hardship if they are done without full consideration of impacts on food production. In a time when policy agendas are crowded with complex problems that have multiple causes, it is important to consider the ways interactions and feedback effects can complicate efforts to address food security. In this way, it is possible to identify strategies wherein efforts in one area of activity can also lead to the enhancement of human livelihoods and well-being. Given the magnitude and persistence of food security problems, there is an imperative need to understand why, despite significant global action, food insecurity remains a complex and enduring problem confronting human societies.

The need for examinations of food security has been underscored by global events in recent years. Rising food prices, natural disasters, and high-profile reports on the likely impacts of climate change have resulted in media organizations, policymakers, international agencies, and nongovernmental organizations devoting attention to the complex causes of food insecurity. A range of causal factors has been identified to explain the sudden re-emergence of high food prices and record levels of, side-by-side, chronic hunger and overweight and obesity including: global population growth, rising demands for resource-intensive products like meat, growing consumer purchasing power in countries such as China and India, changes and variability in climate and severe weather events that reduced harvests of key food crops, high oil prices that increased the costs of producing and transporting food and raised costs of inputs like fertilizers and pesticides, speculation in global financial markets, and impacts on food prices and availability from efforts to promote biofuels from sources such as corn (Ban 2008). At the same time, growing awareness of the contributions of food and agricultural production systems to climate change and the likely impacts that climate change will have on food and agricultural production systems have raised interest in mitigating or reducing the magnitude of impacts, and reducing the vulnerability of human and natural systems to climate change (IPCC 2007). Policy and public interest in the global food system has also been motivated by high-profile cases of food system contamination, raising questions about the advantages and disadvantages of an increasingly global network of food systems that rapidly transfers food from producers to consumers (WHO 2007d). Built on thousands of years of interactions and intermingling between humans and nature, the emerging network of global food systems is a hybrid of natural systems and human societies (Luke 2001b). This book aims to examine the food system as a nexus – and one with a rich history that has shaped both the benefits and dilemmas it poses for us today – that brings together nature, society, and technology. Today's global food problems emerge out of a complex mix of economic, environmental, political, and social factors that impact food security, human society, and nation-states, but also, at the most basic level, determine what ends up (or doesn't end up) on people's plates.

The first chapter reviews connections between food security and security studies and discusses the broadening focus of academic and policy efforts to identify and understand the ways globalization has influenced security threats and vulnerabilities. The chapter first examines the history and various definitions of the food security concept. The chapter's latter sections consider food security in light of the increasing attention paid to relationships between environmental change and security. The chapter then examines how, as understandings of security have shifted, security studies has broadened to consider human security issues. In closing, the chapter reviews the ways modern globalization processes have accelerated the speed and scale of interactions among food systems and resulted in the creation of a global food network.

Chapter 2 traces the long history of interactions between people and environment driven and mediated by food. This chapter examines how changing methods of accessing food have defined shifts in human societies, including the transitions from hunting and gathering to farming and the rise of modern industrialized and globalized food systems. The chapter also uses work by historians and scholars to review how human efforts to obtain sufficient food have affected the environment. In addition to current concerns about climate change, these examinations find that unsustainable food production practices have contributed to many of the worst instances of human-caused environmental degradation.

The food network is a major connector of people and places; increasingly the nature of challenges to ensuring food security has been, and will likely continue to be, profoundly affected by major trends in global affairs. Chapter 3 provides an overview of five trends that are shaping the character of food security challenges: population growth and demographic change, changes in food consumption patterns, rising global food prices, the development and use of new technologies in food production, and global climate change. While each of these trends affects food security, their impacts are magnified by the interactive nature of these trends.

Chapter 4 considers how globalization and global change have amplified the difficulty of optimizing food and agricultural production systems to provide all people with sufficient, safe, and appropriate nutrition. Providing adequate food to all people has been a major challenge to human societies and remains a focus of efforts to improve trade systems and address global development needs. Lack of proper nutrition remains a significant threat to human health and well-being, but this problem is complicated by the existence, contrary to popular perceptions, of undernourishment in developed countries and overnourishment in developing countries. To address this complexity, the chapter considers the ways food insecurity operates along three primary dimensions of malnutrition which present as energy deficiencies, nutrient deficiencies, and excessive net energy intake. The chapter concludes by considering the importance of finding ways to address malnutrition and meet nutritional needs that are in agreement with the aims of human security.

The global food system is also facing a set of challenges related to global environmental change. Chapter 5 explores how better understandings of processes of environmental change have made it clear that food and agricultural production contribute to environmental changes and will likely experience significant impacts as a result of those changes. The impact of environmental and climate changes on agriculture and food production are diverse and widespread. Likely impacts in the future include shifts in the ecological and economic viability of raising crops and animal species in a given environment, increased water scarcity, and acceleration of biodiversity loss, including loss of species that play a key role in food systems such as soil bacteria that help fix nitrogen or encourage water intake or species such as honeybees and songbirds that play key roles as pollinators. The  chapter considers impacts in five major sectors – land and soil, water use and water quality, habitat and biodiversity loss, energy use, and climate change – and also examines how the environmental impact of food and agricultural systems can be lessened by harmonizing with imperatives for sustainable development.

Chapter 6 discusses ways the increasing speed and scale of connections between local, national, and global food systems can serve as vectors to transmit health threats such as infectious diseases, toxic contaminants, or biological weapons. Events in recent decades have raised awareness of the need to ensure food safety, including: experiences with bovine spongiform encephalopathy (BSE), commonly known as mad-cow disease, in the United Kingdom; the rapid emergence and global spread of severe acute respiratory syndrome (SARS), a previously unknown condition, in 2002 and 2003; and high-profile  cases of contamination of spinach, pet food, milk products, and peanut butter. While the global food system largely provides safe and healthful food, food systems can also serve as vectors for diseases from natural processes and accidental contamination but also crime, terrorism or warfare. The chapter argues that while efforts to ensure food safety must address potential nefarious uses of biological agents, they must at the same time be mindful that concerns about potential impacts of threats like biological weapons do not detract from efforts to address the likelier accidental or natural threats that daily impact people. In addition to considering solutions such as increased regulation, centralization, and coordinated oversight of food systems, the chapter concludes by examining strategies such as sustainability and strategic decoupling from global food networks as potential solutions to enhancing food safety.

The book's final chapter discusses the need to develop a global food system that meets the nutritional needs of human populations while fostering the long-term ecological health and security of the planet and its inhabitants. The chapter includes policy implications and directions for future research as well as observations on possible future directions for the global food system. It also reviews some of the greatest obstacles to an ethical, equitable, and sustainable global food system. While processes of global change may make the development of a sustainable global food system more difficult, the rise of global networks could also open new pathways to be used in designing a secure and sustainable global food system. The challenge of creating a sustainable food system is by no means simple, for it must be mindful of human needs, sensitive to current and future ecological conditions, and able to navigate the eddies of complex systems of national and global governance in a time of turbulence and global change. As the final chapter argues, while ensuring food security remains a considerable challenge, there are many reasons for optimism and many opportunities for individuals, states, and the international community to strengthen food security.

1 Food Security and the Global Food System

Ensuring that people have sufficient access to food has been, and remains, a core challenge to the security and stability of communities, states, and the international system. Recent events – including rising global food prices, natural disasters and severe weather events, international food safety episodes, and a global economic crisis – have focused attention on food as a subject of concern for security studies. The beginning of modern interest in food security is often located in World War II, which demonstrated that localized hunger and instability could escalate into problems of global significance. More recent experiences, including rioting and unrest in more than sixty countries over rising food prices, have reminded leaders and international organizations that even in an age of threats from global terrorist networks and asymmetrical warfare, there are few challenges that can cause the widespread and significant security impacts of a lack of basic necessities such as food. Global trends such as population growth, shifting consumption patterns, and climate change strongly suggest that the challenge of food security will remain a pressing concern for individuals, communities, states, and the international system in the future. At the same time that the global significance of ensuring food security has been reinforced by world events, understanding and addressing the challenge is also becoming more complex. Much of this emerging complexity with regards to food security is driven by larger changes in the global security landscape.

The concept of international security was developed during the Cold War as concerns about the shared threats and vulnerabilities of the international system encouraged a move beyond national security. National security is generally taken to refer to the protection of sovereign nation-states from internal and external threats to their vital interests (Robinson 2008). By the middle of the twentieth century, nation-states had developed from their origins in nineteenth-century Europe into the widespread form of political organization. "Commitment to the nation-state ideal shaped and legitimized the wave of decolonization that took place after World War II, and was a cornerstone of the philosophy of the United Nations" (Matthew 2002: 1). Theoretical and political understandings of international security arose during the Cold War period (1945–1991) based on recognitions that in the face of threats from sources like nuclear weapons the security of individual nation-states could only be ensured through international action and cooperation. Since the end of the Cold War, the landscape of national and international security threats has shifted (Matthew 2002; Dannreuther 2007).

Globalization – combined with the reduced capacity of governments to address pressing issues, and the increasing role of nonstate actors in national and international politics – has produced considerable turbulence in world affairs. James Rosenau describes the current global security landscape as one where, "the impact of modern technologies and the many other sources that are rendering the world ever more interdependent, the bifurcated structures and the more skillful citizens are conceived to have fostered such a profound transformation in world politics that the lessons of history may no longer be helpful" (Rosenau 1990: 5). Growing recognition of the changing global security landscape is reflected in a large body of literature that considers the ways this global turbulence, as well as globalization processes themselves, amplify traditional security challenges such as military-to-military conflict and the military use of nuclear weapons, while at the same time creating new threats and vulnerabilities that affect state and human security. Discussions of these changes have found receptive audiences in defense and security communities who are confronting the development and maintenance of traditional war fighting force structures and capabilities while also needing to prepare for an increasing variety of complex operations including: counterinsurgency and counterterrorism missions; aiding in stability, post-conflict and post-disaster situations; supporting civil authorities; and confronting challenges such as climate change and cybersecurity threats (Barnett 2004, 2009; Diehl 2008; NIC 2008; Smil

2008; Krepinevich 2009; United States Joint Forces Command 2010; Ministry of Defense 2010; United States Department of Defense 2010).

Scholars and policymakers are also increasingly aware that some contemporary security challenges operate differently than traditional challenges. In addition to affecting militaries and other aspects of a state's national security, Richard Matthew and George Shambaugh write:

> Many contemporary threats resulting from factors such as infectious diseases like AIDS, drug-trafficking, and terrorism involving weapons of mass destruction are transnational: they cross state borders, but generally cannot be linked to foreign policies or behavior of other states. Rather than being created and controlled by national governments, these threats are situated in a complex, dynamic, and global web created by modern communication, transportation, and information technologies (Matthew and Shambaugh 1998: 163).

In response to these new modes of security threat, scholars, journalists and policymakers have broadened conceptualizations of security to include health, urbanization, information technology, nuclear proliferation, advanced biological technology development, and environmental degradation. This broadened notion of security calls for a concurrent expansion of security studies in order to understand the changing threats and vulnerabilities facing nations and people. To that end, this chapter places food security in the context of the new international security concerns outlined above. Beginning first with a review of the origins and definition of the concept of food security, the chapter will then consider the relationship of food security to environmental degradation before moving to a broader discussion of how the notion of human security can act as a conceptual framework to enhance understandings of this new generation of security challenges. The chapter's final section reviews the rise of a networked society and considers the implications of global change for the world's food system.

Food security: Sufficient, safe and nutritious food for all

Many definitions of food security exist, but at the most general level food security refers to the availability of food and people's ability to access it. As the UK's Department for Environment, Food and Rural Affairs (DEFRA) reports, food security can be a confusing concept, especially in developing countries, because it is a complex, multi-faceted problem involving different yet interlinked aspects (DEFRA 2006). Between 1974 and 2001, organizations issued a succession of official definitions of food security, reflecting the articulation of a gradually more inclusive conceptualization of food security. The 1974 World Food Summit definition focused largely on food supply, defining food security as the "availability at all times of adequate world food supplies of basic foodstuffs to sustain a steady expansion of food consumption and to offset fluctuations in production and prices" (UN 1975: 6). In the early 1980s, the definition of food security used by FAO (1983) was expanded to include both the physical and economic access as vital components of food security, a concern incorporated into later definitions as well, such as the 1996 *Rome Declaration on World Food Security* (Rome Declaration 1996). In 2001, FAO further refined this idea, adding "social access" into food security, establishing the definition used today: "Food security exists when all people, at all times, have physical, social and economic access to sufficient, safe and nutritious food that meets their dietary needs and food preferences for an active and healthy life" (FAO 2009: 8). This emphasis on social access has been adopted at national levels as well. For instance, the US Department of Agriculture (USDA) finds that food security includes the "assured ability to acquire acceptable foods in socially acceptable ways (that is, without resorting to emergency food supplies, scavenging, stealing, or other coping strategies)" (USDA 2007a). Common themes among definitions are not only the availability of food supplies but also the ability of all people to gain access to sufficient amounts of nutritious food for an active and healthy life (Sen 1982; Clay 2002; FAO 2003b; Runge et al. 2003; Barrett and Maxwell 2005; Shaw 2007; Barrett 2010).

Ensuring food security has been a central feature of global

governance efforts to promote peace, prosperity, and stability. Efforts to address global challenges of hunger and malnutrition by improving food production, supply, and trade, and disseminating the findings of early scientific work in nutrition began in the early twentieth century under the auspices of the International Institute for Agriculture and the League of Nations and received a considerable boost during World War II. In May 1943, President Franklin D. Roosevelt convened the United Nations Conference on Food and Agriculture. The roots of the conference can be traced to Roosevelt's 1941 State of the Union address where he described his vision of a world founded upon four freedoms, including what he called the third freedom, "freedom from want – which, translated into world terms, means economic understandings which will secure to every nation a healthy peacetime life for its inhabitants – everywhere in the world" (Roosevelt 1941). The 1943 conference was organized with the specific aim "to consider the goal of freedom from want in relation to food and agriculture" (Shaw 2007: 3). The conference recognized that "freedom from want means a secure, an adequate, and a suitable supply of food" (ibid.) and began discussions of an organization that could address persistent challenges of hunger, resulting in the formal creation of the Food and Agriculture Organization of the United Nations (FAO) on October 16, 1945 (UNDP 1994; Runge et al. 2003; Barrett and Maxwell 2005; Shaw 2007).

With the creation of the FAO, the world community set a goal of ensuring that all people had the food they needed to live a healthy life. Scotsman Sir John Boyd Orr was selected as the FAO's first Director-General and identified the goal and purpose of the organization in an address that recognized that "each nation has accepted the responsibility . . . to provide, as far as possible, food and a health standard for all peoples . . . But something new has arisen. All the governments have agreed to cooperate in a great world food scheme, which will bring freedom from want to all men, irrespective of race and color" (quoted in Shaw 2007: 5). The problem facing the new organization was understood as having two dimensions: first, it required protecting both consumers and producers from severe fluctuations of agricultural prices and production; and second, it involved using agricultural surpluses to assist nations with food production deficits in ways that did not disrupt trade or create disincentives for domestic production improvements. The experiences of the world wars had clearly demonstrated that problems of instability, want, and lack of basic necessities such as food in one nation could become a problem for all nations (Runge et al. 2003; Barrett and Maxwell 2005; Shaw 2007).

During the latter half of the twentieth century, the right to food and an obligation to help all states provide and secure that right was affirmed in many of the foundational agreements of global governance. For instance, in 1948 the United Nations General Assembly adopted the Universal Declaration of Human Rights, which included in Article 25 the statement that "everyone has the right to a standard of living adequate for the health and well-being of himself and his family, including food" (UN 1948). The 1966 Covenant on Economic, Social and Cultural Rights declared "the fundamental right of everyone to be free from hunger" and outlined "the right of everyone to an adequate standard of living for himself and his family, including adequate food" (UN 1966). The importance of finding ways to meet the needs of growing human populations in a way that contributes to environmental sustainability and rural development was highlighted in chapter 14 of Agenda 21 which was adopted by more than 175 Governments at the 1992 United Nations Conference on Environment and Development (UN 1992). The 1996 Rome Declaration on World Food Security confirmed "the right of everyone to have access to safe and nutritious food, consistent with the right to adequate food and the fundamental right of everyone to be free from hunger" (Rome Declaration 1996). These many examples highlight the transformation of food security from a discrete issue of international concern to one fully integrated into the core global governance agenda.

Based on recognitions of the importance of food security to international peace and human security, addressing hunger and malnutrition have been central goals of global efforts to improve health and well-being. In the early 1970s, the world confronted a food crisis driven in the short term by the 1972 decline in world food production (the first drop in two decades), but also by longer-term drivers such as population growth, instability in the volume of world food aid supplies, and rising consumption demands of changing diets in developed and developing countries. In response to the world food crisis, world leaders gathered in 1974 at a World Food Conference and issued a declaration that "every man, woman and child has the inalienable right to be free from hunger and malnutrition in order to develop fully and maintain their physical and mental faculties" (UN 1975: 2). While the 1974 conference represented an important milestone in global recognition of food insecurity as a subject for first order political concern, it did not succeed in laying out an agreed upon global path addressing food security and developing targets and goals. However, the 1974 conference was a catalyzing moment in global concern about food problems, and ushered in the succeeding decades' attention to reducing food insecurity. For instance, the 1996 World Food Summit "established the target of halving the number of undernourished people by no later than 2015" (FAO 2006). In addition to this target, the Millennium Development Goals (MDGs) were articulated in September 2000 when 189 countries agreed to adopt "the UN Millennium Declaration, committing their nations to stronger global efforts to reduce poverty, improve health and promote peace, human rights and environmental sustainability" (UNDP 2003: 15). The first MDG aimed to "eradicate extreme poverty and hunger" by 2015 and includes target 1c which aims to "reduce by half the proportion of people who suffer from hunger." This target is further refined as the two indicators for monitoring progress of halving: (1) the prevalence of underweight children under five years of age; and (2) the proportion of population below minimum level of dietary energy consumption (UN 2008a). The evolving definitions of food security stress the fact that it is not a target to be met (such as ensuring that all people receive 2,000 calories of food per day), but that it is a progressive goal of ensuring access to food that is adequate, safe, and nutritious. Furthermore, refinement in conceptualizations of food security also demonstrate growing recognition that the aim of food security is not just to ensure that people are well fed, but that they have all the necessary requirements to fully flourish as individuals, communities, and societies (Drèze and Sen 1989; Sen 1999; Commission on Human Security 2003; Shaw 2007).

As Dalby (2009) recognizes, concerns over the impacts of

population and scarcity of key resources such as food are not new. Previous discussions of food problems have tended to be from either a neo-Malthusian or cornucopian perspective, and it is useful to briefly review each. Neo-Malthusian, or catastrophist (Smil 2000) perspectives can be traced to the late eighteenth and early nineteenth century work of Thomas Malthus. Malthus foresaw inevitable social problems emerging from the inherent tension he believed existed between differing rates of increase in human population and food supply. In *An Essay on the Principle of Population,* published in six editions between 1798 and 1826, Malthus argued that while "population, when unchecked, goes on doubling itself every twenty-five years, or increases in a geometrical ratio . . . the means of subsistence . . . could not possibly be made to increase faster than in an arithmetical ratio" (Malthus 1826). Malthus's notion that human populations could, under certain conditions, increase at a geometric rate, while food supplies, under optimal conditions, could only increase at an arithmetic rate, has led to considerable discussion and, in recent years, increasing critique and rejection. As Smil (2000) remarks, Malthus himself was guardedly optimistic that human societies could find ways to increase food supplies, commenting in the final chapter of his essay: "On the whole, therefore, though our future prospects . . . may not be so bright as we could wish, yet they are far from being entirely disheartening" (Malthus 1826). Since the publication of his essay, a considerable body of scholarship has developed to refine and extend Malthus's ideas about how finite stocks of natural resources place limits on the growth of human societies and the amount of resources they can consume without triggering effects such as poverty, famine, and conflict (Malthus 1826; Ehrlich 1968; Meadows et al. 1972; Brown 1970, 1977, 2004; Ehrlich and Ehrlich 1990; Brown 2009).

In contrast to these ideas, cornucopians, a term which originates from the Greek myth of a horn of plenty that supplied its owners with endless food and drink, contend that limitless stocks of human ingenuity mean there are few, if any, limits on population growth and resource consumption (Simon 1981; Simon and Kahn 1984; Lomborg 2001). Cornucopians, also referred to as economic optimists, argue that properly functioning markets provide incentives that encourage conservation and substitution of resources and the development of new types of resources and technologies. Julian Simon was a key proponent of the cornucopian perspective. In *The Ultimate Resource* (1981), Simon argued that population increases generally had positive, rather than negative, impacts as they improved the supply of ingenuity available to solve problems and staved off the sorts of collapses predicted by Malthus and his supporters. Over the past few decades, proponents of both the neo-Malthusian and cornucopian perspective have engaged in lively discussions. For example, in 1980 Julian Simon and Paul Ehrlich wagered on a demonstration of the implications of resource scarcity; Ehrlich bet that five metals would increase in price by 1990 as they would become more scarce while Simon bet (correctly) that the prices would go down as innovation and improvements in technology effectively increased the supply of the resources (Regis 1997).

Central to both perspectives of food problems is a sense of crisis. While they differ in their proposed strategies for coping and adaptation, there is general agreement among neo-Malthusian and cornucopian perspectives that human populations face considerable food security challenges. In recent decades, and most noticeably during the food crises of the 1970s and late 2000s, concern about world food problems received a significant amount of attention (Godfray et al. 2010). Observers, such as Lester Brown, point to this confluence of global trends, arguing that the result is that the world is "entering into a new food era. Early signs of this are the record-high grain prices of the last few years, the restriction on grain exports by exporting countries, and the acquisition of vast tracts of land abroad by grain-importing countries" (Brown 2009: 216). A central challenge of this new era will be not just increasing food production to meet human needs – a major scientific goal and achievement during the twentieth century – but also ensuring efficient distribution of existing food supplies as, despite those increasing food supplies in the last century, food did not always reach those who needed it most. For example, Vaclav Smil identifies the underlying challenge of food security as "how can we *best* feed some ten billion people who will likely inhabit the earth by the middle of the twenty-first century" (emphasis added; Smil 2000: ix). The introduction of a special issue of the journal

Science devoted to food security reinforces this focus: "feeding the 9 billion people expected to inhabit our planet by 2050 will be an unprecedented challenge" (Ash, Jasny, Malakoff and Sugen 2010: 797). These observations, however, are merely projections of problems that already exist worldwide. As Sir John Beddington (2009) comments, according to many current projections, global population growth, food demand, and water scarcity could begin to converge to have significant impacts as soon as 2030. As Beddington's observation implies, environmental issues are increasingly at the forefront of investigations of food security, a focus likely to grow as the effects of environmental change become more apparent in the coming years (IPCC 2007; Smil 2008; United States Joint Forces Command 2010).

Navigating a changing security landscape: Environmental and human security

Scholars increasingly recognize that environmental degradation has massive implications for security concerns of all kinds. While integrating new literatures on international and human security, these discussions are grounded in academic consideration of human actions on the global environment that have existed since the mid-twentieth century. Beginning in the 1960s, the environmental movement expanded beyond its roots in the late nineteenth century conservation and wilderness preservation movements to a growing concern for human impacts on nature (Nash 1982). Rachel Carson's 1962 book, *Silent Spring*, which raised questions about the safety of DichloroDiphenylTrichloroethane (DDT) for humans and animals, is often cited as an important origin for this shift. However, Carson's publication coincided with several other important events and trends, all of which shaped the modern environmental movement, including: major environmental disasters such as the 1969 Santa Barbara, California oil spill and the 1969 eruption into flames of the highly polluted Cuyahoga River near Cleveland, Ohio; recognitions of new kinds of global environmental problems that extended beyond what had been considered local problems such as air and water pollution; and a turbulent social and political context where environmental problems had broad appeal to large segments of societies (Nash 1982; Rothman 1997). The development of modern concerns about the impact of humans on the natural world also gave rise to the common usage of the concept of "the environment." The term environment is most often used to refer to a realm of unbuilt nonhumanity including the plants, animals, places, and systems which undergird and surround humanity. However, a great deal of scholarship has developed to consider how the mingling of human labor, ideas, and desires with this natural realm has resulted in a blurring of distinctions between places unbuilt (or first nature) and built (or second nature) (Luke 1997, 1999). During the latter part of the twentieth century, efforts to consider the impacts human actions were having on the environment expanded to include not just questions of wilderness preservation and conservation of wild places, but also questions much more relevant to the places people live and work as well as the air they breathe, the water they drink, and the food they eat (Williams 1973; Nash 1982; Gottlieb 1993; Rome 2001).

The field of environmental security emerged in the 1990s based on broadening conceptualizations of both security and the environment and work by scholars, journalists, and policymakers that explicitly linked the two sets of concerns. Environmental conditions have long imposed constraints on the security of individuals and societies throughout human history, and, while factors like trade and improvements in technology have weakened impacts of the environment on security, they have not removed the environment's influence entirely (Barnett, Matthew and O'Brien 2009). As early as 1974, a national security study memorandum commissioned by then US National Security Advisor and Secretary of State Henry Kissinger warned that factors such as population growth, inadequate food supplies, and the location of natural resources in unstable developing countries could affect the security and national interests of the United States (Kissinger Report 1974). During the 1980s, a number of scholars explored the ways the security of states and their inhabitants were impacted by factors such as environmental change and degradation (Brown 1977; Ullman 1983; WCED 1987; Matthews 1989, 1997; Meyers 1989).

These early expressions of the connections between environment and security foreshadowed the genesis of environmental security in the waning years of the Cold War. In 1991, President George H. W. Bush's administration included threats from environmental degradation in its *National Security Strategy of the United States of America* (Bush 1991). In 1994, journalist Robert Kaplan's article "The Coming Anarchy" focused attention on the security implications of environmental change by declaring "it is time to understand The Environment for what it is: the national-security issue of the early twenty-first century." He argued that the political and strategic impacts of environmental degradation and resulting social effects like mass migration would "be the core foreign-policy challenge from which most others will ultimately emanate, arousing the public and uniting assorted interests left over from the Cold War" (Kaplan 1994). Kaplan's article received wide attention, including from President Bill Clinton who "referred to 'The Coming Anarchy' as 'stunning' and passed it around as recommended reading in the White House" (Lester 1996). Other senior Clinton administration officials also supported the notion that environmental degradation was relevant to security concerns, including Vice President Al Gore (1992), known for his interest in environmental issues, and Secretary of State Warren Christopher (1996). As a result, in the United States "the notion that security necessarily meant the threat of violence and military conflict was widely abandoned and the definition of a national security interest was broadened to include other threats to US interests, such as economics and the environment" (Butts 1999: 109–10). This high level of attention to environmental security concerns prompted a great deal of activity from scholars, governmental agencies, and nongovernmental organizations to examine the ways environmental factors could affect the security of people and states (Brauch et al. 2009; Matthew and McDonald 2009; Dabelko 2008; Conca and Dabelko 2010). Although official and policy interest in environment and security issues waned in the late 1990s and early 2000s, there has been a resurgence of interest in these topics recently, especially with regards to the ways that environmental and climate change are transforming conditions and needs that defense, diplomacy, and development communities will need to be able to operate within (Ministry of Defense 2010; United States

Department of Defense 2010; United States Joint Forces Command 2010).

Since the early 1990s, interest in the security implications of environmental issues has motivated considerable academic and policy activity. Research on the links between environment and security consider connections in a range of areas. One of the major themes of this body of work is the potential for environmental degradation to contribute to violent conflict. A number of researchers have elaborated the pathways by which environmental degradation, often through its social effects, could contribute to or cause conflicts (Gleick 1991; Homer-Dixon 1991, 1994, 1999; Homer-Dixon and Blitt 1998; Klare 2001; Floyd 2008; Dalby 2009). Research has also examined the possibility that resources such as water (Gleick 1991, 1993; Weinthal 2002; Conca 2005) or oil, timber, and minerals (Klare 2001) could be a source for conflict but also a motivator for cooperation (Wolf 1997; Conca and Dabelko 2002; Weinthal 2004). Moreover, researchers have expressed concern about the connections between environment and security including: worries that making such linkages would lead to a securitization of the environment (Kakonen 1994); concerns that links between the two would be difficult to make in ways that would not be counterproductive or analytically misleading (Deudny 1990); and arguing that connections between environment and security could only be understood through site-specific violent conflicts (Peluso and Watts 2001). Simon Dalby writes that while environmental security concerns are driven by the recognition that "climate change and related phenomena are threatening to many ways of life. Less obvious, but at least as important, is . . . the suggestion that environmental change might cause us to rethink what we mean by security" (Dalby 2009: 3). One result of these critiques, and of successive waves of scholarship on environmental security, is a lessening of the focus of environmental security research on the links between environment and conflict and instead a move towards inquiries into how environmental insecurities are intertwined with day-to-day human security problems.

As discussed in the introduction, human security can be broadly defined as freedom from fear and want, or as protecting and empowering the world's most vulnerable people. The concept of human security was the focus of the United Nations Development Program's 1994 Human Development Report which asserted the need to expand discussions of security to recognize that "for most people today, a feeling of insecurity arises more from worries about daily life than from the dread of a cataclysmic world event. Job security, income security, security from crime – these are the emerging concerns of human security all over the world" (UNDP 1994: 3). Human security has two main aspects: "It means, first, safety from such chronic threats as hunger, disease and repression. And second, it means protection from sudden and harmful disruptions in the patterns of daily life . . . the loss of human security can be a slow, silent process – or an abrupt, loud emergency" (UNDP 1994: 23). UNDP identified seven main categories of threat to human security: economic security, food security, health security, environmental security, personal security, community security, and political security. Additionally, the report identifies four essential characteristics of human security: it is a universal concern, its components are interdependent, it is easier to ensure through early prevention rather than later intervention, and it is people-centered (UNDP 1994).

Considerable research and policy activity since 1994 have lent a great deal of credibility to the value of human security and helped expand these early definitions of human security. For instance, the Global Environmental Change and Human Security project further refines the definition of human security "as something that is achieved when and where individuals and communities have the options necessary to end, mitigate or adapt to threats to their human, environmental and social rights; have the capacity and freedom to exercise these options; and actively participate in pursuing these options" (Barnett, Matthew and O'Brien 2009: 18). Similarly, the Commission on Human Security defined human security as the need "to protect the vital core of all human lives in ways that enhance human freedoms and human fulfillment" (Commission on Human Security 2003: 4). This definition of human security built on Commission co-chair and Nobel Prize-winning economist Amartya Sen's conception of capabilities, and emphasized that people's security can be impacted by "critical (severe) and pervasive (widespread) threats and situations" and identified the need to create "political, social, environmental, economic, military and cultural systems that together give people the building blocks of survival, livelihood and dignity" (ibid.). Other recent definitions of human security, such as the Human Security Centre's 2005 Human Security Report, have presented it as a complementary standard to national security: "secure states do not automatically mean secure peoples. Protecting citizens from foreign attack may be a necessary condition for the security of individuals, but it is certainly not a sufficient one. Indeed, during the last 100 years far more people have been killed by their own governments than by foreign armies" (Human Security Centre 2005: vii). While not all scholars agree on the value of the concept of human security, even critics such as Roland Paris recognize that human security provides a useful framework for research that "explores the particular conditions that affect the survival of individuals, groups, and societies" (Paris 2001: 102). This potential is further echoed by Dalby (2009), who argues that human security allows the recognition of new forms of security threats that arise not from deliberate actions of foreign armies or states, but out of the unintended consequences of social, political, economic, and environmental changes.

The expansion of human security definitions adds important amplifications to the meaning and utility of the concept. First, over time the notion of human security has evolved to address vulnerability from threats that are sudden or unexpected (such as war or disaster) as well as threats that are pervasive (such as hunger or ill health). Recognizing these two dimensions of vulnerability is vitally important, as too often attention from policymakers and the media focuses on sudden threats that press themselves onto agendas due to their immediacy or the rapid development of a major crisis while widespread and persistent vulnerabilities remain unaddressed. A second core aspect of human security is the notion that addressing vulnerability requires empowering individuals and communities to take actions on their own behalf. These two elements – protection of basic rights and freedoms and empowering people's ability to act on their own behalf – were recognized as the two keys to human security by the Commission on Human Security (2003). Third, definitions of human security have grown to include communities and not just individuals as important figures deserving of protection, in recognition of the value placed on the collective social group in many societies (Barnett, Matthew and O'Brien 2009). Finally, a fourth core aspect of human security stresses that human security and national security should be mutually reinforcing, and focus on the protection of both states and individuals and not one at the expense of the other (Human Security Centre 2005). Thus the concept of human security as it is most often deployed today is similar to what Drèze and Sen (1989) describe as social security; human security is a comprehensive framework which includes a range of driving forces.

Food security is a fundamental component of human security's effort to ensure safety from both chronic threats and sudden disruptions. UNDP recognized food security as one of seven main threats to human security and stressed that food security "requires not just enough food to go round. It requires that people have ready access to food – that they have an 'entitlement' to food, by growing it for themselves, by buying it, or by taking advantage of a public food distribution system" (UNDP 1994: 27). Improving access to food is a crucial component of addressing food security needs and includes roles for both governments and international agencies. These institutions can play the critically important role of ensuring that the distribution of food supplies is equitable and efficient, which in societies that experience serious food insecurity is often not the case. The Commission on Human Security recognized that millions of people around the world do not have sufficient food: "these people suffer daily hunger, malnutrition and food insecurity even though most national food supplies are adequate. The problem is a lack of entitlement to food and access to an adequate food supply" (Commission on Human Security 2003: 14). Success in achieving food security is thus recognized as both a component of larger efforts to provide human security and a goal that depends on the success of efforts to improve human health and well-being through methods such as poverty alleviation, infrastructure development, education, and improvements in the status of women.

Global change and the global food system

Over the past few decades, local, regional, and national food and agricultural systems have increasingly become intertwined in an emerging global food system, a complex network of relations that includes the production, harvest, processing, transport, and consumption of food. Today, there are malnourished people in developed and developing countries. This global food network is filled with pockets of both abundance and scarcity and its emerging shape does not map onto many of the traditional political science models of the world such as North/South, East/West/Nonaligned, Developed/In Transition/Developing, or Rich/Poor. The creation of a global food system has happened as the result of amalgamated decisions in a wide variety of locations including farm fields, scientific and commercial laboratories, governmental agencies, and international negotiations. While increasingly interconnected, agricultural and food production systems are not a fully incorporated system in the sense that they are an integrated whole, but are perhaps best discussed as a network, or a set of interconnected systems.

Interest in the rise of networks is not solely confined to the food system. In response to the increasing closeness of disparate places and people, the notion of a "network" has gained increasing salience among scholars who use it to clarify the complexities of this evolution in global connectivity and to describe the evolving structure of relations between people, places, and things. Networks, at the most general level, are an interconnection of systems that allow sharing between systems and contain regularized interactions between nodes of activity (Castells 1996; Held et al. 1999; Watts 1999, 2003; Buchanan 2002; Barabási 2003; Barney 2004; Matthew and Shambaugh 2005). Physicist Albert-László Barabási writes, "We increasingly recognize that nothing happens in isolation. Most events and phenomena are connected, caused by, and interacting with a huge number of other pieces of a complex universal puzzle. We have come to see that we live in a small world, where everything is linked to everything else" (Barabási 2003: 7). Many types of networks support contemporary human interactions, from information networks like the World Wide Web to transportation networks like the air transit system.

One of the key features of networks is that they collapse distances, though not in a traditional, geometric sense. In networks, the shortest distance between two points often involves traveling through a hub, rather than directly from node to node. While networks can continue to function with the loss of some or many nodes, disruption of a hub can have significant impact on the overall network and can have cascading impacts on other networks (Watts 1999, 2003; Buchanan 2002; Barabási 2003; Homer-Dixon 2006). The rise of global networks has affected many areas of daily life from transportation to telecommunications, security to health, the practice of law to the sorts of foods people eat (Garrett 1994, 2007; Zacher and Sutton 1995; Deibert 1997; Matthew and Shambaugh 1998, 2005; Slaughter 2004).

As an increasingly networked world has emerged, observers have expressed concerns that increased connectivity creates new forms of threat and vulnerability that are even further amplified as systems become increasingly complex and brittle (Matthew and Shambaugh 1998; Homer-Dixon 2000, 2006; Flynn 2007). As Thomas Homer-Dixon writes, "networks are particularly vulnerable to intentional attack: if someone wants to wreck the whole network, he simply needs to identify and destroy some of its hubs" (Homer-Dixon 2006: 118). For Homer-Dixon, this feature of networks is why the world's increasing connectivity creates significant sources of threat and vulnerability. "Greater connectivity tends to make already dominant hubs even more dominant . . . Once a hub is damaged, intentionally or otherwise, its problems can spread quickly far and wide" (ibid.). While networks collapse distances and are efficient in moving people, goods, and information, this decreased functional distance between once far-flung people and places amplifies traditional security challenges and creates new forms of threat and vulnerability that can impact human security.

While local, regional, national, and international food systems are interconnected, they are not, as stated above, an integrated system but instead a network of systems with distinct hubs and nodes. This lack of coherent integration – even while it functions with great efficiency to move things rapidly from place to place often across vast distances in a matter of hours or days – is perhaps the key feature of the global food system. Moreover, while the global food network is transnational in the sense that it crosses the borders of states, its behavior cannot be explicitly linked to the policies or behaviors of states. And yet the behavior of the global food network is greatly influenced by policies and actions of states, such as subsidization of certain types of agricultural production and the creation or reduction of trade barriers. It is, furthermore, affected by the actions and interactions of international organizations such as FAO, the World Food Program and the World Bank, as well as by a variety of substate and nonstate actors including farmers, fishermen, consumers, scientists, boards of directors, and activists.

The global food system has both nodes and hubs, some of which are distinct to the food network and some of which are shared with other networks, such as transportation systems like ports and airports for transportation, power plants and transmission lines for energy, and information systems used for trading agricultural commodities. The presence of shared hubs also means shared vulnerabilities, so that the food network could be affected or impaired by events at a shared hub such as a port, airport, or power plant. In this way, the food network shares common vulnerabilities with other sorts of networks that we increasingly depend on to deliver daily life necessities (Matthew and Shambaugh 1998; Homer-Dixon 2000, 2006; Flynn 2007). In addition to shared hubs and nodes, the network of global food systems also has distinctive hubs and nodes of its own that provide opportunities for accidental or intentional disruption. Examples of major hubs in the food network include grain silos, large-scale livestock production facilities, slaughterhouses, or milk treatment and bottling facilities. These hubs are integral to the operation of the system as they allow for increased efficiency and functioning of the network (Nestle 2003; Homer-Dixon 2006). However, the existence of hubs also creates new forms of threat and vulnerability for the global food network. Silos can provide efficient sites for grain storage and transportation, but they are relatively undefended, difficult to secure, and, in times of rising prices, can also be an ideal target for thieves (California Farm Bureau Federation 2007). Milk silos provide benefits for the processing and treatment of milk supplies from various production sites, but, under the proper circumstances, they could also be used to transport a weaponized biological agent to large numbers of people (Wein and Liu 2005). In addition to direct impacts on humans, the loss of a key hub in the food network can also have significant social, economic, and political impacts, especially if the loss impacts something like the power necessary to keep food frozen or the rapid transportation necessary to move fresh fish or produce from producers to consumers.

The global food system, like other networks, must balance security concerns against economic and political demands. Many global networks, such as air transportation, mail and cargo, energy systems and information technology systems, must maximize the positive aspects of network connectivity while yet minimizing the connectivity's drawbacks. As in other sectors of the global economy, such as manufacturing or the apparel industry, the global food system is confronted with the need to develop systems to reduce transaction costs and opportunistic behavior and effectively govern global value chains (Gereffi and Korzeniewicz 1994; Gereffi, Humphrey, and Sturgeon 2005). Globalization has made possible dramatic increases in the productivity and distribution of food, leading to tremendous increases in the variety of food available in almost all parts of the world and having an array of impacts on human health and nutrition (Pinstrup-Andersen 2007). Globalization has allowed a similar mix of positive and negative effects on human security more generally, where processes of global change have amplified old sources of threat and vulnerability (such as infectious disease), and created new forms of vulnerability (such as advanced biological weapons that could be developed using genetic engineering technologies). Perhaps most importantly in the coming decades, processes of global change have amplified one form of threat – environmental degradation – to such an extent that it now presents a qualitatively different challenge in the form of global climate change (Easterling et al. 2007; IPCC 2007).

Efforts to ensure food security are enhanced by the nested nature of systems, in that the global food network is embedded in, acting upon, and dependent upon other global networks. The embedded nature of the global food network has a number of impacts. The impact of shared threat and vulnerability from common hubs was discussed above. But there are other impacts on the food network, such as shared social and political history. For example, one significant challenge to food security remains the legacies of processes of decolonization and the enormous inequalities that these processes often encouraged, including corruption among elites who control economic systems and the distribution of food resources; conversion of local agricultural systems into production for export-oriented crops; and lack of development (or intentional deprivation) that impacts the poorest people in societies, which often forces them into informal economic activities and illegal actions such as poaching and overfishing in an effort to gain access to the food necessary for survival. As will be discussed further in the next chapter, globalization is a major transformative factor impacting the shape of the global food system.

2 From Local to Global: Shifts in World Food Systems

Humans in the twenty-first century are not the first to face significant challenges related to security, safety and nutrition of food supplies. Human societies have dealt with food problems through a variety of strategies to limit or reduce constraints imposed by food scarcity and local environmental conditions including migration and the establishment of trade networks and development of technologies and social processes to improve food production, transportation, and storage (Barnett, Matthew and O'Brien 2009). While contemporary globalization may be unique in its speed, scale, and depth of change, it is not the first era in human history that is defined by changes in technology, mobility, or flows of trade. Calls, such as Timothy W. Luke's, for a greater understanding of the "hybridities of Nature/Society at sites which intermix the natural and the social," require a full consideration of human interactions with nature, not just contemporary comprehension (Luke 2001b: 2). Michael Pollan (2001) writes that food is an artifact, a thing reflecting human will and that the foods selected and savored by societies, as equally as those spurned, reflect human choices. In this way, analysis of the global food system aids us in understanding not only how human choices have shaped natural systems but also the impact the systems we have created to produce and distribute food will have on our future choices. As one of these hybrids of nature and society, the global food system is precisely the kind of nexus that Luke and Pollan urge us to examine.

Understanding the relationship between food and security seems more pressing in light of developments in the food system in recent years: recent rises in global food prices and global impacts of localized natural disasters and severe weather events have shown how globally interconnected our food system has become. These developments illustrate the accelerated connections between the world's places and peoples and highlight the important links between how humans produce, distribute, and consume foodstuffs and pressing social, political, and environmental issues. The ways human populations gain access to food is a defining feature of human civilizations, and today food is a major part of global trade flows and a primary driver of global change processes like land clearance and climate change. While fishing remains an important source of food for many people, the majority of food consumed by humans comes from farming (especially if we take farming in its broadest sense to include the structured production of crops, livestock, and increasingly marine organisms through aquaculture). Agriculture also provides important resources for human societies, from fibers such as wool and cotton to materials such as timber and bamboo. Today's global food system looks remarkably different from the agricultural and food production systems of previous decades. Despite these distinctions, it is vital to recognize that all these food systems – even the most primitive ones – were shaped by the mingling of human choices and natural systems.

This chapter asserts that much of the human relationship to nature has historically been mediated by food, and will also seek to show that today's food system encounters unique challenges on a massive scale. As such, this chapter begins with an exploration of the concept of globalization as a foundational force in global affairs that is transforming not only security, but also many aspects of social, political and economic life. Next, the chapter moves on to briefly consider the development of human societies from hunters and gatherers to agricultural societies to the modern age. This overview enables us to understand that, first, agriculture and food production systems are networks that humans have shaped to reflect our physical, economic, political, and social needs and desires, and, second, that having enough food to eat (the most basic definition of food security) has long been a central political challenge for human societies. The final section of the chapter considers how one of the most far-reaching and pressing global phenomena – global environmental change – is testing our ability to sustain and manage the global food network and what lessons we might draw from our historical relationships to food and the environment in order to further inform that discussion.

Globalization

Since the 1970s, and especially since the end of the Cold War, processes of economic, political, and social globalization have brought increased interconnectedness, mobility, and access for transnational flows of people, goods, and information. As Gereffi, Humphrey and Sturgeon (2005) note, the global economy has undergone significant transformation in recent decades due to globalization. Trade and production have become more dispersed across geographic boundaries. These activities have also become more coordinated as transnational corporations moved from vertically integrated businesses into more dispersed operations that have reduced direct ownership of many business functions such as manufacturing and support services. A wide variety of definitions of globalization exist. Held et al. conceptualize globalization as "the widening, deepening, and speeding up of worldwide interconnectedness in all aspects of contemporary social life, from the cultural to the criminal, the financial to the spiritual" (Held et al. 1999: 2). Ulrich Beck describes modern globalization as a set of processes "through which sovereign national actors are criss-crossed and undermined by transnational actors with varying prospects for power, orientations, identities, and networks" (Beck 2000: 11). Thomas Friedman explains globalization as "the inexorable integration of markets, nation-states and technologies to a degree never witnessed before," and continues that this integration is occurring "in a way that is enabling individuals, corporations and nation states to reach around the world farther, faster, deeper, and cheaper than ever before, and in a way that is enabling the world to reach into individuals, corporations, and nation states farther, faster, deeper and cheaper than ever before" (Friedman 1999: 9). While the wording of definitions may vary, all contain key common elements that help us gain a better understanding of globalization: a notion that globalization involves interconnections between diverse parts of the world; that these interconnections are increasing in speed and scale; that the interactions operate through networks that exist within and between states; and that these interconnections are having impacts on many aspects of life including economic, political, and social systems (Held et al. 1999; Gereffi, Humphrey, and Sturgeon 2005).

Attention to globalization has given rise to a great deal of scholarship and debate about the meaning, origins, and even existence of globalization (Harvey 1989; Friedman 1999; Held et al. 1999; Beck 2000; Luke 2001b; McNeill 2008). In an effort to provide a systematic approach to understanding globalization, Held et al. (1999) identify three major approaches to conceptualizing globalization: hyperglobalist, skeptical, and transformational. The hyperglobalist approach sees globalization as defining a new period in human history where nation-states become units in a global economy as increasingly global economic processes de-nationalize economies by establishing transnational networks of production, trade, and finance (Wriston 1992; Ohmae 1995; Guehenno 1995; Held et al. 1999). The skeptical approach draws on historical and economic information about world trade flows, largely from the nineteenth century, to argue that contemporary levels of economic interconnection are not unprecedented, but rather are merely an extension of interactions between economies that remain largely national or regional, especially given the development of regional trading blocs in North America, Europe and Asia-Pacific (Ruigrok and van Tulder 1995; Boyer and Drache 1996; Hirst and Thompson 1996; Hirst 1997; Held et al. 1999). The transformational approach contends that globalization is the primary driver of rapid changes that are reshaping social, economic and political systems (Giddens 1990; Scholte 1993; Castells 1996; Held et al. 1999). For transformationalists, contemporary globalization processes are unprecedented and are leading to the creation of a world where there is no longer a meaningful distinction between international and domestic realms or states and nonstates (Rosenau 1990; Ruggie 1993; MacMillan and Linklater 1995; Held et al. 1999).

As Held et al.'s categories indicate, a critical discussion in the study of globalization is whether modern globalization processes are new or represent the persistence of historical trends that date back centuries or even millennia. When taking historical perspectives into account, particularly in relation to food and food networks, it becomes clear that modern globalization processes are the continuation and amplification of a long series of processes that have created closer connections between all parts of the world. For instance, historian William McNeill describes globalization as the way changes in "transport and communications have tied humankind in all parts of the world together more closely than ever before" (McNeill 2008: 1). Yet, McNeill writes that modern changes are a continuation of a long-standing process of global change whereby the "human past can plausibly be understood as a series of thresholds when new conditions of life rather abruptly accelerated the pace of resulting change" (ibid.: 2). McNeill includes among these thresholds the control of fire, the ability to move across large bodies of water, and the development of agriculture. While discussions of globalization often emphasize that increasing levels of connectivity mean that the current moment in global relations is somehow unique, it is valuable to recognize that, as McNeill asserts, "from the long term point of view . . . recent mass migrations and widespread disruption of village patterns of life by roads, trucks, buses, radio, TV and computers look more like another wave of intensified human interaction, comparable to its predecessors and far from unique" (McNeill 2008: 5). This recognition usefully reminds us that current processes of global change are not entirely unique and in fact represent a continuity with patterns of global change that have altered human life in significant ways throughout our history (Crosby 1986; Diamond 1999; McNeill 2000; McNeill 2008).

To recognize these continuities between modern processes of global change and previous periods of global change, however, is not to suggest that there is nothing distinctive about the current era of global change. While there may be continuities with previous eras of global change, there are also features of this era of change which make it distinctive. Certainly, the character of human societies have been altered in the past by the development of technologies such as fire which allowed human beings to modify their environments or navigation devices such as the compass which allowed sailors to leave the sight of land and return safely, but so too are the characteristics of human societies being altered by modern innovations such as the personal computer. The development of the personal computer and the information networks that connect them have allowed very rapid changes in the ways that people store, access, and process information. The spread of personal computers has occurred very rapidly and much faster than some would have believed. For example, Bill Gates (2007) reports he was regarded as optimistic for predicting in 1982 that IBM would sell 200,000 personal computers that year. The number turned out to be 240,000. By 2007, global sales of personal computers had experienced a thousand-fold increase and topped 250 million worldwide. Computer sales are just one example of the increasing speed and scale of global interconnection. Today's globalization processes build upon previous periods of intense globalization, such as between the mid-1800s and 1920s, when the rate of connections between places and peoples also increased rapidly as a result of industrial revolution technologies like the steam engine. However, while globalization may be a long-term phenomenon, there is a general sense that there is something distinctive about what Thomas Friedman (1999) calls "this era of globalization" as rapid advances in technology and transportation have combined to dramatically increase the speed, scale, and density of interactions between people and places (Friedman 1999; Held et al. 1999; Luke 2001b; Gereffi, Humphrey, and Sturgeon 2005; McNeill 2008).

In considering the perspectives of all three of Held et al.'s approaches to understanding globalization (hyperglobalist, skeptical, and transformational), as well as discussions about the historical nature of these processes, we can thus further refine the definition of globalization employed by this book. Held et al. offer a revised conceptualization of globalization as "a process (or set of processes) which embodies a transformation in the spatial organization of social relations and transactions – assessed in terms of their extensity, intensity, velocity and impact – generating transcontinental or interregional flows and networks of activity, interaction and exercise of power" (Held et al. 1999: 16). In reviewing these many ideas and definitions of globalization then, we can understand globalization as a phenomenon that has certain key elements:

- *Rate* – globalization increases the speed of interactions
- *Magnitude* – globalization increases the scale of interactions
- *Structure* – globalization operates through networks of systems
- *Effect* – globalization is transforming economic, social and political systems

Collectively, globalization can be understood as a set of processes involving increasing speed and scale of interactions that operate through networks and that are transforming many aspects of daily life (Held et al. 1999; Matthew and Shambaugh 2005).

Modern globalization brings new opportunities for improving human livelihoods and well-being, but also brings greater recognition of the persistent sources of human insecurity from threats such as a lack of sufficient food. Globalization may be increasing the speed and scale of transnational interactions, but the effects, both positive and negative, of globalization remain unevenly distributed. Timothy W. Luke writes that "globalization is a very long-running series of cultural, economic, and social processes, and for the most part, some of them are leading toward real material improvements in everyday life. Yet, these improvements are not being shared equally" (Luke 2001b: 6). One of the key challenges then is to ensure that improvements brought by globalization reach all human beings. In addition to persistent sources of insecurity, such as malnutrition, globalization has also resulted in the creation of new sources of insecurity, such as cyber-threats (Flynn 2007; United States Department of Defense 2010; United States Joint Forces Command 2010), and the amplification of existing sources of insecurity such as infectious disease (Garrett 1994, 2007; NIC 2000; Brower and Chalk 2003; Smolinski et al. 2003). One significant impact of globalization is an expansion of the types of phenomena that are seen as sources of security threats and vulnerabilities. While food security has long been a concern of human societies, globalization has made addressing this challenge much more complex as it is no longer a matter of confronting localized food insecurity with local resources, or even of alleviating localized food insecurity with resources from the broader network, but instead of managing the complex feedback between local food insecurity and the entire global food network. In attempting to understand the difficulty of solving world food problems, it is helpful to review the long history of human efforts to produce sufficient, safe, and nutritious food to enable people to lead active and healthy lives.

Humans and food: Transitions to agriculture and the modern era

For the majority of human history, humans obtained food through hunting and gathering foods that could be stored for limited amounts of time. The history of food during this early period is extraordinarily difficult to research and understand. One important implication of this long, unknowable history is that much of human physiology was shaped during this early time and not since the beginning of settled agricultural societies around 10,000 years ago (Kiple 2007). Discussions of food security today must be mindful of the ways in which the history of humanity's efforts to gain access to sufficient food continue to have real impacts on the character of food security in the present. For example, our origin as highly mobile and active hunter-gatherers helped shape our physiology and is a factor in the growing global prevalence of overweight and obesity as more and more of humanity gains access to energy-dense, nutrient-poor foods while increasingly adopting lifestyles with reduced levels of physical activity.

As scholars have increasingly turned toward "big picture" phenomena such as the environment, economic exchange, or gender relationships in their study of history, one major topic of inquiry has been the development and spread of agricultural practices (Crosby 1986; Ponting 1991; McNeill 1998, 2008; Diamond 1999; Garnsey 1999; Christian 2004; Fogel 2004; Federico 2005). For instance, Jared Diamond's 1997 bestseller, *Guns, Germs, and Steel*, has at its core – despite the title's indications otherwise – a narrative of the emergence and development of agriculture. As Diamond writes, "food production was indirectly a prerequisite for the development of guns, germs, and steel," and his book seeks, in part, to sketch the development of agriculture from its beginnings about 11,000 years ago (Diamond 1999: 86). This turn toward big picture history has helped shed new light on the origins of agriculture and the circumstances promoting the transition from hunter-gathering to farming. Though often described in bleak circumstances, life in hunter-gatherer societies was fairly good. People tended to eat well and in many cases had more varied and nutritious diets than humans in settled agricultural societies. "It would seem that the lives of our hunter-gatherer ancestors, living in a state of nature, were not 'poor, nasty, brutish, and short' as Thomas Hobbes pithily put it in his *Leviathan*. Instead they were a relatively healthy lot – at least those that managed to survive a rigorous selection process" (Kiple 2007: 4). Given these findings, it is useful to ask how and why agriculture developed.

Jared Diamond, relying on other scholars, lays out the five areas of the world where food production arose independently. Agriculture began not in one location, but independently in five: Southwest Asia (the Fertile Crescent), China, Mesoamerica, the Andes (and perhaps some neighboring regions), and the eastern US (Diamond 1999: 98). The recognition of these multiple independent origins for settled agriculture raises the question of why people in so many different geographical locations would, at around the same time period in human history, begin to try new ways of getting food. As Jared Diamond and many others have asserted, there is nothing logical about the leap from hunter-gatherer to farmer. Agriculturalists work, on average, considerably longer hours than do hunter-gatherers, and archeological evidence shows that early agriculturalists died younger, had more diseases, and were less healthy than hunter-gatherers. Why the switch, then? Diamond's story is, at its base, a scatological one. As Diamond notes, hunter-gatherers, consciously or not, influenced their environments as they roamed. They used fire to clear areas to allow easier hunting and shape the movements of prey species, they selected the biggest and most appetizing fruits and vegetables to consume, and after staying in places would leave behind the seeds of these favorite foods in their latrines and waste areas. These seeds would often lead to the creation of unplanned gardens awaiting the return of more humans to consume the food and continue this process. However, eventually something pushed hunter-gatherers to settle down in one place. The transition to agriculture may have been aided by a confluence of circumstances, such as the end of the last great Ice Age and resulting rise of sea levels (which restricted population movements and closed off safety valves that allowed excess numbers to move on to new areas) and the development of a more stable climate that was favorable to the spread of wild cereal plants and the raising of certain kinds of animal species. Diamond lists five key factors that influenced this transition: declining availability of wild foods; depletion of wild game; the development of food collection, preservation and storage technologies; rising population density; and, eventually, the displacement of hunter-gatherer populations (Diamond 1999; see also, Fernandez-Armesto 2002; Kiple 2007; Christian 2008).

Early agricultural production, however, only arose in the handful of places listed above. What was particular about those regions, Diamond asks, that they became centers of food production, spreading their technological know-how, eventually, to neighboring (and sometimes quite distant) regions? Diamond posits that there are only two explanations for the failure of the many other places on the map to independently develop agriculture: people problems, or plant problems. While he makes short work of the notion of "people problems" – asserting that all peoples were capable of and interested in making use of useful plants and foods around them – Diamond complicates the notion of "plant problems." As he shows, some areas had domesticable plants (like apple trees) that were never domesticated. His fundamental argument is that the reason agriculture arose earlier in some places than in others was due to the "entire suite" of plant and animal species available in that region – just a few domesticable plants were not enough to entice hunter-gatherers into settling down (Diamond 1999).

The transition to agriculture was not immediate or without reversals; nor was it a uniform success that brought benefits to all the societies that tried it. The work of a number of scholars, including Diamond (1999) and Armelagos (1998), has demonstrated clear links between the rise of agriculture and a shifting landscape of health challenges facing human populations (this topic is discussed in more detail in chapter 6). Agriculturalists not only kept grain stores – havens for rodents and other pests – but also domesticated animals, the source of many diseases, as well as living in increasingly dense population clusters. The emergence and growth of cities further intensified disease exchanges, not all of which were unintentional. The close relationship of disease to imperialism, particularly in the Americas, has also been written about by historians such as Alfred Crosby (1986). Moving from hunting and gathering to settled agriculture also led to a decline in the variety of human diets and the rise of health conditions related to nutritional deficiencies. Following transitions to agriculture, humans began to deal with problems such as rickets (caused by a deficiency of vitamin D), scurvy (caused by a deficiency of vitamin C), and anemia (caused by a deficiency of iron). Evidence also indicates that hunter-gatherers had lower rates of tooth decay and repetitive motion injuries to joints and tended to be taller than humans from agricultural societies. Yet, despite these new kinds of threats to health and well-being, agricultural societies flourished. Surpluses of food and the freeing of significant portions of populations from work in food production led to the creation of more complex forms of social, political, and economic organization and advances in art, language and technology (Diamond 1999; Fernandez-Armesto 2002; Kiple 2007; Christian 2008).

The next major inflection in human history came as recently as 250 years ago. Though often dated to the start of the industrial revolution around 1750, the roots of the modern era's intensification of global interactions, population growth, and technological development stretch back earlier, perhaps to around 1500 or before, and build on successive advancement in technology, governance, and social organization. Historian David Christian (2008) comments that it is easier to quantify and track major trends of the modern era as it is the first to generate large quantities of data that allow the identification of major trends, including increases in population and productivity, urbanization, the development of complex and powerful governments, growing gaps between rich and poor, and improvements in the status of women. During the modern era, high rates of innovation and development of new technologies have transformed many aspects of daily life. Despite some early predictions, improvements in food production have more than kept pace with the expansion of human populations. For example, during the period from 1800 to 2000, the population of the world grew from less than one billion people to six billion, while world agricultural productivity increased as least tenfold (Federico 2005). Robert Fogel (2004) finds that one result of improvements in technology and public health has been a dramatic improvement in nutrition and increase in human lifespans, as well as physiological changes such as increased body size and improvements across a range of health indicators. Though the modern era is often associated with industrial development, many of the transformations of the era were fueled by improvements in producing, storing, and transporting food supplies (Fogel 2004; Federico 2005; Christian 2008).

While settled agriculture and the transition to the modern era eventually led to greater stability in food sources, obtaining food and distributing it appropriately has been a persistent challenge for states. Some scholars have asserted, in fact, that through examinations of food (and the related issues of land distribution, land cultivation, and government trade policies concerning food) we can illustrate the distinct end-goals of varying states' policies. For instance, historian R. Bin Wong (1997) argues that, between the seventeenth and nineteenth centuries, the "reproduction and transformation of an agrarian state" was the primary goal of Chinese rulers. The "agrarian empire" social order, Wong asserts, rested largely on keeping a rural population on the land with farming as their primary occupation. To do so, in addition to trade policies that encouraged commerce (even while cornering the market on some luxury items, like tea, and heavily taxing others, like salt), the Chinese state established a series of granaries throughout the countryside, relying on local elites for donations in order to maintain the system. These granaries sustained the rural economy, as farmers could borrow seeds from them when necessary, and stores of grain could be transferred from them in times of famine (Will and Wong 1991). The Chinese state also utilized the market to ensure that famine areas received sufficient grain. In part, Wong attributes the Chinese state's stability and longevity to its emphasis on ensuring that food was distributed to areas in need, preventing except in the most desperate times the kinds of food riots that regularly roiled Europe during the early modern period (Wong 1997).

Food has been an important driver of processes of globalization and efforts to open new routes or improve access to new food sources have had marked impacts on diets and societies. The globalization of food has resulted in the spread of a number of important food sources from their points of origin. From their disparate origins, just four crops make up almost three quarters of global food sources:

rice (30 percent), wheat (18 percent), corn (13 percent) and cassava (12 percent). Rice, a member of the grass family, includes a number of wild species distributed throughout tropical areas of Africa, Asia, Central and South America, and Australia (all of which are thought to descend from a common progenitor that developed prior to the second major fracturing of the supercontinent Pangaea in the Early Cretaceous period more than 130 million years ago) and two cultivated species, one of which – common or Asian rice – is now grown in 112 countries (Chang 2007). Wheat, also a member of the grass family, emerged in the nitrogen poor soils of the Near East and has come to flourish in a wide range of environments (McCorriston 2007). Corn, or maize, originated as a grass at a variety of altitudes and climates in Central and South America and has spread across Africa, Europe and Asia (Messer 2007). Cassava, or manioc, is a tropical root crop that developed as a woody shrub in Brazil or possibly in Central America or the Amazon region (Karasch 2007).

The spread of rice, wheat, corn, and cassava are only four examples of the impact that the spread of foods have had on economic, social, and political systems. Historians such as Philip Curtin (1984) and Jerry Bentley (1993) have looked at the way cultural exchanges – of religious values, political systems, and language – spread along trade routes. They find that while luxury goods like silk and glass traveled from one side of a continent to the other, the trade routes were actually sustained by short-range trade of food goods and other staples. The popular story of European exploration credits a European desire for cheaper spices, and in particular cutting out the Indian Ocean and Middle Eastern middlemen who brought them to Europe, in order that food might not be so bland. And the global trading networks that grew out of the colonial system were built, at least in part, on the consumable goods trade – sugar and rum in the Atlantic, for instance, tea and eventually opium in Asia. In the metropoles, such as London, too, new foods had an impact on more than just traders' pocketbooks, but were incorporated into culture and society. For example, sugar was combined in England with another colonial product – tea – to create a new pick-me-up for the British laboring in factories and doing other kinds of physical labor (Mintz 1985; Pomeranz 2000).

Recent studies indicate that the introduction of these new products had more than an anecdotal cultural impact on the British population, particularly as trade grew in the nineteenth century. In his comparative study of Europe and China, Kenneth Pomeranz (2000) notes that Britain vastly outpaced the rest of the European continent in sugar consumption. In 1800, for instance, British per capita consumption of sugar was 18 pounds, more than four times the per capita consumption one hundred years earlier (Pomeranz 2000). Even with this increase, Britain did not match Chinese sugar consumption levels until the late nineteenth century. Regardless, Pomeranz argues that in England (and eventually in the other parts of Europe as well), sugar made a transition from "highly desired 'spice' to staple carbohydrate" (Pomeranz 2000: 125), filling a nutrient gap for British workers at the same time that British agricultural productivity fell: "An environment in which calories were unusually scarce and many of the poor were also struggling to adapt to new rhythms of work (including having their midday meals at their job) was a perfect one for the penetration of sugar into the core of the English diet" (ibid.: 126). Through expansion of trade and improvements in technology, globalization of the food system meant that foods that were once luxury or specialty goods rapidly became dietary staples (Mintz 1985; Pomeranz 2000).

Scholars have recognized that food also plays an important role as a signifier of values, class, and nationality. As Arjun Appadurai (1988) shows in research on the spread of cookbooks outside their home regions in India, food can sometimes bridge class, ethnic, and language divides. Even as foods spread and appear to transcend cultural boundaries they can be understood quite differently in different contexts. In recent years, Americans have come to see the fast food restaurants that began in the 1950s as emblematic of major problems with America's eating habits, food system and culture (Schlosser 2002). In contrast, as anthropologist Yan Yunxiang (Yan 2000) noted in a study of McDonald's in Beijing, China, while Chinese patrons perceived McDonald's food and the design of its restaurants as quintessentially "American," they also saw McDonald's as serving healthy, safe food in an environment that provided equality of leisure, gender, and age groups.

This brief review of the halting, tenuous, and failure-prone nature of human transitions to agricultural and more modern changes in food systems provides some explanation as to why human beings in many places, despite great advances in science and technology, still have difficulty producing and gaining access to enough food. Discussions of food security are at their core about the amount, variety, and types of foods humans need to live healthy lifestyles. It is vitally important to be mindful of this rich and complex history of interactions between nature and humans in search of food. As the next section will discuss, human efforts to provide sufficient food have also been a major factor in human interactions with the environment and a driving force of global environmental change.

Agriculture, food production, and environmental change

Throughout history, the ways in which people satisfy their needs for food – including hunting, gathering, fishing, farming, and raising livestock – have been significant contributors to human impact on the environment. Transitions from hunter gathering to agriculture, the development of settled societies, and the increasing industrialization and intensification of agriculture in the modern era have all resulted in significant localized impacts that have increasingly aggregated into global impacts. Historically, unsustainable agricultural and food production practices have driven many of the worst instances of human-induced environment change and have contributed to the decline of many civilizations (Worster 1979; Diamond 2005). In recent decades, greater attention to the environmental impacts of agriculture and food production have revealed that activities related to the production, transportation, and consumption of food make significant contributions to processes of global change. Food production will in turn experience significant impacts as a result of those processes of environmental change (Steinfeld 2006; Easterling et al. 2007; IPCC 2007). The acceleration of connections between the world's places and peoples has highlighted the important links between how humans produce, distribute, and consume foodstuffs and pressing social, political, economic, and environmental issues.

As discussed above, though not an easy or always successful transition, human societies that cultivated crops and domesticated livestock flourished, and food became one of the major drivers of trade and globalization. Agriculture and food production thus became major sources of significant and widespread impacts on the environment. For example, Anne Osborne describes how the introduction of New World crops (particularly sweet potatoes and peanuts) led to significant environmental changes in the prosperous Chinese Yangtze River Delta in the nineteenth century. Prior to the introduction of New World crops, the primary agriculture occupation in this region was rice-cropping. As they could be grown on the previously wild hilltops and highlands above the rice fields, crops from the New World opened up new agricultural possibilities. However, once cleared and planted, the hillside soil was rapidly exhausted and when the migrant farmers who had cleared the hills moved on, the soil from the cleared hillsides ran into rice fields, streams, and eventually into waterways. The runoff, coupled with decreased government spending on dredging and waterway maintenance, contributed to the increased flooding and other water conservancy problems China experienced during the nineteenth century (Osborne 1994). Historical studies are also valuable in that they demonstrate the errors in seeing the lower classes and others on the margins as always eking out their existence at the expense of the environment. As Madhav Gadgil and Ramachandra Guha explain, the caste system in India to some degree (and for a certain period of time) ensured the conservation of natural resources. When a single caste's livelihood was dependent on a single resource – timber, say – the caste group worked to preserve it. Colonial policies in India, however, undermined some of those traditional systems, increasing the exploitation and then destruction of India's natural resources. This environmental degradation led, in part, to the widespread famines in the late nineteenth century (Gadgil and Guha 1996).

Mike Davis further explores the environmental causes of those late nineteenth-century famines, arguing that these devastating but largely forgotten famines resulted from the combination of weather pattern shifts (specifically an El Niño/Southern Oscillation that changed rainfall patterns across the Middle East, South and

Southeast Asia, and in the Americas in 1876–1878) and the forced incorporation of local economies into increasingly global markets. As Davis notes, the droughts of the late 1870s were only "the first of three global subsistence crises in the second half of Victoria's reign" (Davis 2001: 6). There were again droughts in 1889–91 and in 1896–1902 that affected broad swaths of the globe, triggering massive famines without regard to national boundaries, and often followed by "epidemics of malaria, bubonic plague, dysentery, smallpox and cholera" that "culled millions of victims from the ranks of the famine-weakened" (ibid.: 6–7). Davis estimates the combined death toll for the late Victorian famines as at least 30 million and perhaps as high as 50 million. Though changing weather patterns are central to explaining these famines, Davis emphasizes that bad weather alone cannot account for the high death tolls. Instead, he notes that the famine's effects were most deeply felt in places where the state lacked either the capacity or the will to aid famine victims. In many cases, that state capacity was limited by the emerging global economy, which had impoverished states once capable of dealing with internal famines (such as Qing China), making them increasingly vulnerable to colonization (and under colonial rule, states were even less likely to be responsive to local needs, as they were fundamentally extractive enterprises, such as in British India) (ibid.).

While many of the negative impacts of human activities on the environment have been unintentional, as Davis indicates, some of the most significant impacts have been the result of economic and political processes that were working as intended. Historian James Scott argues that elements of the modernist project – or perhaps rather its underlying logic of mapping and standardizing the environment – have led to both human and natural disasters. Scott makes a particular point of the potentially negative consequences of the modernist project in regard to nature and agriculture, and especially in its efforts of "administrative ordering of nature and society" (Scott 1998: 4). As he notes, monocultures are "more vulnerable to . . . disease and weather than polycultures" (ibid.: 21), and the emphasis on productivity and technology that encouraged the shift to monoculture has not actually achieved the levels of consistent productivity promised in the twentieth century. As Scott argues, monoculture has not only created a multitude of further vulnerabilities but also "has failed in important ways to represent the complex, supple, negotiated objectives of real farmers and their communities" (ibid.: 262).

Similarly, environmental historian Donald Worster argues that while many of the worst instances of environmental degradation may not have been intentional, they were not entirely unintentional either but were rather the result of intensified use and exploitation of the environment and natural resources. Worster notes that unsustainable agricultural practices have driven many of the worst instances of human-induced environment change. Notable examples of human driven changes include: the deforestation of China's uplands around 3000 BC, the deforestation of Mediterranean vegetation over the course of many centuries of human habitation, and the more recent example of the North American Dust Bowl during the twentieth century (Worster 1979: 4). In the United States and Canada during the late 1800s and early 1900s, intensive cultivation led to the dust storms of the 1930s. Dust storms darkened skies from the Great Plains to as far away as Washington, DC and hundreds of thousands were left without homes and livelihoods as soil blew into the Atlantic Ocean and banks foreclosed on loans farmers could not pay. However, unlike previous instances of human-induced environmental change, the Dust Bowl "cannot be blamed on illiteracy or overpopulation or social disorder. It came about because the culture was operating in precisely the way it was supposed to. Americans blazed their way across a richly endowed continent with a ruthless, devastating efficiency unmatched by any people anywhere" (ibid.: 4). Worster continues that while some of the worst instances of environmental degradation may come from natural causes, such as hurricanes, "others are the slowly accumulating effects of ignorance or poverty. The Dust Bowl, in contrast, was the inevitable outcome of a culture that deliberately, self-consciously, set itself the task of dominating and exploiting the land for all it was worth" (ibid.). The memory of the Dust Bowl lives on in the photos of Dorothea Lange, John Steinbeck's novel *The Grapes of Wrath,* and songs by Woody Guthrie, Nanci Griffith, and Bruce Springsteen, but also in continued concerns that unsustainable agricultural and food production practices could prove to be major factors in providing new generations with memories of dust bowls, floods, changing climates, or other forms of environmental change that will have major impacts on human security and well-being.

Intensified agricultural and food production were made easier by the development of technologies such as the steel plow and innovations in irrigation that allowed fewer people to farm more land while also increasing productivity. Intensification and changing technology also increased the environmental impacts of agriculture. Jason Clay locates the beginnings of major changes in global agriculture to the invention of the steel plow by John Deere in 1837: "As the plows and the machines that pulled them got bigger, more and more land could be farmed by fewer people. Every increase in scale and intensity, however, had environmental impacts as well. Over time it has become apparent that agricultural practices, more than any single factor, have determined the state of the global environment" (Clay 2004: 1). Agricultural practices also play a role in reducing the ability of natural ecosystems to provide useful services such as regulating climate and filtering water as well as using renewable natural resources, such as soil, at rates that are not renewable. For example, one estimate finds that soil is being depleted at a rate of one to two orders of magnitude (between 10 and 100 times) greater than it is being replenished (Montgomery 2007). Agriculture and food production contributes to localized environmental changes, but is also a factor driving the large-scale process of global change. Agricultural practices can contribute to a considerable share of many countries' emissions of greenhouse gases, including gases such as carbon dioxide from land clearance and deforestation and also gases that result from crop and livestock production like methane, nitrous oxide, and ammonia (FAO 2003a; Clay 2004).

Although food is produced around the world in a variety of ecological, social, and political circumstances, it is possible to identify similarities in methods of production. In their 1987 report, the World Commission on Environment and Development (WCED) recognized the emergence of three broad types of agricultural systems: industrial agriculture, Green Revolution agriculture, and resource-poor agriculture. Industrial agriculture is capital and resource intensive, tends to be large scale, and favor large producers. This form of agriculture is primarily found in developed regions and in some small areas in developing regions. Green Revolution agriculture is a system of production that developed during and following the "Green Revolution," the period from the early 1940s to 1970s where implementation of research-based agricultural methods and new technologies allowed significant increases in global agricultural production, especially in developing countries (Brown 1970; Evenson and Gollin 2003; Shaw 2007). Green Revolution agriculture is typically found in flat, irrigated and resource-rich areas in developing countries such as Mexico, India, and Pakistan. While this type of agriculture was initially adopted on larger farms, its technologies and methods are increasingly accessible to smaller producers. Finally, resource-poor agriculture usually occurs in difficult-to-farm areas, such as drylands, highlands, and forests, in developing countries. Resource-poor agricultural production often occurs in areas with fragile soils and depends on rain water for irrigation of crops. Despite their differences, each of these three types of agricultural systems is similar in that all three systems of food production face signs of crisis that threaten their ability to continue to produce food (WCED 1987; Shaw 2007).

Improvements in methods of agricultural production, storage, and transportation during the twentieth century allowed significant increases in global agricultural production, especially in developing countries. Assessing the impacts of these improvements in agricultural production, Peter Hazell writes that "the story of English Wheat is typical. It took near 1,000 years for wheat yields to increase from 0.5 to 2 metric tons per hectare, but only 40 years to climb from 2 to 6 metric tons per hectare" (Hazell 2002: 1). By the early 1970s, however, production improvements had begun to level off and a series of severe weather events that occurred simultaneously in many parts of the world contributed to a global food crisis that revealed how unpredictable and fragile the world food security situation remained (Shaw 2007). In recent decades, increases in agricultural production have begun to level off while a growing body of work has documented the many local and global environmental impacts of agricultural and food production activities. These developments have focused attention on the need to advance and use technologies and methods that reduce the environmental impacts of agriculture and food production while also finding ways to address persistent sources of food insecurity through the sustainable intensification of food production (Royal Society 2009).

When considering challenges to food security, it is important to recognize the tremendous benefits that have arisen from the intensification and industrialization of agriculture and food production. Most notably, the increases in agricultural productivity have so far allowed circumvention of the kinds of food shortages Thomas Malthus predicted, as described in the previous chapter. As Vaclav Smil writes, "that our ingenuity has been able to feed this ever larger and ever-faster growing population has been humanity's most important existential achievement" (Smil 2000: 2). While the increasing speed, scale, and density of food production practices have had significant impacts on the global environment, these processes have also resulted in tremendous gains in human well-being and livelihoods. Improvements in food and agricultural production have allowed not just for an increase in the number of people on the planet, but also general improvements in diet and human health, including significant reductions in chronic malnutrition (Fogel 2004). Since the global food crisis of the 1970s, the speed, scale, and density of interactions in food and agricultural production systems have been accelerated by the globalization process and, as discussed in chapter 1, have resulted in the rise of a network of global food systems. Recent global experiences with food price crises and global economic disruptions have once again focused attention on the significant challenges that remain to making certain that all people have enough food to lead healthy lives. But, as will be discussed in the next chapter, the world has begun to change economically and demographically and these processes of global change are dramatically transforming the food security landscape. Trends such as global population growth, urbanization, changing patterns of production and consumption, and global climate change pose considerable challenges to ensuring food security.

3 Global Trends Impacting Food Security

As discussed in previous chapters, globalization and global environmental change are having dramatic impacts on many aspects of daily life; the global food system has been and continues to be considerably transformed by the increasing speed, scale, and density of global interactions. Efforts to ensure food security are linked into a range of current global issues. This chapter reviews five major trends that are having significant impacts on food security. The chapter begins by discussing rising global population rates and changes in patterns of population demographics. Next it considers the impact of changing diets and food consumption patterns. Then, it reviews concerns about rising prices of food. The fourth section covers the development of new technologies in the biological sciences, including genetic modification, which have become rapidly integrated into agriculture and food production activities. The chapter's final section discusses global climate change and the impacts that climate change could have on food security. In addition to assessing the effects that each of these trends is having on global security, the discussions in this chapter provide an orienting foundation for more detailed examinations later in the book of three core sets of challenges to food security.

Population growth and demographic change

In the coming decades, food security will be impacted by global population growth and changing demographic patterns. Global population has been growing steadily over the past few centuries and saw significant increases during the twentieth century growing from 1.7 billion in 1900 to just over six billion in 2000. While demographers do not expect that the twenty-first century will see a "population explosion" like the twentieth century did, the number of people on the planet will continue to increase over coming decades from around 6.8 billion people in 2009 to an estimated 9.2 billion people by 2050 according to the United Nations Population Fund (UNFPA) "medium-variant" scenario. At the same time that the size of global population is growing, the demographic composition of world population is also shifting. Much of global population growth is expected to occur in developing countries, with estimates that 90 percent of world population will live in less developed regions by 2050. The world's population is also becoming increasingly urban, with more than half of the world's population now living in urban areas (for the first time in human history), and urban areas are expected to absorb almost all the projected global population increase through 2050. World population is also growing older, with expectations that, by 2050, nearly one in three people in developed countries will be aged 60 or older (UNDP 1999; Smil 2000; UNFPA 2009).

The character of population growth in the twenty-first century will be largely shaped by its location primarily in urban areas in developing regions. As Jack Goldstone writes, international security in the coming decades "will depend less on how many people inhabit the world than on how the global population is composed and distributed; where populations are declining and where they are growing, which countries are relatively older and which are more youthful, and how demographics will influence population movements across regions" (Goldstone 2010: 31–2). The nature of demands on the global food system will be shaped by increasing numbers of people, but also heavily impacted by the composition and distribution of global population growth. Population growth that is centered in urban areas in the world's poorest countries will also likely see amplification in the number of urban poor living in slums. Already, one out of every three people living in cities, or about 1 billion people (around one sixth of the world's population) live in slums and over 90 percent of slum dwellers today are in the developing world (UNFPA 2007). "In sub-Saharan Africa, urbanization has become virtually synonymous with slum growth; 72 percent of the region's urban population lives under slum conditions, compared to 56 per cent in South Asia. The slum population of sub-Saharan Africa almost doubled in 15 years, reaching nearly 200 million in 2005" (UNFPA 2007: 16). An increase in urban populations, especially with regards to increasing populations living in slum conditions, will likely lead to a continuation, if not acceleration, of trends associated with rapid urban growth in the nineteenth and twentieth centuries, including insufficient sanitation, education, and public health systems (UN Habitat 2007).

In reviewing such population statistics and trends however, it is important, as Betsy Hartmann (2009) cautions, to be mindful about uncritically taking on assumptions with regards to population growth that reinforce stereotypes about destructive and dangerous poor by deterministically linking population growth with social ills such as increased rates of migration, environmental impact, and poverty. However, it is also vitally important to recognize the very real inequalities between people in the world who live in developed countries and those that live in developing countries. As Richard A. Matthew and Anne Hammill write, "a vast gap between rich and poor persists that can be expressed in a single, widely affirmed, measure: roughly 80 per cent of the natural resources used each year are consumed by about 20 per cent of the world's population" (Matthew and Hammill 2009: 2). This inequality shapes the character of development challenges in years and decades to come, with the most persistent challenges to development faced by "the bottom-billion," the people in the world who live in countries that "coexist with the twenty-first century, but their reality is the fourteenth century: civil war, plague, ignorance" (Collier 2007: 3). As Paul Collier describes, these bottom billion live in societies that are caught in four traps: the conflict trap, the natural resources trap, the geographical trap of being landlocked with bad neighbors, and the trap of bad governance and economic policies in a small country.

Food security will thus face a challenge from a growing global population while also facing the need to come to terms with the impacts of global climate change on food and agriculture. These trends indicate a need for sustained effort to examine the variety of local and global factors – including food production as well as challenges such as poverty, governance, and trade issues – that contribute to food insecurity. In many of the places where food security is a pressing problem, efforts will also need to be mindful of the long legacy of previous efforts that have failed to fully eliminate food insecurity.

Current projections indicate that world agriculture and food production will likely be able to produce sufficient food to meet population growth (Godfray et al. 2010). However, understanding the probability that food production can meet needs should not deter us from recognizing that ensuring food security will involve significant economic, ethical, political, social, and technical challenges. Efforts to address food insecurity involve many important questions related to defining what needs global food production is seeking to satisfy. Far from philosophical discussions, the ways in which human needs are defined will lead to many questions such as choices about the sorts of food that will be grown, the methods and impacts of food production that will be used, and what sorts of standards for diet, nutrition, and access will guide efforts. Given likely trends in population growth through the middle of this century, efforts to feed a growing human population will remain a significant source of pressure on the food system for the foreseeable future (WCED 1987; Smil 2000; Pinstrup-Andersen 2002; FAO 2003a; UNFPA 2007; Beddington 2009; United States Joint Forces Command 2010).

Changing diets and food consumption patterns

Food security is also being impacted by changes in global patterns of wealth and prosperity which are altering patterns of food production and consumption and increasing the environmental impacts of agricultural and livestock production. People with increased purchasing power, often in developing countries such as Brazil, China, or India, are able to pay more for staple crops and, as they become wealthier, they are adding more meat to their diets. In the 1990s, less than half of all meat consumed worldwide was eaten in developing countries; by 2006, this figure had risen to nearly 60 percent, although consumers in the developed world continue to eat the most meat per person (Nierenberg 2006). In response to this demand, global rates of meat and poultry production have been steadily increasing. In 2006, 83.7 million tons of poultry was produced worldwide, and this figure was expected to increase in 2007 by 3 percent to more than 86 million tons. With regards to beef, there were 66.2 million tons of beef produced in 2006 and it was expected that this amount would increase by 1.3 percent in 2007 to 67.1 million tons. Overall, global meat production doubled between 1977 and 2003 and by 2002 developing countries had overtaken industrialized countries as meat producers (Nierenberg 2003). Consumption patterns are also driving continued record-high fish catch rates. In 2003, 132.5 million tons of seafood were harvested; much of the catch came from lakes, rivers, and oceans (77.7 million tons), but a growing portion (54.8 million tons) came from aquaculture which has become an increasing method to supplement declining ocean and freshwater fish stocks (Halweil 2006; Nierenberg 2006; FAO 2007).

Increasing livestock production has also enlarged the amount of resources devoted to producing animal protein as well as the impacts of livestock production. Increased production of meat means that increasing amounts of grain – the majority of corn and soybeans produced globally – are used to raise livestock. Increased production of livestock and aquaculture has been linked to increases in air and water pollution and concerns about health threats from concentration of animal wastes, impacts on land, soil, and water, and it contributes to problems such as the creation of antibiotic resistant microbes and rising levels of pharmaceutical residues in water supplies. Recognition of environmental and health impacts of large-scale livestock raising operations is an excellent example of the real and significant political, economic, and social challenges involved in ensuring food security in a sustainable manner. Producers must struggle with the need to address growing consumer demands for meat and dairy products while also facing pressures to keep costs as low as possible. At the same time, there are significant pressures related to the environmental impacts of raising livestock that must also be considered (Halweil 2006; Nierenberg 2006; Ellis and Turner 2007; FAO 2007).

Balancing competing demands from the need to sustainably intensify food production to meet growing demands for food while also responding to consumer demands for more meat and dairy products will be a significant challenge for food systems in coming decades. Changing diets and food consumption patterns have a number of impacts on outcomes like nutrition, livelihoods, and well-being.

Shifting consumption patterns are also considerable determining factors on the environmental impacts of agriculture and food production activities. Appraising the amount of cropland available for use by food production activities, Vaclav Smil points out that "total land requirements in a world of nine to ten billion people will depend heavily on the composition of their average diets" (Smil 2000: 38). Questions about whether there is land or water in the world to provide enough food for all people to be secure are thus intimately linked to questions about what sorts of diets people consume. For example, the amount of land needed per person varies enormously based upon diet. Smil (2000) estimates that the average diet in many developed countries that includes a large portion of meat and dairy products requires up to 4000 square meters per person of land while a largely vegetarian diet produced through high-intensity agriculture could require around 800 square meters per person of land. Even within typical diets in developed countries, the amount of resources required vary considerably if meat is provided primarily by chicken and pigs (1,500 m^2/capita) or whether it comes from large amounts of beef in diets (3,000 m^2/capita). Similar patterns exist with regards to demands on water resources, requirements for crop nutrients, and impacts on agroecosystems (Smil 2000; Clay 2004; Brown 2009).

A key component of efforts to ensure food security must thus involve discussions about the sorts of diet that people will consume. Questions about the full impacts of changing diets are complex and must take into account the full impacts of choices; they must also be able to address the many political and economic questions, such as the impact of subsidies and trade barriers on prices for meat, that impact dietary choices. Given the complexity of the global food system, it is also imperative to be highly skeptical of notions that less meat in diets would deterministically lead to reductions in environmental impacts and improvements in food security. As Erik Stokstad (2010) points out, crops such as corn or soybeans, which are staples in the diets of livestock raised in developed countries, are not staple crops in diets in many parts of the world where food insecurity is a problem; thus, freeing up grain production in developed countries would not deterministically lead to improvements in food insecurity. Such recognitions, however, should not deter further investigations into the connections between diet and food security. There are many cultural, economic, historical, political, and social factors that are involved in dietary choices. Returning to the guiding principles of human security, it will be vitally important that individuals and communities be involved in discussions about desired diets. In increasing numbers of places in both developed and developing countries, policymakers, experts, and the public have begun conversations about the long-term and widespread impacts on health and well-being of transition to diets made up of energy-dense but nutrient-poor foods, especially on children. Such conversations should also be expanded to incorporate discussions about the environmental impacts of dietary choices and food preferences to encourage individuals, communities, and states to develop strategies that address world food problems that are not driven solely by economic efficiency, but which also take into account questions of justice, equity, and sustainability (Smil 2000; Brown 2009; Stokstad 2010).

The global food price crisis of the early twenty-first century

By the spring of 2008, political figures, media outlets, and international forums confirmed what many around the world had been feeling for months; global food prices were on the rise. Rarely the subject of front-page stories or special reports, the global food price crisis pushed food insecurity onto political, media, and economic agendas. Prices for many staple foods including corn, wheat, cooking oil, and meat experienced a steady increase beginning in late 2006 and rising sharply during 2007. FAO's Food Price Index (FFPI), a weighted average of six commodity price indices, rose from 115 in 2005 to 122 in 2006 to 154 in 2007 before peaking at 208 in June 2008 (this index had fallen to 162 by March of 2010). Tracking the price trend for specific commodities tells a similar story of rapid increases to record levels. For instance, the price per ton for wheat doubled between May and September 2007 from $200 to $400 (setting a new world price record) while corn rose to over $175 per ton (another world record), a price that was more than 50 percent higher than the

2006 price (*The Economist*, December 7, 2008). The complex, interactive and networked-based nature of food insecurity in the twenty-first century was clearly demonstrated by the range of causal factors identified to explain the rise in global food prices.

A range of causes and driving forces, including economic, political, social, and environmental factors, were identified as contributing to rising food prices. Among the factors identified were: global population growth; increasing prosperity among consumers in economies like China and India who are able to pay more for food, eat bigger meals, and are transitioning to diets that include more meat; changes and variability in climate and severe weather events that reduced harvests of key staples in many parts of the world; declining world food stockpiles; the imposition of export restrictions by countries such as Argentina and the Ukraine which restricted exports in an effort to lessen local impacts of global price rises; global financial trends as investors fled from bad mortgage and credit markets and sought stability in commodities like wheat and rice; unintended impacts from efforts to promote biofuels; and rising global oil prices which made running food production and transportation more expensive while also increasing the costs of key food inputs such as fertilizers and pesticides (Ban 2008; Beddington 2009; FAO 2009). As this range of factors demonstrates, the causes of rising prices are fundamentally interlinked with other major trends in the global food system and major global problems.

Along with recognition of problems came awareness that factors driving price increases were not primarily anomalies, and that resulting higher food prices were likely to persist for years to come. In April 2008, Robert Zoellick, the president of the World Bank, called for governments to meet the World Food Program's (WFP) call for $500 million in emergency aid by May 1, 2008. In addition to meeting short-term needs for immediate food aid to help millions of people deeply affected by rising prices, Zoellick commented "This is not just a question of short term needs, as important as they are . . . This is about ensuring that future generations don't pay a price too" (*CNN*, April 13, 2008). Recognition of the likelihood that causal factors will persist for some years to come have prompted calls for action to help protect the poor from rising food prices, including strategies such as:

emergency increases in food aid programs, and providing inputs to stimulate production of staple crops, such as corn or rice, in the most impacted countries; as well as commitments to increase the budget available to relief programs.

The impacts of rising food prices were considerable and included rapid and dramatic increases in the number of hungry people in the world (as discussed in chapter 4, estimates released in late 2009 indicate there are now more than a billion people in the world who do not have enough to eat on a daily basis), changing consumption behaviors as people try to cope at individual and family levels. For example, Pascal Joannes, a procurement manager for WFP in the Sudan, reported that prices for white beans rose from $235 to $1,160 for a metric ton in just two years (*Los Angeles Times*, April 1, 2008). In China, the price for pork, the most commonly consumed meat, rose 60 percent between early 2007 and early 2008, with the prices for cooking oil, rice, and other staples also seeing a significant increase (*AFP*, April 8, 2008). Rising food prices contributed to rioting and unrest in over sixty countries, including Burkina Faso, Cameroon, Egypt, Ethiopia, India, Indonesia, Italy, Ivory Coast, Mauritania, the Philippines, Senegal, Thailand, Uzbekistan, and Yemen (Clinton 2009). At the same time that many people in the world, especially the world's poor, face higher prices for food, there has also been a convergence of factors that are magnifying the impact of these price rises.

Rising food prices have also had considerable knock-on effects, including reducing aid flows and making banditry and piracy more lucrative. Such factors include reduced foreign direct investment; reduced flows of remittances, the crumbling of many coping and insurance schemes that had developed, and also reduced giving and support for aid agencies. For example, in 2009 the United Nations Refugee Agency (UNHCR) reported a 30 percent gap between food and fuel supply and demand for refugees (UNHCR 2009). Contributing to this gap were increases in banditry and hijacking directed at aid flows. In 2005 the United Nations Security Council cited pirate attacks on food aid shipments as a factor that prevented UN efforts to provide food aid to nearly 2 million people impacted by a drought in Somalia (*UN Daily News*, March 15, 2006). In April 2008, the UN World Food Program announced that it might be forced to reduce food rations for more than 3 million people because of attacks on trucks carrying food aid. WFP said that at least 60 trucks had been hijacked in Western Sudan since the start of 2008, resulting in a halving of deliveries of food rations during a crucial period of raising stocks prior to the commencement of Sudan's rainy season. In many parts of the world, rising food prices combined with impacts of the global economic recession to have widespread effects on health and well-being (WFP 2008; FAO 2009).

Although global food prices have eased somewhat from their highest levels in 2008, they remain substantially above pre-crisis levels in many parts of the world. The continuation of high food prices may be explained by noting that many of the long-term drivers which have been identified as contributing to rising food prices – such as global population growth, changing patterns of food demand and consumption, and global environmental change – remain unabated. The complex causes of a rise in food prices and the trends related to those causes mean that food prices are unlikely to fall significantly in the near term. These trends underscore the persistence of challenges to food security and highlight the complex sets of interconnected drivers which must be addressed to effectively reduce the local and global factors that inhibit people from having sufficient food to lead healthy lives.

Impacts of new technologies on agriculture and food production

Advances in technology – from increasing sophistication in crop breeding methods to improvements in irrigation methods to replacing human and animal power with machinery – have made extensive contributions to improvements in food production and enhancements in human well-being. In previous decades, there have been numerous developments in a range of fields that have contributed to improving the quantity and quality of food supplies. Reviewing the results of these developments, a 2009 report by the Royal Society found "the biological processes relevant to productivity of food crops can now be dissected more completely and there is an unprecedented opportunity to translate this research into the genetic improvement of crops or changes in crop management" (Royal Society 2009: 21). Many of these technological advances related to improved ability to undertake genetic analysis, identify a gene or set of genes that could be used to develop novel crop management techniques, or the ability to use genetic modification to make improvements in crops. Beyond boosting crop yields, these improvements in technologies could be essential to combating weeds, viruses, and fungi – such as stem rust and potato blight – that represent major biological threats to food supplies and food security (Royal Society 2009; NRC 2010; Pennisi 2010).

Although based on techniques originally developed in the early 1970s, genetic modification (GM) did not emerge as an issue of global concern until the late 1980s with the release of the first genetically modified organisms (GMOs) or products developed using genetic modification techniques. Genetic modification – also referred to as agricultural biotechnology or genetic engineering – can be broadly defined as any technology associated with the manipulation of biological organisms to make products that benefit human beings. This collection of technologies and methods includes techniques that begin with the identification and analysis of genes and deoxyribonucleic acid (DNA) using molecular biology, and include techniques to isolate, extract, and clone fragments of DNA or genes. These techniques also include gene splicing, which is used to separate DNA fragments and connect fragments from different sources as well as the ability to transfer or insert DNA into the cell of a higher plant or animal, and then use the altered cells to recover and reproduce a new organism that contains the introduced DNA. If a gene is inserted into the DNA of an organism under the right conditions, it is possible to force an organism to express proteins, even if those proteins were not originally part of their genome. These expressions are called "novel proteins." Such proteins could be ones that provide resistance to herbicides, cause the production of insulin, or prevent the maturation of seeds (Grace 1997; McHughen 2000; Royal Society 2009).

In the field of agriculture, GM has been rapidly adopted because it offers the potential to reduce the time required to produce new plant cultivar (crop plant) varieties. Conventional breeding methods involve crossing one variety of cultivar with another to introduce a desired trait to the original cultivar. For instance, a common example is the development of a variety of rice that can produce more grains of rice, but thus becomes so heavy that the tops of the plants fall onto the ground where they are more susceptible to pests and diseases. A breeder then might cross the high-producing rice with a dwarf rice plant to produce a high-producing plant that is shorter and thus not as likely to fall over. The complication with conventional breeding methods is that along with the desired protein to produce shorter plants may come thousands or tens of thousands of proteins for other traits that are not as desirable. Breeders must spend years breeding out the undesirable traits in a new line of crop plants. Understandably, such a process becomes even more complex if breeders are seeking to combine products from multiple varieties of plants. The appeal of GM is that it allows a breeder to select the individual desired trait, and introduce only the DNA fragment necessary to produce that trait. The average time required to develop a new cultivar through conventional breeding is twelve to thirteen years, while genetically modified cultivars can be developed in six years (McHughen 2000). Some crops, such as potatoes and bananas which are not grown from seed, are also very difficult to breed (Royal Society 2009). Genetic modification technologies allow the identification, insertion, and transfer of genes within species in shorter time periods than conventional plant breeding (McHughen 2000; Lambrecht 2001; Royal Society 2009).

Beyond facilitating cross-breeding of related species, genetic modification also allows the transfer of genes between species of plants. As DNA and genes are instructions for assembling amino acids into proteins, and since all cells contain the same twenty amino acids, most organisms are able to assemble a wide variety of proteins if given the proper genetic recipe. Thus, it is theoretically possible to insert DNA from a fish into a tomato, and the tomato will contain a protein created by the fish DNA fragment. Additionally, inserting multiple gene fragments raises the possibility of creating plants that are able to express traits from multiple species. For example, such plants could produce their own insecticides and fertilizers, have enhanced frost tolerance, and last longer once picked. It is the ability to transfer DNA across species boundaries that underlies many concerns about genetic modification technologies, as many groups and individuals express unease about the ability of science to develop and deliver products to the market that may contain genes one would not normally expect to find in foods (McHughen 2000; Lambrecht 2001; Royal Society 2009).

Almost immediately after the introduction of the first genetically modified crops in the late 1980s, scientists, citizens, farmers, and activist groups raised a variety of questions about the impacts of the introduction of genetically modified organisms on food systems and food security. These groups cited concerns that included questions about lack of transparency and access to the national and international forums where topics related to genetic modification were being debated. Concerns about GMOs were one of the issues which helped motivate the protests directed against a 1999 ministerial conference of the World Trade Organization (WTO) in Seattle, Washington. Other concerns about GMOs include market concentration in the seed industry; intellectual property rights; biological security concerns about a range of topics including, but not limited to, transfer of modified genes into microbes or pest species, transfer of allergens, mutation of genes, transfer of traits such as sterility; and impacts on animal welfare and biodiversity. A central aspect of these concerns revolves around the impacts of releasing products tested in controlled laboratories or field sites into much more complex ecological systems and the complexity involved in trying to achieve some form of bioremediation if it is found that genes have indeed escaped into wild populations. While such concerns have not halted the use of genetically modified crops, they have raised significant questions about how and where biotech foods will be grown, traded, and consumed. Questions about genetically modified organisms inspired international legal efforts that attempted to define and regulate the use of genetic modification techniques, including the Cartagena Protocol on Biosafety and the Codex Alimentarius Intergovernmental Task Force on Foods Derived from Biotechnology (Grace 1997; Gottweis 1998; McHughen 2000; Shiva 2000; Lambrecht 2001; NRC 2002; FAO 2003a).

These concerns, however, have not prevented the rapid adoption of GM in the United States and around the world. Since its introduction, GM has rapidly become a large segment of the global agricultural sector. By 2002, GM products accounted for 66 percent of land area planted as crops in the United States, and the global area planted with transgenic crops has grown rapidly, from 27.5 million acres in 1997 to 145 million acres in 2002 (Pew Initiative on Food and Biotechnology 2003). By 2007, the US National Agricultural Statistics Service reported that 86 percent of all corn, 89 percent of all soybean, and 92 percent of all upland cotton were varieties that had been genetically modified (NASS 2007). By 2009, genetically modified crops accounted for 85 percent of all corn, 91 percent of all soybeans, and 88 percent of all cotton acreage being grown in the United States (NRC 2010).

One outcome of the debates over genetically modified food was the emergence of a new, more complex form of environmentalism that links concerns about environmental degradation with concerns about social justice and human security. In the mid-1990s, concerns about genetic modification emerged, alongside concerns for environmental justice and pro-poor conservation, as code words for a more inclusive conceptualization of environmentalism that includes concerns previously seen as external to environmental politics such as race, class, and poverty alleviation. These concerns include topics such as development, human rights, security, and linkages between urban livelihoods and rural conditions. Concerns about GM and GMOs also resonated with a notion gaining support in the late 1980s and early 1990s that when the consequences of human actions are unclear, they should be guided by the Precautionary Principle. Adopted as Principle 15 of the 1992 Rio Declaration on Environment and Development, the Precautionary Principle holds that "where there are threats of serious or irreversible damage, lack of full scientific certainty shall not be used as a reason for proposing cost-effective measures to prevent environmental degradation" (UNEP 1992b). These disparate sets of actors have been using questions about genetic modification as a way to look at the world and identify what it was they sought to change and pointed to growing awareness of global climate change as an example of the significant impacts human action could have on the environment.

The rise of questions about the social, ecological, and political impacts of genetically modified organisms also emerged at a time when consumers in many developed countries were expressing growing interest in foods produced using organic or sustainable methods. The emergence of GMOs that did not seem to offer immediate benefits to consumers also seemed at odds with the growing movement around good, healthy, natural foods represented by writers such as Michael Pollan (2001, 2006, 2009a, 2009b), Maria Rodale (2010), and Eric Schlosser (2002) as well as social movements such as the Slow Food Movement which was founded in 1989 by Italian Carlo Petrini "to counteract fast food and fast life, the disappearance of local food traditions and people's dwindling interest in the food they eat, where it comes from, how it tastes and how our food choices affect the rest of the world" (Slow Food Movement 2010). As will be discussed in more detail in chapter 5, while many questions remain about the safety, utility, and benefits of technologies such as genetic modification, there is growing consensus that advances in biological science represent an important component of efforts to address food insecurity. Beyond imperatives to meet rising demands from growing populations and changing diets, one of the most pressing challenges confronting the global food system will be the need to confront impacts on food and agricultural production from global climate change.

Climate change and food security

There is now enormous evidence and scientific agreement that human activities have contributed to changes in the earth's climate system. The impacts of changes in our planet's climate system could be far reaching and will have effects on people, societies, and security in all parts of the world. In general, climate is used to refer to the average weather, or a statistical description of the mean (average) and variability of relevant quantities (such as precipitation and temperature) over a given period of time (anywhere from months to millions of years, though the standard period used by the World Meteorological Organization is 30 years). The term "climate" is also used to describe the overall state of the climate system, which consists of five components, the atmosphere, the hydrosphere, the cryosphere, the land surface and the biosphere, and the interactions between the components. This climate system changes over time in response to its own internal dynamics and external factors such as volcanic eruptions. The state of the climate, however, can also be altered by human-generated factors (often referred to as forcings) such as changes in land-use and cover patterns (such as deforestation) and changes in the composition of the atmosphere. The concept of climate change thus refers to a statistically significant variation in either the mean state of the climate or in its variability. As noted above, these changes can be driven by the internal dynamics of the climate system or by external forces which can be either human caused (often referred to as anthropogenic) or arise from natural sources such as volcanic eruptions (IPCC 2007).

A great deal of scientific effort has gone into understanding the impacts of human activities on the global climate system. The Intergovernmental Panel on Climate Change (IPCC) is an international governmental organization formally established in 1988 by the World Meteorological Organization (WMO) and the United Nations Environment Program (UNEP) to examine the risk of human generated changes in the earth's climate systems. In its Fourth Assessment Report in 2007, IPCC concluded that "warming of the climate system is unequivocal, as is now evident from observations of increases in global average air and ocean temperatures, widespread melting of snow and ice, and rising global average sea level" (IPCC 2007). The Stern Review (2007) found that "the scientific evidence that climate change is a serious and urgent issue is now compelling" (Stern Review 2007: xiii). In 2009, the Met Office, the UK's National Weather Service, reported that if greenhouse gas (GHG) emissions continue to rise, the likely impact of global warming could be greater than four degrees (centigrade) by the end of the twenty-first century (Met Office 2009). In December 2009, WMO projected that 2009 was likely to rank in the ten warmest years on record since the beginning of climate recording in the 1850s, and that the decade 2000–2009 was warmer than preceding decades (WMO 2009). These findings from a variety of organizations reflect the strong scientific consensus that climate change is occurring and can be attributed to human actions which are generating noticeable and significant impacts on the climate system.

Based on the growing evidence that human actions are changing the global climate, prominent global leaders have called for recognizing climate change as one of the highest priority issues facing the international community. In 2006, UN Secretary-General Kofi Annan stated: "Global climate change must take its place alongside those threats – conflict, poverty, the proliferation of deadly weapons – that have traditionally monopolized first-order political attention" (Annan 2006). In 2007, UK Foreign Secretary David Miliband identified climate change as one of the three great insecurities facing the world (*NPR*, September 29, 2007). In addition to official attention, a number of efforts have been made to increase public awareness of climate change. Perhaps one of the most impactful efforts in the United States was *An Inconvenient Truth*, a 2006 film presented by former US Vice President Al Gore and directed by Davis Guggenheim which won the 2006 Academy Award for Documentary Feature. The general importance to human well-being of efforts to both continue to refine the scientific understanding of climate change and raise awareness of the problem was demonstrated in October 2007 when it was announced that the IPCC and Al Gore would share the 2007 Nobel Peace Prize (Nobel Foundation 2007). These recognitions also demonstrate a growing understanding that addressing climate change will be a process that involves actions in both scientific and political domains.

Notwithstanding the growing consensus of scientific information on climate change, there remains a considerable disconnect between agreement among international bodies and scientific experts and the understandings of the general public and political leaders. Despite what many consider to be general agreement on the scientific evidence of climate change, there remains considerable division among publics in many countries, including the United States (DiMento et al. 2007). For example, a December 2009 ABC News poll found rising levels of public doubt about scientific information on the environment, with four out of ten Americans (including 58 percent of self-identified Republicans and 40 percent of self-identified Independents) indicating they place little or no trust in information from scientists about the environment (*ABC News*, December 18, 2009). The impact of such divisions is moderated, however, by a continued willingness among Americans to support the regulation of greenhouse gas (GHG) emissions. For example, in the same ABC News poll, majorities of Americans support regulation of more stringent regulation of GHG emissions, even if such regulation leads to higher energy costs. These divisions were amplified by the release of hacked e-mails revealing discussions among climate scientists (dubbed "Climategate" by the global media) and the turbulence surrounding the 15th Conference of Parties meetings in Copenhagen which failed to produce a legally binding framework for climate change mitigation.

The impacts of climate change are expected to be widespread and felt in a range of sectors, including water resources, health, and food production. The likely impacts of global warming trends include regional changes such as contraction of snow cover, increased thawing of permafrost regions, and decreases in sea ice; increases in frequency of heat waves, and heavy precipitation; increased tropical cyclone intensity; and increase in precipitation at higher latitudes with likely decreases in precipitation in subtropical land regions. The Stern Review identified a number of mechanisms through which climate change will impact people including melting glaciers, declining crop yields, ocean acidification, rising sea levels, and a variety of impacts on ecosystems and species. Reviews of the potential impacts of climate change have also identified a number of threats from climate change to basic human livelihoods. One of the conclusions of the Stern Review is that "climate change threatens the basic elements of life for people around the world – access to water, food, health, and use of land and the environment" (Stern Review 2007: 65). There is growing recognition that climate change impacts will not be equally distributed. Areas such as Africa and Asia will face increasing levels of water scarcity, compromised food production, and impacts to coastal areas that could reduce fisheries and tourism revenues; regions like North America could see a 5 to 20 percent increase in agricultural yields, at least in the near term (IPCC 2007).

While global models about the impacts of climate change continue to be refined, there remains significant agreement about the probability of climate change. However, there is less understanding about the way that change and variability in the climate system will impact particular places. Gregg Easterbrook writes that "climate change could bring different regions of the world tremendous benefits as well as drastic problems. The world had been mostly warming for thousands of years before the industrial era began, and that warming has been indisputably favorable to the spread of civilization" (Easterbrook 2007). Easterbrook continues that the impacts from climate change could be significant, widespread, and uneven and could lead to significant changes in a global political geography that is largely organized based on a climate that has prevailed since the Middle Ages (ibid.). It is becoming increasingly clear that the impacts of climate change will have significant ramifications for national and international security as well as on the human security of individuals and communities.

Climate change has also been receiving an increasing amount of attention from security thinkers. A 2007 report by the CNA Corporation's Military Advisory Board (which is composed of retired senior US military officers), identified climate change as a serious risk to the national security of the United States. They concluded that climate change has the potential to add new hostile and stressing factors, act as a threat multiplier for instability in volatile regions of the world, draw the US more frequently into efforts to provide stability, and could even add tensions in stable regions of the world (CNA 2007). The German Advisory Council on Global Change found that "without resolute counteraction, climate change will overstretch many societies' adaptive capacities within the coming decades. This could result in destabilization and violence, jeopardizing national and international security to a new degree" (WGBU 2008: 1). A series of scenarios developed by a group of experts working under the auspices of the Center for a New American Security and the Center for Strategic and International Studies found that expected impacts of climate change (a global temperature increase of 1.3°C (2.3°F) by 2040) could lead to increased tensions, resource-driven conflict and increased pressures on failed and failing states while higher warming rates (5.6°C (10.8°F) by 2100) could have what scenario authors describe as abrupt and catastrophic effects, including more powerful, longer lasting and increasingly common hurricanes, droughts, heat waves and floods that impact the food, water, and national security of millions of people (Campbell 2008). The Joint Operating Environment 2010 also recognized climate change as an important trend that is likely to influence global security by having impacts on the coastal areas that house one-fifth of global population, contributing to rising tensions between Arctic nations, and increasing demands on US forces to respond to natural disasters caused or intensified by climate change (United States Joint Forces Command 2010).

It is vital to recognize that the impacts of climate change are not predetermined to be harmful and disruptive to peace and security. Recent security-focused analyses of climate change have recognized that shared threat and vulnerability from climate change could prove an effective motivator for cooperation and collaboration in activities that address climate threats and also enhance human health, security, and well-being. As the WGBU comments, "climate change could also unite the international community, provided that it recognizes climate change as a threat to humankind and soon sets the course for the avoidance of dangerous anthropogenic climate change by adopting a dynamic and globally coordinated climate policy" (WGBU 2008: 1). In its analysis, CNA (2007) recommends strategies which focus on technology and readiness of the US military and intelligence establishments. These strategies include incorporating climate change into national security and intelligence planning processes and assessing the vulnerability to US forces and facilities from climate change impacts, as well as outlining the need to use technology and improvements in logistics to improve the energy efficiency and operational capacities of US combat forces. However, CNA also recommends that the US "should commit to a stronger national and international role to help stabilize climate changes at levels that will avoid significant disruption to global security and stability," and that the US "should commit to global partnerships that help less developed nations build the capacity and resilience to better manage climate impacts" (CNA 2007: 46–7). Assessing the need for increased response by the US military forces, the United States Joint Forces Command (2010: 33) finds "the ability of US military forces to relieve the victims of natural disasters will impact the reputation of the United States in the world . . . perhaps no other mission performed by the joint Forces provides so much benefit to the interests of the United States at so little cost."

Thus, even while analyses focused on the national security implications of climate change make important recommendations for enhancing the ability of national security apparatuses to address threats and implications of climate change, they also recognize that climate change will require action beyond the spheres of traditional security activities. Richard Matthew (2007) argues that vulnerabilities introduced by climate change demonstrate the need to improve human security by addressing core vulnerabilities to human security threats. The need to respond to likely impacts with broad efforts that improve human security across a range of indicators is highlighted by the fact that while climate change may involve benefits to some – such as those countries and groups able to utilize newly navigable shipping channels or mineral, oil, and gas deposits revealed by retreating ice flows – it is becoming increasingly clear that the negative impacts from climate change are likely to fall disproportionately on the world's poorest and most vulnerable people. There is thus considerable irony in the likely pattern of impacts of climate change: the peoples who have done the least to contribute to and benefited the least from the processes that are driving climate change are both the least likely to benefit from changes and the most likely to be negatively impacted. Addressing threats from climate change will thus need to involve not only efforts to come to terms with changes in earth's climate system, but also finding ways to address persistent threats to human security, such as ill health and malnutrition, that will likely be amplified by and interact with climate change (Matthew 2007; Giddens 2009; Stern 2009).

As awareness has grown about the certainty and likelihood that climate change will have significant effects on all aspects of life on earth, an increasing amount of attention has been focused on identifying steps that can be taken to reduce the magnitude of climate change impacts. The most significant action that can be taken with regard to climate change is to reduce the GHG emissions that drive climate change. Taking into account current efforts to limit emissions and promote sustainable development, the IPCC reports that global GHG will continue to grow over the next few decades, perhaps by as much as 25 to 90 percent between 2000 and 2030 (IPCC 2007: 6). However, warming trends would continue even if drastic methods were taken to reduce emissions. The IPCC finds that "anthropogenic warming and sea level rise would continue for centuries due to the time scales associated with climate processes and feedbacks, even if GHG concentrations were to be stabilized" (IPCC 2007: 13). Thus, even under the most ideal circumstances that saw dramatic reductions in global GHG emissions, efforts will be necessary to moderate the effects of climate change. The IPCC reports that "societies have a long record of managing the impacts of weather and climate related events. Nevertheless, additional adaptation measures will be required to reduce the adverse impacts of projected climate change and variability, regardless of the scale of mitigation undertaken over the next two to three decades" (IPCC 2007: 14). Aside from efforts to reduce GHG emissions to lower the magnitude and impacts of climate change, there are a number of strategies that can be employed to reduce the effects of climate change and variability.

Efforts to reduce the magnitude of climate change and minimize the impacts of changes involve both adaptation and mitigation. IPCC defines adaptation as "initiatives and measures to reduce the vulnerability of natural and human systems against actual or expected climate change effects. Various types of adaptation exist, e.g. anticipatory and reactive, private and public, and autonomous and planned" (IPCC 2007: 76). Mitigation is defined as "technological change and substitution that reduce resource inputs and emissions per unit of output. Although several social, economic and technological policies would produce an emission reduction, with respect to climate change, mitigation means implementing policies to reduce greenhouse gas emissions and enhance sinks" (ibid.: 84). Thus, both adaptation – actions that reduce vulnerability to climate change effects – and mitigation – actions aimed at reducing the magnitude of global warming – are necessary to develop strategies to address impacts from global warming. In addition to adaptation and mitigation, recognition of the likely impacts of climate change has also spurred interest in the prospect of using geoengineering techniques to alter the earth's reflectivity and help absorb greenhouse gasses from the atmosphere (Caldeira 2009; Levitt and Dubner 2009). While geoengineering strategies include a range of ideas, proposals are often presented by proponents as solutions that will be easier to achieve than climate mitigation or adaption efforts. However, as a number of analyses have revealed, the difficulty, cost, long time frames involved and uncertainty associated with geoengineering proposals should not be underestimated (Blackstock 2009; Deudney and Grove 2009; Homer-Dixon 2009; Luke 2009).

As this chapter has discussed, the character of food security in the twenty-first century is being impacted by a variety of trends operating at multiple levels of activity, from individual, to domestic, to international, to global. Each of these trends is having an impact on food security, but considerable interactive effects among these trends also multiply their total impacts. For example, population growth, urbanization, changing consumption patterns, and climate change are all likely to place significant new stresses on the environment. The development of more sustainable and adaptive agricultural systems, in addition to providing strategies to address climate variability and change, could also provide an array of benefits to reduce the environmental impact of agriculture and food production by providing comprehensive frameworks that address problems such as impacts on land, water, and energy use while also ensuring food security, providing livelihoods and helping maintain health and well-being. As the next three chapters review, these trends, combined with the aggregate impacts of globalization, have transformed the character of food security as a global problem. Food security is being recognized as an area of first-order global political concern. Ensuring food security in the twenty-first century requires: addressing the three major categories of malnutrition that affect people; effectively confronting the impacts of global environmental change; and meeting the challenge of ensuring that food supplies and the global food system remain safe from contaminants, toxins, and harmful diseases.

4

Ensuring Proper Nutrition: The Challenge of Malnutrition in an Era of Global Change

Despite global agreement and the establishment of firm targets for hunger reduction, the number of malnourished people in the world has increased sharply in recent years. Rising global food prices, changing diets, natural disasters, severe weather events, and the global economic crisis have reinforced that one of the pressing challenges in the new millennium remains the age-old problem of food security. While improvements in food production and global health during the twentieth century allowed human societies to flourish – including dramatic increases in global population size, life expectancy, and reductions in infant and child mortality rates – malnutrition remains a widespread form of food insecurity that impacts billions of people on a daily basis. Malnutrition is more than just the physical sensation of hunger, but is the collective term applied to a variety of forms of poor nutrition.

Beyond significant problems from energy deficiencies, also called chronic hunger, malnutrition concerns are complicated by a significant number of individuals worldwide who are micronutrient deficient (because their diets do not provide proper vitamins and minerals) as well as increasing numbers of children and adults, in both developed and developing countries, that are overweight or obese. World food problems related to malnutrition in the twenty-first century thus remain focused around the threefold challenge to ensuring proper nutrition for all people: energy deficiencies, nutrient deficiencies, and excessive net energy intake. In a globalizing, networked world, a major requirement for food security is the need to develop a global food system that is able to adequately address the causes and drivers of each form of malnutrition. Providing all people with sufficient, safe, and nutritious food will require meeting short-term needs (like ensuring people get physical, social, and economic access to food) as well as long-term needs (such as making sure that people are able to make food choices that allow them to lead active and healthy lives). Malnutrition is only one aspect of food security (two other core challenges to food security will be addressed in the following chapters), but it is the foundational one.

Malnutrition has a broad range of direct and indirect impacts on human health and well-being. In addition to causing ill health, malnutrition undermines economic growth, perpetuates poverty, complicates education efforts, and increases vulnerability to and magnifies the impact of health threats such as infectious diseases and parasites. As will be discussed in more detail below, the causes of malnutrition are much more complex than just food availability; ensuring proper nutrition also requires confronting factors such as poverty, access to clean water and sanitation, good health, food choices, cultural traditions, and gender dynamics. Understanding the complex, multifaceted causes and forms of malnutrition is essential to developing efforts and policies that can halt and reverse the alarming growth in people impacted by all three forms of malnutrition. As will be discussed in the final section of the chapter, some of malnutrition's causes – like food choice – can best be addressed at the individual or household level, while others – like poverty – are often the result of domestic, interstate or even global trends and stresses. Moreover, some of these causes, such as international trade policies or global climate change, are factors which require action across multiple levels of analysis.

This chapter shows that while the character of challenges to ensuring all people receive proper nutrition may have shifted, food security continues to have significant impacts on the national security of states and the human security of people. The chapter is divided into three sections. The first section outlines current trends and data on the three forms of malnutrition. Many organizations have recognized the new dimensions of malnutrition challenges – which are not easily divided by regions of the world (for example, the popular notion that we would find primarily undernourishment in sub-Saharan Africa and primarily overnourishment in the United States). Instead, as the gap between the rich and the poor has escalated around the world in the past two decades, people who suffer from overweight and obesity often exist in the same countries, and sometimes even in the same households, with people who experience energy and nutrient deficiencies. The second section discusses the multiple causes and impacts of malnutrition. Finally, the last section considers the need to develop solutions that can address malnutrition at multiple levels of action, including the individual/household and the community level, as well as national or international factors that impact food availability, food prices, and food choices.

Malnutrition: A persistent challenge to food security

Globalization and global environmental change have given rise to a global food system that has amplified the magnitude of malnutrition problems. One result of this globalization of food insecurity is that there are pockets of abundance and scarcity in developed and developing countries and rates of chronic hunger and overweight/obesity are higher today than at any time in recent decades. A full discussion of malnutrition must thus encompass not just classical food security problems of chronic hunger (people who do not receive sufficient energy from their diets), but also must consider problems related to people who do not receive an adequate supply of vitamins and minerals and nutrients from their diets (micronutrient deficiencies) as well as people who have excessive net energy intake (also called overweight or obesity depending upon the severity of the condition). While popular discussions of malnutrition tend to focus on the immediate and highly impactful challenge of people who do not receive enough food, examinations of food security have long sought to raise understandings of the full range of malnutrition challenges. While the causes and specific impacts of malnutrition may vary between the underweight, the micronutrient deficient, and people who are overweight, each form of malnutrition has significant negative health impacts. For example, people who are underweight are susceptible to poor maternal and infant health, reduced childhood growth and health, and compromised mental development. Those who are overweight or obese have increased incidence of chronic diseases such as strokes, hypertension, cardiovascular disease, type-2 diabetes, and certain forms of cancer. In addition to their impacts on the lives of individuals and communities, these forms of malnutrition aggregate into major sets of economic, political, and social concerns (Khan 2006; Pinstrup-Andersen 2007).

The most recognized form of malnutrition is energy deficiency or chronic hunger. Around the world, many people are chronically hungry because their diets do not provide enough energy for them to lead active and healthy lives. Historical analyses have found that chronic energy deficiencies have long been widespread in human societies (Diamond 1999; Fogel 2004). Recent events, including a rise in global food prices and the global economic crisis, have led to dramatic increases in the number of hungry people in the world. Estimates for 2009 indicate there are more than 1 billion hungry people in the world, up sharply from 915 million hungry in 2008. If these estimates are correct, FAO reports that "this will represent the highest level of chronically hungry people since 1970" (FAO 2009: 11). In addition to this increase in the number of hungry people, the past few years has also seen a reversal of the steadily decreasing proportion of hungry people in developing countries (ibid.). These trends represent significant increases in both the number and proportion of undernourished people in the world. The recent food crisis has been especially impactful as it is affecting many parts of the world at once and thus reducing both national and subnational coping mechanisms. At the same time, food insecurity has been impacted by successive global crises, such as the food price crises of 2006–8 and the more recent global economic crisis, while levels of chronic hunger are also being driven by developing countries' greater commercial and financial integration into the world economy (FAO 2009).

Global figures provide a useful aggregate measure of chronic hunger, but it is also worth reviewing the regional dimensions of challenges with regard to diet-based energy deficiencies. While chronic hunger impacts all regions of the world, not all world regions are impacted equally. Sub-Saharan Africa is the world region with the highest levels of food insecurity. The number of undernourished there doubled between the 1970s and 2000s (from 92.8 million to 206.2 million), an increase attributed to multiple factors such as "long-term deterioration in livelihoods coupled with civil strife, sharp inequalities in resource endowment, and occasional adverse climate events" (Diriba 2007). According to FAO (2009) data from the period 2004–6 (the most recent period available at the time of writing), the number of people undernourished in sub-Saharan Africa has increased to 212.3 million. Data for the Near East and North Africa also show an increase in the number of people undernourished from 19.1 million in 1990–2 to 33.8 million in 2004–6. There have also been decreases in other world regions, such as Latin America and the Caribbean (from 52.6 million in 1990–2 to 45.3 million in 2004–6) and Asia and the Pacific (from 585.7 million in 1990–2 to 566.2 in 2004–6). It is also important to recall that these figures do not yet fully reflect the impact of the food price crisis of 2006–8 and the global economic crisis (Diriba 2007; FAO 2009).

While the vast majority of malnutrition from energy deficiencies occurs in developing regions of the world, they are not the only parts of the world where malnutrition from inadequate access to food occurs; significant numbers of hungry people are present even in the more developed portions of the world. FAO estimates that, for the period 2001–3, there were 25 million undernourished people in transition countries and 9 million undernourished people in the industrialized countries (FAO 2006). In the United States, USDA reports that during 2008, 14.6 percent of all households (around 49 million people or one in six Americans) lacked food security at some point during the year, an increase of almost one-third over the previous year and the highest number observed since USDA began tracking household food security in 1995 (USDA 2009). In the United States, food insecurity does not necessarily mean that people are not able to access sufficient food, as coping strategies often involve reducing the variety of food sources or relying on staple foods. In the most extreme cases, households that had very low food security (6.7 million or 5.7 percent of all US households) adopted coping strategies such as adults forgoing meals or eating a less balanced diet to ensure that children had access to needed food (ibid.). While poor households were more likely to be food insecure, many of the factors that can influence food insecurity – such as job loss, illness, change in marital status, or other unexpected events – are not always captured by annual household income and some US households experienced food insecurity even though their annual incomes were well above the poverty line (Gunderson and Gruber 2001; Nord and Brent 2002). Other measures of the severity and widespread nature of food insecurity in developed countries can be found by looking at nutrition assistance programs. A November 2009 investigation by *The New York Times* (November 29, 2009) found that one in eight Americans and one in four children in the United States were using nutrition assistance programs to gain access to food. These discussions reiterate two key points: that lack of food security involves both the supply of food and people's ability to access food, and that malnutrition from energy deficiencies is a problem in all regions and countries in the world.

The persistence of energy deficiencies has made it a continued focus of global efforts to address malnutrition. At the World Food Summit (WFS) in November 1996, more than 180 nations pledged to eradicate hunger and set as a goal halving the number of undernourished people worldwide between 1990 and 2015 (FAO 2006). According to FAO's (2009) update, *The State of Food Insecurity in the World 2009*, there has been no progress toward meeting this goal. The number of undernourished people in the world has actually increased over the periods used by FAO to assess progress towards the reduction goal, beginning at 845 million for 1990–2 and ending at 872.9 for 2004–6 (FAO 2009: 48). Efforts during the 1970s and 1980s demonstrated that dramatic reductions in the number of undernourished people are possible: the 1970s saw a reduction of 37 million undernourished, while the 1980s saw a reduction of 100 million undernourished people in developing countries (FAO 2006). Not only is a reduction of the number of undernourished people in developing countries not being achieved, but the most recent information available indicates that the number of undernourished is actually increasing. Such trends will make achieving the targets set for hunger reduction by 2015 very difficult to achieve (Pinstrup-Andersen 2007).

A second major standard for addressing chronic hunger comes from the Millennium Development Goals. The first MDG seeks to "eradicate extreme poverty and hunger" by 2015 and one of the targets of the goals is to halve the proportion of those suffering from hunger (UN 2008a). As with the World Food Summit standard of reducing numbers, progress towards meeting the MDG standard of halving the proportion of people who suffer from hunger has not been as effective as world leaders had hoped. In 1990–2, 20 percent of people in developing countries were undernourished so achieving the hunger reduction target set by the first MDG would require reducing the proportion of chronically hungry to 10 percent. In 2006, this number had been reduced to 17 percent (FAO 2006). As with targets to reduce the number of chronically hungry people in the world, the impact of rising food prices and global economic crisis has resulted in a reversal of declines made in previous years. Estimates for 2008 and 2009 indicate that the trend of a decline in the proportion of undernourished people in developing countries has ended and is likely to increase in coming years (FAO 2009). While the world in 2010 is still five years from the deadline for reaching targeted reductions, the recent rise in global food prices has raised awareness that it may be very difficult to meet either the WFS or the MDG targets for reduction of hunger and malnutrition. Even in the event of significant efforts that allowed the meeting of both WFS and MDG targets, the world will still be faced with 412 million people (or 10 percent of people in developing countries) who are undernourished and, as a result, concerns about chronic hunger resulting from diets that do not provide people with sufficient energy will remain a persistent challenge for decades and generations to come.

Sufferers of malnutrition include significant numbers of people who experience micronutrient deficiencies in their diets from a lack of key vitamins and minerals such as vitamin A, iodine, iron, zinc, and folate. A 2004 study jointly produced by the United Nations Children's Fund (UNICEF) and the Micronutrient Initiative found that despite significant efforts 15 percent of people in the world lack adequate iodine, more than 40 percent of children under five in the developing world have compromised immune systems as a result of a deficiency of vitamin A, and iron deficiency reduces the health and productivity of 40 percent of people in the developing world (UNICEF 2004). Iodine has a major effect on the brain development of fetal cognitive development. According to a 2006 report from the World Bank, one-third of the world's population (almost 2 billion people) suffers from various forms of iodine deficiency disorders

(World Bank 2006). The problem of micronutrient deficiency is "a problem of diet. Throughout the developing world, the poor live mostly on a monotonous regime of starchy staples to which small quantities of more nutritious foods are added as money and availability allow" (UNICEF 2004: 4). While staple foods such as wheat, rice, corn, or millet provide calories, they do not on their own provide enough vitamins and minerals for a healthy diet (World Bank 2006; Micronutrient Initiative 2009).

Micronutrient deficiencies have a range of impacts including: lowering intellectual capacity, impairing mental development, and compromising the immune systems of those impacted. The human development related effects of micronutrient deficiencies are especially marked in children as they can have lasting impacts at key stages of mental and physical development. Solutions to addressing micronutrient deficiency include strategies such as fortifying table salt with both iodine and iron, improving efforts to distribute vitamin and mineral supplements to vulnerable groups such as women and children, and improving education and disease control efforts. In 2008, the Copenhagen Consensus ranked the provision of micronutrients as the best investment for development, determining for instance that providing vitamin A and zinc supplements to children would cost US $60 million per year but return a value of more than US $1 billion (Micronutrient Initiative 2009: iv). It is also worth stressing that micronutrient deficiencies are not an exclusive form of malnutrition; there is considerable overlap between groups who are energy deficient and those who experience micronutrient deficiencies (World Bank 2006; Pinstrup-Andersen 2007; Micronutrient Initiative 2009).

At the same time, the world is confronted by serious and persistent malnutrition challenges from excessive net-energy intake. Changing global diets mean that more and more people are consuming diets composed of energy-dense, nutrient-poor foods while also transitioning to lifestyles that involve lower levels of physical activity than in the past. This global "nutrition transition" means that many nations are now not only confronted by health and nutrition challenges from undernutrition but also from increasing rates of overweight and obesity (World Bank 2006). A person is considered to be overweight if they have a body mass index (BMI) of 25 to 29.9 kg/m^2

and obese if they have a BMI greater than 30 kg/m^2. However, overweight and obesity are not mutually exclusive, since obese persons are also overweight. In general, a BMI of 30 is considered to be about 30 lb (14 kg) overweight and is roughly equivalent to 221 lb (100 kg) in a 6'0" (1.8 m) person and to 186 lb (84 kg) in a person that is 5'6" (1.7 m) (NIH 1998). Overweight and obesity can have a number of health impacts including increased incidences of chronic diseases such as type-2 diabetes, cardiovascular disease, and hypertension (WHO 2003). WHO estimates that over 1.6 billion adults are overweight and more than 400 million are obese, and projects that these numbers will increase such that by 2015 there will be 2.3 billion overweight adults and more than 700 million who are obese (WHO 2006). In the United States, obesity rates have increased significantly over a relatively brief period of time. In 1990, no US state had a prevalence of obesity in the adult population greater than 15 percent. By 2008, 32 states had prevalence equal to or greater than 25 percent, with six of these states having a prevalence of obesity equal to or greater than 30 percent (CDC 2009b).

Problems from overweight and obesity are truly global, occurring in both developed and developing countries. As the World Bank reports, contrary to popular perception, overweight can exist even in very poor countries where undernutrition is widespread (World Bank 2006). Overweight and obesity are especially alarming in that they impact all countries and regions. For example, "in Mexico, rates of adult male obesity have tripled since 1988; in China more than 200 million adults are affected . . . ; in South Africa in 1998, 29 percent of men and 56 percent of women were overweight or obese" (ibid.: 49). In addition to occurring in the same countries, overweight and obesity often occur in the same household as energy and nutrient deficiencies. Research by Colleen Doak et al. (2000, 2005) suggests that there is a rising frequency of what are called "dual burden households," which are households that contain both an underweight and an overweight member. Rates of dual burden households include 7 percent of households in the United States, 8 percent in China, 9 percent in Russia and 11 percent in Indonesia (Doak et al. 2005).

The World Health Organization characterizes the growing prevalence of overweight and obesity as one of the most visible yet neglected public health problems. A number of health consequences related to overweight and obesity have been identified, including increased risk of cardiovascular disease, cancer, and other noncommunicable diseases, as well as endocrine and metabolic disturbances, debilitating health problems, and psychological problems. Growing recognition of the global prevalence of people who are overweight, obese, or suffering from diet-related noncommunicable diseases has led to increasing calls to analyze obesity as a public health threat rather than an individual health condition. These calls gain support from recognitions that overweight and obesity are also strongly linked to other pressing social and political challenges such as reducing healthcare costs. For example, in the United States, one recent estimate finds that spending on obesity-related conditions (diabetes, heart disease, and other serious ailments) now accounts for 9.1 percent of all medical spending and could amount to $147 billion per year in 2008 (Finkelstein et al. 2009).

Global obesity problems, especially the impact of the obesity epidemic on children, have begun to receive attention from scholars, doctors, and public health officials as well as celebrities and political figures. English chef Jamie Oliver has embarked on a number of initiatives to encourage people in the US and UK to make changes in their lifestyles and diet and received a 2010 TED Prize for his wish "to create a strong, sustainable movement to educate every child about food, inspire families to cook again and empower people everywhere to fight obesity" (TED Prize 2010). In early 2010, First Lady Michelle Obama helped launch "Let's Move," a major new initiative that seeks to eliminate childhood obesity in the United States within a generation. Writing in *Newsweek* (March 14, 2020), Mrs. Obama describes the initiative as:

> Families making manageable changes that fit with their schedules, their budgets, and their needs and tastes. It's about giving parents the tools they need to keep their families healthy and fit, and getting more nutritious food – more fresh fruits, vegetables, and whole grains, and less sugar, fat, and salt – into our nation's schools. It's about helping grocery stores serve communities that don't have access to fresh foods, and finding new ways to help our kids stay physically active in school and at home.

As this statement makes clear, addressing problems of overweight and obesity will involve engaging on sensitive topics such as food choices, exercise habits, and cultural preferences for certain foods. Recognition of the impacts from overweight and obesity comes not just from a public health perspective. For instance, in a March 2010 report, a group of retired military officers expressed concern that more than one-quarter of Americans between the ages of 17 and 24 are unable to join the military because they are physically unfit, explicitly pointing to obesity as a problem that compromised national security (Mission: Readiness 2010). Discussions about overweight and obesity may be difficult, as they touch on deeply personal issues such as diet, exercise, genetic predispositions, and family and cultural history. However, such discussions, as well as structural changes to improve access and information about food, are vitally important to the health and security of states and peoples. As the next section examines, while individual and family choices are an important aspect of malnutrition, explaining all three forms of lack of proper nutrition also involves social, economic, political, and technological factors at national, international, and global levels.

Understanding the causes of malnutrition

Malnutrition is caused by food availability, but also a number of other factors such as health, infrastructure, and cultural practices. One of the perennial debates with regard to malnutrition is whether food insecurity is the result of an inadequate food supply or unequal distribution of food supplies. Such efforts to locate a root cause of food insecurity are not just academic, as different causes point towards different solution sets. As D. John Shaw writes, "after the world food crisis in the early 1970s . . . the continued tendency was to equate the world food security problem with the world food problem," and thus policymakers focused their efforts on increasing food production (Shaw 2007: 383). However, arguments locating the source of malnutrition in inadequate food supplies are undermined by many examinations which conclude that global food supplies are sufficient for current human needs at both the present time and in the foreseeable future. Assessing the role of food supplies in causing threats to human security, UNDP concluded that "the overall availability of food in the world is not a problem . . . The problem often is the poor distribution of food and a lack of purchasing power" (UNDP 1994: 27). Per Pinstrup-Andersen finds "current global food supplies are sufficient to meet nutritional requirements of all people, if the food were distributed according to needs" (Pinstrup-Andersen 2002). According to FAO (2002), the world produces sufficient food to provide everyone in the world with at least 2,720 kilocalories (kcal) per person per day. The global food system "produces 17 percent more calories per person than it did 30 years ago, despite a 70 percent population increase" (ibid.: 9). Looking ahead, FAO also believes that world agriculture would be able to continue to feed the projected population of the world without "putting excessive pressure on prices or the environment" (ibid.). Recent global food price increases and the economic crisis have returned attention to increasing food production to keep up with population growth and rising demand, but analysis continues to emphasize that food insecurity and malnutrition arise from a larger basket of causal factors than just food supply.

Thus, truly addressing the challenges of malnutrition along all three of the dimensions discussed above requires moving beyond notions that all malnutrition problems can be solved by simply increasing food production. UNDP recognized food security as a major threat to human security and emphasized that access to food is far more complex than simply supply of food. "The availability of food is thus a necessary condition of security – but not a sufficient one. People can still starve even when enough food is available – as has happened during many famines" (UNDP 1994: 27). Throughout human history and up to the present day, hunger and malnutrition have been present at times when food supplies were abundant (Sen 1982). Even where lack of food is a component of malnutrition, lack of proper nutrition is rarely driven by insufficient amounts of food in the global food system, but instead stems from unevenness in accessing food because of poverty, lack of infrastructure, or other social and political barriers such as war or ethnic conflict (Sen 1982; UNDP 1994; Messer et al. 2001; FAO 2002).

Lack of food is rarely the only, and frequently not even the primary, driver of malnutrition. At the individual level, people become malnourished for one of three reasons: inadequate or inappropriate dietary intake, ill health, or a combination of these two factors. Factors involving diet and health are particularly impactful when they exist in a negative feedback where health conditions reduce appetite and ability to eat while at the same time increasing nutrient requirements, and where inadequate quantity or quality of food increases people's susceptibility to health problems – which include both sudden threats like starvation and chronic threats like diabetes and high blood pressure (WHO 2000a; World Bank 2006). Individual causal factors of malnutrition are often amplified at the family, community, and national level. Variables that influence food intake and ill health are impacted and reinforced by broader deficiencies in infrastructure, education, and health care. These factors operate along three dimensions:

- *Food* – access to food but also choices about what foods are consumed and structural forces affecting food prices and availability;
- *Health* – inadequate availability of care and access to it, as well as more structural problems from lack of clean water, sanitation, and energy;
- *Care* – household and individual level decisions about child care (such as decisions about whether to breastfeed) and nutrition and eating behaviors.

Thus, while malnutrition, and especially the challenge of energy deficiencies, is often discussed as resulting from insufficient food, malnutrition can rarely be addressed solely by increasing food supplies or food intake. Malnutrition is a multi-causal problem, and addressing malnutrition links food security efforts into broader efforts to enhance human security by improving health, infrastructure, education, and the status of women. However, this should not be taken to mean that targeted action designed to address malnutrition cannot have significant impacts. Malnutrition can be meaningfully addressed through efforts that combine strategies such as improved education about nutrition with interventions such as improving maternal health, knowledge, and feeding practices (World Bank 2006).

Improving nutrition requires action by parents, families, and communities that is supported by local and national efforts to address key contributors to malnutrition, especially water treatment and sanitation. Food intake is certainly an important component of malnutrition, but so too are lack of clean water, bad sanitation, and disease which lead to diarrheal illnesses that can rapidly dehydrate victims and are especially devastating to children. Efforts to improve nutrition using targeted, coordinated programs have proven to be very successful over relatively short time frames and can also provide an important boost to development, education, and poverty alleviation efforts. Improving nutrition is not always resource intensive and is feasible on a large scale, especially in poor countries. Many developing countries have made considerable progress in addressing malnutrition even in times of economic hardship through the targeted use of the right technologies, policies, and methods. Especially effective are high-impact, low-cost solutions such as mass vaccination efforts to improve resistance to diseases, programs that encourage breastfeeding, and the provision of iodized salt, vitamin supplements, or oral rehydration solutions to reduce the impact of diarrhea (Pelletier et al. 1995; Haddad et al. 1995; Haddad and Smith 1999; Smith et al. 2005; World Bank 2006).

As the preceding discussion explored, addressing malnutrition involves a number of complex factors aside from just increasing food supplies. Certainly, the quantitative dimensions of food production remain an important part of addressing hunger and malnutrition, but there are also significant qualitative dimensions of the food system. Qualitative questions about how food is grown, processed, transported, prepared, and consumed are as important to solving malnutrition challenges as quantitative questions of how much food is being produced or can be produced. In seeking to address malnutrition, it is important that discussions include not only questions of whether, how, and where to grow more food, but also topics such as what kinds of foods are produced or not produced, who benefits from food production, if foods are produced in ways that provide the most benefit to people and do the least harm to the environment, and whether the foods we produce enhance, support, or undermine human health? We must also consider what kinds of food we grow and to what ends those foods are used. Highly nutritious crops like soybeans can be used to feed humans as well as livestock. Corn is a relatively low-cost staple source of nutrition but it can also be transformed into corn syrup and used in the manufacture of other foods, used as livestock feed, and even converted into biofuels. These are just two examples of the ways in which food crops are not just used to meet human nutritional needs but are artifacts whose history and use are products of human cultural, political, and economic systems. As Pollan (2001) and Luke (2001b) indicate, food's status as an artifact at the nexus of nature, technology, and society is one of the principal reasons why solutions to malnutrition must involve discussions and actions across a range of sectors.

Developing solutions to malnutrition

This chapter argues that proper understanding of malnutrition is essential to developing solutions to food insecurity. Too often, discussions of food insecurity tend to gain global prominence only at moments of crisis. As food riots, front-page stories, and high prices fade, global attention shifts away from the many important questions that must be addressed to reduce food insecurity. Malnutrition is linked to considerable pain, suffering and death; the pressing need to address food insecurity cannot be given too much attention. Focus on energy and nutrient deficiencies are especially necessary given the troubling indications that earlier progress in reducing the global number and proportion of chronically hungry people has reversed in recent years. In the short term, strategies to address malnutrition include providing targeted food aid and micronutrient supplements, establishing community-based nutrition and health services, integrating nutrition education into microcredit programs, and improving maternal health and education about care and feeding of children (World Bank 2006). Longer-term strategies include improvements in water and sanitation systems, developing local fruit and vegetable markets, creating recreation programs and areas, improved regulation of food systems, infectious disease control, and health services provision, improvement in the education and status of women, optimization of agricultural subsidy systems, and reductions in trade barriers (Pinstrup-Andersen 2002; Clay 2004; World Bank 2006).

Many solutions to malnutrition will require individual behavior changes such as improving food choices and making lifestyle changes such as eating and exercise behaviors. While actions at the individual or household level can address some causes of malnutrition, other drivers are more widespread and will require national, international, and nongovernmental efforts. For example, while individual food choices are a component of all three malnutrition dimensions, individual choices are often influenced by larger structural forces. The foods that people have access to have much to do with the types of foods that are produced, the ways in which foods are distributed, and the means that people have to access foods. For example, in many low-income neighborhoods in the United States, in both urban and rural areas, people live in "food deserts" and face significantly reduced menus of food choices and often find it easier to access energy-rich, nutrient-poor foods than fruits, vegetables, and whole grains. Addressing the root causes of malnutrition will require education of individuals and households about food choices, but also steps to address the structural factors which limit the range of choices available to those individuals.

The global significance of addressing malnutrition has been underscored by recognitions of the significant impacts of global economic crisis and rising food prices. The L'Aquila statement on global food security which emerged at the 2009 G8 summit endorsed five principles that should guide future efforts to address food insecurity: invest in partnerships around country-led plans to identify needs, obstacles and strategies; address the underlying causes of hunger through comprehensive approaches, including research, infrastructure, and recognizing the vital role of women small farmers (who produce over 70 percent of agricultural production in low-income countries); improve coordination; leverage benefits of multilateral institutions to support and fulfill country plans; and the need for long-term assistance commitments, based on accountability, of years and decades needed to enact changes (Clinton 2009; L'Aquila 2009). These principles demonstrate that successfully addressing food insecurity requires renewed willingness on the part of developed and developing countries to work towards a new food system. The principles offer a few useful yardsticks for measuring progress in their recognition that plans must consider the conditions and needs of countries, must build capacity among small producers (especially women small producers), and must make and sustain commitments of resources over the long periods needed to develop robust and resilient food systems.

Efforts to address malnutrition are also tied to conflict reduction and peacebuilding. Recent events, including unrest in more than sixty countries over high food prices, have highlighted the connection between food and security. In September 2009, at a food security event co-hosted with UN Secretary-General Ban Ki-moon, US Secretary of State Hillary Clinton (2009) stated, "we want to make sure that enough food is available, and that people have the resources to purchase it. That is a key foreign policy objective of President Obama and our administration. This is an issue that affects all of us, because food security is about economic, environmental, and national security for individual homelands and the world." In recognition of the importance of food and security, the Obama administration has announced plans to shift the focus of food security programs towards efforts that help farmers improve output and make technology and infrastructure investments to make agriculture "more productive and profitable" in developing countries. These efforts recognize that conflict and insecurity are both cause and effect of malnutrition and have a range of impacts related to food security that drive malnutrition, including loss and displacement of population, destruction of infrastructure, livestock and crops, and amplification of other factors, such as disease (Messer et al. 2001).

Efforts to improve malnutrition are a vital component of efforts to improve human security by enhancing global health, addressing persistent failures of development, providing education, and advancing the status of women. In considering each of these goals, efforts to address malnutrition must be especially aware of feedback effects and opportunities for dual-benefit solutions so that policies, programs, and technologies designed to address malnutrition also achieve other human security goals. For example, people who are properly nourished are more resilient across a range of health indicators while children who have a proper diet are less likely to be sick and thus more likely to attend school and be able to take advantage of educational opportunities. Spill-over debates about food safety and the potential impacts of genetically modified foods can also affect efforts to address malnutrition. For example, global debates about food safety of biotech crops has led to increased discussion of the content of, though rarely the rejection of, food aid (Clapp 2005; Clapp and Fuchs 2009). As discussed in chapter 3, food security is thus also enmeshed in efforts to resolve key questions in debates about new technologies such as genetic modification, especially with regards to different standards and perceptions of risk in rich and poor countries.

A significant factor that contributes to malnutrition is poverty and the lack of sustainable livelihoods, especially in rural areas. In the coming decades, reducing undernourishment will depend largely on addressing hunger among the rural poor. According to the World Bank, 75 percent of poor people in developing countries live in rural areas (World Bank 2007). FAO concludes that "no sustained reduction in hunger is possible without special emphasis on agricultural and rural development" (FAO 2006: 6). Addressing hunger and malnutrition in rural areas involves creating vibrant rural economies and implementing successful poverty alleviation efforts. This will entail a willingness to consider alternatives to established notions of development. Vandana Shiva writes that "monocultures of the mind make diversity disappear from perception, and consequently from the world. The disappearance of diversity is also a disappearance of alternatives . . . how often in contemporary times total uprooting of nature, technology, communities and entire civilization is justified on the grounds that 'there is no alternative'" (Shiva 1993: 5). The creation of diverse forms of sustainable rural livelihoods must be understood not as a precondition but a vital part of food insecurity reduction.

Vibrant rural economies and agricultural systems are a prerequisite for hunger reduction, but not simply because they produce more food. As FAO (2006) notes, in rural-based economies, agriculture is the most important economic driver and so investments in agriculture not only raise production but also augment the entire local economy. Addressing malnutrition also improves health, education, and productivity and can thus begin a cycle of positive feedbacks where improvements in nutrition and development reinforce each other (Gore 1999; FAO 2006; World Bank 2006). At the same time, the majority of the world's population lives in cities and so efforts to address hunger and malnutrition must also take into account urban food insecurity challenges. Urban poverty and food insecurity tend to be linked to the decline of rural livelihoods that drive migration to the cities (FAO 2006). The urban poor use a variety of informal systems to access food supplies, including use of reciprocal trade agreements or short-distance migrations for hunting of animals for bush meat. Studies of the impact of urban agricultural have demonstrated how sustainable urban agricultural systems can help provide key sources of food including fresh fruits and vegetables (Mougeot 2005; FAO 2006). Urban food insecurity could also be significantly improved through the development of rural livelihoods that could ease, and perhaps even reverse, migration patterns.

Another factor with major impacts on food supplies and food security are the agricultural subsidies that shape the global food system. Historically, a central goal of states has been to keep staple food prices low and promote agricultural self-sufficiency among their populations, thus ensuring political and social stability. In modern times, many states have resorted to agricultural subsidies – providing incentives for the production of certain crops – to accomplish this goal. Subsidies are used by almost every developed country to allow producers to sell crops at prices lower than would otherwise be possible, while also generating a desired return on investments. In addition to encouraging crop production, subsidies can also force unsubsidized producers in other countries out of production, as they are unable to compete with the artificially low prices of subsidized production. In the United States, subsidization of crops began in 1929, and is a key component of farm bills that are brought up for renewal by Congress every five years. In 2002, the Farm Bill increased subsidy payments despite increasing awareness of potential negative impacts of subsidies and potential strategies to reduce them. The 2007 Farm Bill was a subject of even greater public discussions yet the final version that passed in 2008 did little to address concerns about the negative impacts of subsidies. Subsidies can also emerge as solutions in other policy areas, such as energy bills that seek to encourage production of biofuels from crops like corn (Clay 2004; Donner and Kucharik 2008).

While the topic of agricultural subsidies generates a great deal of debate and discussion, since global agricultural and trade systems have been shaped by subsidy programs for many years, at the present time there do not appear to be immediately viable alternatives to some forms of agricultural subsidies. Without subsidies, prices for food would be subject to great volatility and could thus have significant negative and unpredictable impacts on producers and consumers. At a time when global populations are increasingly urbanized, the priorities of most governments remain providing food, largely produced in rural areas, to largely urban and peri-urban populations; subsidies have provided a great deal of assistance towards achieving this goal. The lack of real alternatives to subsidizing production, however, does not mean that there is no room to improve the use of subsidies and refine the goals served by such practices. For example, subsidies can be used to advance other goals aside from lower food prices and protection of domestic production. Reformulated subsidies can play an important role in encouraging conservation of rural landscapes, maintenance of wild and natural habitats on farms, protection of waterways, transitions to sustainable methods, and development of urban gardens and farmers' markets. Subsidies could also play an important role in encouraging production of foods that aid in proper health and nutrition such as fruits and vegetables. Discussions of the uses of subsidies would benefit from increased transparency and participation, and will involve a need for a complex balancing of national versus global interests and careful evaluation of the political, economic, and social needs that subsidies advance (Pinstrup-Andersen 2002; Clay 2004).

As this chapter has reviewed, addressing food insecurity by optimizing nutrition – especially if significant progress is to be made prior to the 2015 deadline set by the Millennium Development Goals and the World Food Summit – will require major effort, sustained will, and considerable resources. The evolving complexity of malnutrition in a networked world means that strategies must address all dimensions of the challenge and cannot simply focus on one type of malnutrition at the expense of others. The range of strategies utilized must include efforts that operate at multiple levels of analysis, from individuals and households to communities and nations, and should be optimized to take advantage of opportunities for dual-benefit and high impact scenarios. Nonetheless, ensuring that the global food system provides all people physical, social, and economic access to sufficient, safe, and nutritious food remains a fundamental requirement of human security's goal to ensure safety of individuals and communities from both chronic threats and sudden disruptions. As will be discussed in the next chapter, such food systems must also be sensitive and adaptive to the expected impacts of environmental and climate changes.

5

Managing Global Environmental Change: The Environmental Impacts of Agriculture and Food Production

The previous chapter explored malnutrition's central role in a human security understanding of food security challenges. This chapter considers a second core challenge to ensuring food security, environmental change, and specifically looks at how environmental change results from and can in turn cause changes in the agriculture, fishing, and food production practices that are the basis of the global food network. As discussions of global environmental change have increasingly entered popular discourse in recent years, commentators and advocates have focused on energy sources and usage and proposed solutions such as improving car fuel efficiency or shifting to energy-efficient light bulbs. As Maria Rodale writes, "the debate over the climate crisis and environmental destruction has been almost completely focused on energy usage . . . We haven't yet made the full connection between how we grow our food and the impact it can have on the climate crisis and our health crisis" (Rodale 2010: 5). Though it is a prominent feature in the scientific literature on climate and environmental change, popular and political discussions of global environmental change rarely raise food as a generative factor, likely area of impact, or possible source of solutions to global environmental change. As reviewed in chapter 3, this absence is significant given that land use and food production practices account for more than 30 percent of human-induced greenhouse gas emissions (Scherr and Sthapit 2009). Agricultural and food production systems are linked in that food systems drive environmental changes which in turn impact food systems which leads to further environmental changes and so on.

The environmental impacts of food and agriculture continue to be significant drivers of related environmental issues such as soil and water degradation, which can further complicate efforts to address climate change. Global agriculture, according to FAO

(2003a), consumes more water than any other industry, and is also the primary source of nitrate and ammonia pollution. Agricultural practices are closely linked to problems such as land clearance, degradation, and increased salinization of soils, increased stresses on water resources, impacts on water quality from agricultural runoff, and the development of antibiotic-resistant microbes. This chapter examines how this "vicious cycle" of food system-induced environmental degradation could be harmonized with imperatives of sustainable development to create a "virtuous cycle" that enhances environmental quality, promotes human security, and ensures food security (Gore 1999; UNEP 2002; FAO 2006).

Drawing on the great wealth of information that now exists on the causes and impacts of global environmental change, the chapter reviews the environmental impacts agriculture and food production practices have had on the environment. The chapter considers environmental impacts in five major sectors: land and soil; water use and water quality; habitat and biodiversity loss; energy use; and climate change. The chapter concludes with a discussion of ways to reduce the environmental impact of agriculture and food production. This discussion focuses particular attention on the need to develop food systems that provide for human needs while also aiding efforts to both mitigate and adapt to processes of global environmental change, a process that I argue can be harmonized with efforts to increase agricultural sustainability.

Impacts on land and soil

Covering only about one-third of the earth's surface, land is indispensable to agriculture and livestock production. These land resources, according to a definition by UNEP (2002) include soil, land cover, and landscapes. Land and soil provide a range of additional benefits, including regulating hydrological cycles and aiding in the preservation of biodiversity, carbon storage, and other ecosystem services (the resources and process provided by natural systems that are beneficial to human livelihoods and well-being). Though finite, the functional amounts of land and soil resources, along with water and nutrients, are, as Smil (2000) asserts, variable with management practices that considerably affect their quality and efficiency of use. Many current agricultural practices reduce the ability of ecosystems to provide goods and services such as carbon sequestration and soil retention and absorption of water. The amount of land under agricultural cultivation has increased steadily in developing regions while remaining largely constant in developed regions, with the largest gains in cultivable land made in the mid-twentieth century (UNEP 2008). Degradation and pollution of land resources, such as the overuse of fertilizers and other chemicals, has also occurred as a result of policy failures and unsustainable agricultural practices (UNEP 2002). Human induced land modification, largely related to agricultural activities, has impelled significant environmental changes (Smil 2000; UNEP 2002, 2008).

Changes in land and land use patterns have positive and negative effects on human well-being, the environment, and the provision of ecosystem services. "The enormous increase in the production of farm and forest products has brought greater wealth and more secure livelihoods for billions, but often at the cost of land degradation, biodiversity loss and disruption of biophysical cycles such as the water and nutrient cycles" (UNEP 2008: 86). Since the early 1970s, efforts to increase food production have been the main factor increasing pressure on land resources. Other pressures on land resources include increasing human population and population density (especially in urban and peri-urban areas), increased productivity, higher incomes and changing consumption patterns, climate change and variability, and changes in technology. Land resources provide the overwhelming majority of food including 98 percent of food energy and 93 percent of dietary protein (Smil 2000). Changes in land and land use patterns can have impacts on a range of factors relevant to human security including the environment, human livelihoods, human health and safety, and socioeconomic dimensions (UNEP 2002, 2008).

Soil loss is an especially key component of impacts of agriculture and food production on land resources. While soil erosion is a natural cycle, soil loss can become a problem when land management practices or activities such as mining, urban development, and infrastructure development accelerate rates of erosion. Jason Clay notes that since 1850 humans have "converted close to 1 billion hectares of forests, grasslands, and wetlands to farmlands," dramatically increasing soil erosion in the process (Clay 2004: 46–7). Soil erosion can lead to reduced productivity as soil loss means not just the loss of organic matter, but also the loss of nutrients, reduced water retention capacity, and the loss of biodiversity including species of bacteria and other organisms that can aid in water and nutrient retention. Although soil is a renewable resource, many current agricultural and food production practices use soil at nonrenewable rates. According to some estimates, around one-third of all cropland in the United States has been abandoned due to soil erosion since 1950 (Hawken et al. 1999). A 2007 study estimated that soil is being depleted at rates that are one to two orders of magnitude (between 10 and 100 times) greater than it is being replenished (Montgomery 2007). The very long time periods for soil formation have led to calls that soil be regarded as a nonrenewable resource. For instance, Wes Jackson writes that "soil is as much of a non-renewable resource as oil" (Jackson 1996: 83). While soil can be replaced, the processes involved in converting organic matter into topsoil take very long periods of time, which suggests the need for efforts to conserve as much soil as possible. Negative impacts on land and soil are not unavoidable. Cases of conversion to sustainable agricultural practices have demonstrated that losses to soil and soil nutrients can be reversed (Hawken et al. 1999). Even in the absence of full conversion to sustainable methods, a number of techniques exist to reduce erosion from agricultural activities such as no-till agriculture, use of shelterbelts to protect fields from wind and water, and methods that leave some forest and vegetation cover, or use cover crops such as clover, on fields (Jackson 1996; UNEP 2002, 2008).

Salinization, or salt buildup, in soil is another key threat to land resources. Salinization, when salt is present in agricultural land or water sources that humans wish to use, occurs due to inadequate rainfall, improper irrigation, and poor drainage. Salt appears naturally in soil, streams, rivers, and groundwater, and concentrations of salt increase as plants intake water but leave the salt it carried in the soil. In high concentrations, salt can cause a range of problems, from inhibiting water absorption in plants and animals to corroding metal. Build-up of salt can be caused through irrigation methods which apply more water than crops can use and more water than would be provided to an ecosystem through natural rainfall or flooding. Perhaps the most dramatic example of irrigation-induced salinization can be found in the Aral Sea. Extensive irrigation, using water from the lake, has caused the volume of the lake to fall by 90 percent since 1960, and the land irrigated with the water has lost fertility due to salt buildup. Salinization can also occur when seawater is introduced to depleted or overdrawn coastal aquifers or when water-intensive crops and pastures replace native vegetation. The latter process, also known as dryland salinity, means that, as less water is used by crops and pastures, more water infiltrates groundwater stores, which results in the rise of more saline water into streams and onto the surface through the evaporation processes. Eventually, this process may create a crust of salt on the surface of soils. More than 20 percent of the arable land in West Asia has been degraded by salinization of soil. Globally, studies indicate that as much as 20 percent of irrigated land has reduced productivity due to salinization (FAO 2003a; Clay 2004; UNEP 2008).

Soil nutrient depletion is another major environmental impact from agricultural practices. Soil nutrient depletion refers to a decline in soil fertility based on reductions in soil of the levels of plant nutrients, such as nitrogen, phosphorus, potassium, and organic matter. Healthy soil contains a great deal of biodiversity and biomass, sustaining varied life such as microbes and organisms like earthworms, millipedes, spiders, snails, beetles, and centipedes. Organic matter – the decaying remains of plants and animals, animal wastes, and microbes – is a key indicator of soil quality and health. Organic matter is crucial for maintaining soil fertility and soil structure. Soil structure allows water and plant roots to penetrate soil and soil that loses its structure can become hard, brittle, and very difficult for water and roots to penetrate. The depletion of nutrients in soil operates through a variety of mechanisms. The conversion of land from forests, wetlands, or other natural habitat can also lead to significant decreases in soil fertility, as just a few decades after turning to cropland, carbon rates in soil decline by 30 to 50 percent. Conversion to cropland disrupts fertility in a number of ways. By its very purpose, cropland is intended to produce crops which will be harvested and thus removed from the soil, rather than returned to the soil as plant matter is in forests and natural ecosystems. Cultivation of crops also involves tilling and aeration, processes which speed up decomposition rates of organic matter in soil. In attempting to understand soil nutrient loss, it is thus important to look holistically at the health not just of fields and farms, but of entire agricultural ecosystems, as losses or gains in nutrient composition of soil in one area can impact others. In addition to increasing capital costs for agricultural activities, the addition of inputs, combined with soil nutrient loss, can also affect water resources and water quality as nutrients that are leached out of or washed off soil enter into water systems (Smil 2000; Clay 2004; UNEP 2008).

Impacts on water use and water quality

Agricultural practices have a range of impacts on water use rates and water quality. While three-quarters of the earth is covered by water, most of this water is not fresh. As Hawken et al. estimate, only a tiny percentage of fresh water is available for use, as the majority is frozen in glaciers and icecaps (Hawken et al. 1999). Limited freshwater sources have been tapped by an increasing global population and growing irrigated agriculture. Some observers estimate increases in water use as high as "sixfold in the last century (from 579 to 3,750 cubic kilometers per year)" (Clay 2004: 54). These massive increases in freshwater use reflect the centrality of irrigation as a method used in the twentieth century to increase food production; according to some estimates, irrigation alone bears responsibility for the majority of world food production increases in the middle decades of the twentieth century (Hawken et al. 1999). Use has not diminished in recent decades; currently, agriculture is responsible for almost 70 percent of global freshwater withdrawals (Smil 2000; FAO 2003a; UNEP 2008).

Rates of freshwater use have raised concerns about possible stress on water resources. At the present time, "1.6 billion people, or almost one quarter of the world's population, face economic water shortage (where countries lack the necessary infrastructure to take water from rivers and aquifers)" (UN Water 2007: 4). Trends such as global population growth as well as impacts from climate change are likely to increase pressure on water resources. UN Water reports that regional water shortages are the greatest concern, as "by 2025, 1.8 billion people will be living in countries or regions with absolute water scarcity, and two-thirds of the world population could be under conditions of water stress" (ibid.: 10). The impact of rising rates of water scarcity will be varied and will certainly interact with other trends. For example, one of the major ways that water is transported around the world is in food. In some circumstances, to circumvent localized water shortages, it is easier for countries to grow food in other places and transport it back to feed their populations. Pakistan has recently attempted to capitalize on this interest in overseas farmland by offering their farmland to water-strapped Gulf nations. While this strategy may bring financial benefits to Pakistan, it also has costs (including the need to develop a new 100,000 strong agricultural security force) and could lead to exacerbations of water scarcity in Pakistan and the prospect of food-insecure Pakistanis watching food grown and watered in Pakistan shipped to wealthy Gulf states (Kugelman 2009). This is but one example of the ways that water and food can interact in security-relevant ways. A large literature explores the possibility that water could act as both a cause of increased conflict and a driver of improved cooperation (Gleick 1993; Conca and Dabelko 2002; Wolf et al. 2005).

Agriculture uses a large portion of global freshwater. All freshwater comes from rainfall, most of which is captured by soil and returned to the atmosphere by evaporation. Only 11 percent of freshwater is available as stream flow and groundwater that can be used for agriculture, consumption, or urban and industrial uses. Of that small available percentage, almost 70 percent is used for agriculture. However, use of freshwater varies by region and ecosystem. Almost three-quarters of irrigated land is in developed countries where it is used to produce crops such as rice (34 percent of crops produced on irrigated land), wheat (17 percent) and cotton (7 percent). The efficiency of water use varies greatly depending on the region and whether water is being used to grow crops or raise livestock. In general, livestock and aquaculture require markedly more water than crops, perhaps as high as 80 times as much for livestock (ibid.). Improved management of water resources must not only address water stress threats, but also ensure that agricultural production keeps pace with population growth and changing consumption patterns (Smil 2000; FAO 2003a; Clay 2004; UNEP 2008).

Agriculture and food production, in addition to affecting water usage rates, also have significant impacts on water quality. Hawken, Lovins and Lovins assert that "agriculture is America's largest, most diffuse, and most anonymous water polluter" (Hawken et al. 1999: 197). Agricultural inputs such as pesticides and fertilizers frequently escape from their application site and flow onto other lands and into waterways. In addition to impacting water quality, agricultural runoff can harm human health and other organisms. Many studies have documented the negative impacts of agricultural pesticides on birds, insects, mammals, and amphibians (Carson 1962). Water quality can also be impacted by improper storage or disposal of agricultural and livestock waste products. For example, one estimate of the waste impacts of large-scale livestock production facilities, also known as concentrated animal feeding operations (CAFOs), found that while the vast majority of operations work to meet environmental and health standards, "heavy rains or accidents can cause lagoons where liquefied animal waste is stored to eventually break or leak into the surrounding soil and watersheds, releasing dangerous levels of trace heavy metals and bacteria into drinking water" (Ellis and Turner 2007: 23). In addition to the direct impacts that waste can have on water resources by asphyxiating fish and aquatic life, waste products also contain medicines and can contribute to problems such as the development of antibiotic resistance among microbes (Garrett 1994; FAO 2003a; Clay 2004).

Beyond impacts on fresh water and water quality, food production is also a significant driver of impacts on the world's oceans. Oceans represent 97 percent of all water on earth and are the source of much of the moisture that falls as precipitation. Oceans also perform a number of vital services through circulation of waters. Ocean circulation is driven by differences in seawater density (determined by water temperature and salinity) and moves warm water towards the poles and cold water towards the equator. This circulation process has a number of effects, including helping to sequester carbon dioxide (CO_2) from the atmosphere into the ocean, distributing heat and nutrients, and influencing the climates of areas, such as the United Kingdom, which would be much colder without the infusion of warm waters. Changes in the world's oceans are having a number of impacts including altering precipitation patterns, and negative effects on marine life and aquatic ecosystems. There is also concern that climate change could alter global circulation patterns and increase the acidity and amount of carbon in oceans which could affect marine life (UNEP 2006, 2008).

Food and agriculture are indirectly affecting oceans by accelerating global climate change, but they are also having many direct and significant impacts on the state of the world's oceans. Agricultural runoff and other pollutants are major contributors to the increase in the number and size of deoxygenated areas (also called dead zones) in the world's oceans. According to UNEP (2006), the number of such areas has risen rapidly, doubling every decade since the 1960s, and there are now an estimated 200 dead zones in the world, compared with 149 in 2004. Such areas are a major threat to fish stocks and the many people who depend on marine life for food and livelihood. Marine life is also being heavily affected by fishing and food production activities. Population growth, changes in consumption rates, and changes in technology have all helped fuel significant increases in global fish catch which rose to 141 million tons of seafood in 2005, a figure that represents an eightfold increase over global seafood harvests in 1950 (Halweil and Nierenberg 2008). Moreover, agricultural runoff contributes to the destruction of coastal wetland and coral reef areas; agricultural runoff is expected to rise 14 percent globally by 2030 compared with the mid-1990s (UNEP 2006).

As with soil and land resources, food, fishing and agricultural activities do not necessarily require unsustainable use of freshwater flows or unacceptable impacts on water quality and oceans. A range of methods, policies, and technologies can improve the efficiency and sustainability of water use. Some solutions involve the use of new varieties of crops that require less water to grow. Another solution is improving the efficiency of water use. In the United States, water use efficiency has been steadily increasing since the 1980s. Even with a growing population and economy, the efficiency of water use in the United States has been improving in recent decades. For example, "the amount of freshwater withdrawn per American fell by 21 percent during the years 1980–1995 . . . over twice as fast as energy efficiency improved" (Hawken et al. 1999: 216). Improvements in water use efficiency can come through a variety of methods, such as drip irrigation systems or methods that allow for better information about soil moisture levels that can guide how much water is needed in a given area, or even sub-area, of a farm. Other ways to improve water use efficiency include better efforts to capture and use rainfall at the sites where it falls. Using catch basins, cover crops, and substances that can be mixed into soil to increase water intake all provide ways to increase water use efficiency and reduce runoff. Efforts to improve management of fisheries and develop sustainable aquaculture can provide ways to improve local livelihoods and attract foreign investment but also need strong action to reduce fishing practices that harm fish stocks and should identify species and techniques for aquaculture that do not require substantial inputs, such as fish meal, and do not produce new sources of waste and pollution (WCED 1987; Hawken et al. 1999; Clay 2004; UNEP 2006, 2008).

Impacts on habitat and biodiversity loss

Agricultural activities are a major driver of land modification and deforestation activities that lead to habitat and biodiversity loss. Estimates from FAO concluded that as much as 13 million hectares of forest are lost to agriculture land expansion in developing countries each year. Forests serve a variety of functions, many of which have direct and indirect benefits for humans. "In addition to directly supporting industries such as timber, pulp, and biotechnology, all forests provide a range of ecosystems services. These services include prevention of soil erosion, maintenance of soil fertility, and fixing carbon from the atmosphere as biomass and soil organic carbon" (UNEP 2008: 88). Beyond providing economic uses and ecosystem services, "forests host a large proportion of terrestrial biodiversity, protect water catchments and moderate climate change. Forests also support local livelihoods, provide fuel, traditional medicines and food to local communities and underpin many cultures" (ibid.). Land modification activities also affect habitats other than forests, such as waterways and "edge habitats," or the areas close to human settlements and farms. The loss of woodlots, hedgerows, and windbreaks combined with the draining of wetlands and altering of the course of waterways encroaches on wildlife habitat, breeding grounds, and migration routes. The loss of such habitat also affects human populations. As Donald Worster (1979) describes, one of the most destructive and widespread impacts of efforts to increase cropland and increase productivity were the North American dust storms of the 1930s. In addition to loss of habitat, practices such as shorter fallow periods, soil erosion, and soil nutrient loss, as well as poor water management practices, contribute to degradation of habitats (FAO 2003a; Clay 2004; UNEP 2008).

Destruction of habitat, frequently for conversion into agricultural lands or livestock pasture, results in loss of biodiversity and the ecosystem functions provided by natural habitat and is a significant contributor to biodiversity loss. The 1992 Convention on Biological Diversity (CBD) defines biodiversity as, "the variability among living organisms from all sources including, inter alia, terrestrial, marine and other aquatic ecosystems and the ecological complexes of which they are part; this includes diversity within species, between species and of ecosystems" (Convention on Biological Diversity 1992). Other definitions of biodiversity stress that it includes all forms of life, but also includes diversity among human cultures (UNEP 2008). Biodiversity is a key component of human and nonhuman systems. "As the basis for all ecosystem services, and the foundation for truly sustainable development, biodiversity plays fundamental roles in maintaining and enhancing the well-being of the world's more than 6.7 billion people, rich and poor, rural and urban alike" (UNEP 2008: 160). The CBD asserts that biological diversity has a range of values, including the intrinsic value of biological diversity as well as ecological, genetic, social, economic, scientific, educational, cultural, recreational, and aesthetic values (UNEP 1992a). Agricultural practices play many roles in the loss of biodiversity, including conversion of natural habitat into agricultural lands, deliberate eradication of species that threaten livestock such as wolves, and reduction of competition among native species by creating habitats that favor some species over others (Clay 2004; UNEP 2008).

Loss of species and declines in biological diversity can have a range of impacts on humans, agriculture, and ecosystems. Species exist in complex relationships with their ecosystems and other organisms. Often, humans have attempted to improve on the functioning of ecosystems for human ends, such as sport hunting or raising livestock, by removing predator species such as wolves, only to find that the removal of key species can have significant negative impacts on the health of an ecosystem. Aldo Leopold writes about one occasion where he was with a group that happened on a pack of wolves:

> In those days we had never heard of passing up a chance to kill a wolf. In a second we were pumping lead into the pack . . . When our rifles were empty, the old wolf was down and a pup was dragging a leg into impassible slide-rocks. We reached the old wolf in time to watch a fierce green fire dying in her eyes. I realized then, and have known ever since, that there was something new to me in those eyes – something known only to her and to the mountain. I was young then, and full of trigger itch; I thought that because fewer wolves meant more deer, that no wolves would mean hunters' paradise (Leopold 1949: 130).

Leopold goes on to describe how over time he observed the ecological impacts of species removal. Without wolves, rather than a bountiful supply of deer for hunting and a range ideal for cattle grazing, deer populations boomed, leading to over-foraged vegetation and, eventually, to a significant starvation induced die-off among the deer population. For Leopold, the lesson was that people needed to learn to "think like mountains," considering how their activities impacted the health of ecosystems and thus the long-term health and prosperity of human and nonhuman communities, rather than just considering short-term human interests (Leopold 1949).

Biological diversity has also been reduced by changes in the culture and methods of agriculture and food production. The industrialization of agriculture has resulted in significant increases in global food production, but has also led to major declines in the biological diversity of key food sources. For example, out of the approximately 30,000 species of edible plants, only 7,000 of them have been used as food while just fifteen species produce more than 90 percent of all food. In the last century, more than 75 percent of biodiversity among crop species has been lost, including 80 percent of the varieties of corn that existed in the 1930s and 94 percent of pea varieties once grown in the US (*New York Times*, February 29, 2008). Recognition of the impact of biodiversity loss has prompted renewed effort to create a global network of plant and seed banks to store samples and information about genetic resources of plant species (Smil 2000; Clay 2004). Domesticated animal breeds also have reduced biological diversity, though not as dramatically as the reduced diversity of crop species. However, Clay (2004) estimates that in the last hundred years, one in six of the domestic animal breeds have gone extinct.

Biodiversity loss also affects insects such as spiders and ladybugs which are enemies of pests, and honeybees and song birds which play key roles as pollinators. The economic value of such species has gained attention as a result of recent dramatic declines in honeybee populations. Beginning in 2006, close to a quarter of beekeeping operations in many parts of the United States and other countries lost up to 50 percent of their bee populations to a mysterious condition called Colony Collapse Disorder (*Science*, March 16, 2007). The loss of key ecosystem and economic services provided by species such as pollinators can have significant effects such as the lost value of the services they provide as crop pollinators (a service estimated to be valued at $14–20 billion each year). The cost and difficulty of replicating the pollination role of honeybees demonstrates the importance of protecting habitat and biological diversity, especially with regards to key crops and species (Smil 2000; Clay 2004; UNEP 2008).

Impacts on energy use

The many processes involved in producing, transporting, preserving, preparing, and consuming food utilize a great deal of energy. Figures related to the use of energy in agriculture and food production vary widely, often depending on whether they focus on direct and indirect uses in agricultural production or take a broader look at the total energy cost of food. One estimate of total energy consumption found that the food sector uses 10 to 15 percent of the energy consumed in developed countries (Hawken et al. 1999). Direct energy uses include farm-level uses, including energy use to run machinery and equipment. "In 2002, the US agricultural sector (encompassing both crops and livestock production) used an estimated 1.1 quadrillion Btu of total direct energy. This represents slightly more than 1% of total US energy consumption of 98 quadrillion Btu in 2002" (CRS 2004: 2). With regards to indirect energy uses, or energy used to manufacture fertilizers and pesticides, estimates are that "in 2002 agriculture accounted for about 56% (12 million out of about 21.4 million metric tons) of total US nitrogen use . . . In addition, the US Environmental Protection Agency (EPA) estimates that US agriculture accounted for 67% of expenditures on pesticides in the United States in 2001" (ibid.: 4). In addition to energy use on farms and in production of pesticides and fertilizers, much of the energy used by the global food system is involved in processes related to processing, manufacturing, and distributing food.

Transportation is a major factor in food-related energy use and includes the energy used in producing food and transporting it to consumers, but also must take into account the energy that consumers use in trips to markets and restaurants. Jason Clay writes that a German study "suggests that the production of 0.24 liters (a typical cup) of strawberry yogurt entails 9,093 kilometers (5,650 miles) of transportation . . . In the United States, the food for a typical meal has traveled nearly 2,092 kilometers (1,300 miles)" (Clay 2004: 59). Travel distance is only one useful measure of the energy cost of food, however, as methods of transportation greatly impact the amount of energy used. Foods transported by rail or ship use far less energy than foods transported by air, truck, or car. For example, a 2009 lifecycle assessment of salmon found that frozen salmon had significantly lower environmental impact than fresh salmon; in some cases the impact of frozen salmon was almost half that of fresh salmon as fresh salmon is almost always transported by air (Pelletier et al. 2009). As this discussion suggests, understanding the energy impacts of food and identifying which sorts of foods are more sustainable than others is a complex endeavor (Hawken et al. 1999; CRS 2004).

Impacts from climate change

Food production and land use are important drivers of processes of global climate change and account for almost one-third of greenhouse gas emissions. Agriculture and food production contribute a substantial share of many countries' GHG emissions, including gases such as carbon dioxide from land clearance and deforestation, as well as methane, nitrous oxide, and ammonia that result from crop and livestock production (FAO 2003a). "Of the total human-induced GHG emissions in 2004 (49 billion tons of carbon dioxide equivalent), roughly 31 percent –15 billion tons – was from land use. By comparison, fossil fuel burning accounts for 27.7 billion tons of CO_2-equivalent emissions annually" (Scherr and Sthapit 2009: 9). Greenhouse gas emissions from land use include contributions from sources such as soil fertilization, biomass burning, irrigated rice production and livestock manure. Though burning of fossil fuels for transportation and energy production are often a focus of significant attention in climate change discussions, it is important to recognize that land use GHG emissions represent an amount of annual emissions that is more than half of the amount provided by burning of fossil fuels (FAO 2003a; Scherr and Sthapit 2009).

The impacts of climate change on agriculture will vary significantly, and, at least in the near term, will likely be both positive and negative. Overall, the global food system will face significant impacts from climate change through, for example, extending growing seasons in some places and reducing them in others. FAO finds that "there are large uncertainties as to when and where climate change will impact agricultural production and food security" (FAO 2003a: 357). In general, the agricultural sector is extremely sensitive to climate variability and food security could be compromised by rising temperatures and more frequent droughts and floods (Chan 2008). Climate change could also have significant consequences on food security through increased frequency of heat stress, drought, fires, and flooding events which could decrease crop yields and have impacts on livestock. Climate change will have both direct and indirect impacts on food production and food security. Direct impacts of climate change on agriculture could include impacts on crops, forests, increased water scarcity, biodiversity losses to animal and fish populations that provide key sources of nutrition, and sea level rise. It is also important to recognize that climate change impacts will likely not be limited to human populations, but could also have impacts through increased biodiversity loss in plant and animal populations. Climate change impacts could accelerate other negative environmental consequences of agriculture and food production activities such as increased soil erosion, nutrient depletion, and impacts on water quality caused by increased rainfall and extreme weather events. Climate change could also have indirect impacts on food security such as through effects on the availability of resources such as oil, thereby increasing costs for transportation, and also the prices of inputs such as synthetic pesticides and fertilizers or through mechanisms such as exacerbation of global health challenges through mechanisms such as changing the range of pests and pathogens (FAO 2003a; Clay 2004; Easterling et al. 2007; IPCC 2007; Schmidhuber and Tubiello 2007).

While agriculture and food production are often discussed as drivers of climate change, they could also play an important role in efforts to mitigate climate change. The recognition that agriculture is both a driver and a means of addressing climate change is compatible with more general recognition that agricultural practices can have positive impacts on the environment. As Scherr and Sthapit (2009: 12) write, "we face a unique opportunity to achieve 'climate-friendly landscapes.' These include, for example, large expanses of agricultural land, interconnected with natural habitats that are managed to minimize greenhouse gas emissions and maximize the sequestration of carbon in soils and vegetation." Agriculture, land use, and forestry can, under certain conditions, help provide and enhance environmental services such as water storage and purification and the preservation of rural landscapes. In addition, using croplands both more sustainably and more intensively provides a means to reduce pressures to develop forests, grasslands, and other natural habitats. FAO finds "there is a growing appreciation of agriculture's positive contribution to climate change mitigation through carbon sequestration and the substitution of biofuels for fossil fuels" (FAO 2003a: 358). Using certain methods, crop and livestock production can play a significant role in sequestering carbon in soil organic matter. For example, in the United States, altering agricultural practices to reduce the impacts of tilling, improve management of crop residue and implementing land restoration, could sequester about 140 million tons of carbon or nearly 10 percent of total United States emission of all GHGs (FAO 2003a; Scherr and Sthapit 2009).

Aside from mitigation efforts, agriculture can also play an important role in efforts to adapt to the effects of climate change. Adaptations can be divided into two broad categories: "*autonomous adaptation*, which is the ongoing implementation of existing knowledge and technology in response to the changes in climate experienced, and *planned adaptation*, which is the increase in adaptive capacity by mobilising institutions and policies to establish or strengthen conditions favourable for effective adaptations" (Easterling et al. 2007: 294). Adaptation efforts will involve a range of activities at various levels of action. At the local level, activities focus on helping farmers adapt to changes and variations in weather conditions. Efforts could include systems to distribute better weather information, especially in areas of the developing world where weather forecasts can be difficult to access. Adaptation efforts could also include programs to transition to more ecologically appropriate forms of crop production and the development of agricultural production systems that are more resilient to impacts from climate change and variability. Programs to encourage adaptation also need to take into account the likely large-scale impacts of climate change, such as increased incidence of extreme weather events, drought, salinity, and aridity. Under such conditions, a range of adaptive measures may help lessen the impacts of climate change, including actions such as: maintenance of broad genetic diversity among crops; developing traits such as drought resistance, tolerance for greater temperature extremes, and salt tolerance in crop cultivar varieties and livestock breeds; encouraging use of agricultural practices such as sustainable agriculture and agroforestry that make use of and enhance genetic diversity; improving the efficiency of on-site freshwater use, especially capturing rainwater, which can both improve water management and reduce runoff; and developing systems to manage floodwaters and address sea level rise. Such actions could help reduce the effects of current climate variations, as well as providing resilience in the face of expected future changes (FAO 2003a; Easterling et al. 2007; Matthew and Hammill 2009).

Reducing environmental impacts through sustainable intensification of food production

This chapter has discussed the ways food production activities have had significant, though often unintentional, impacts on the global environment. Activities intended to provide people with sufficient food have been, and continue to be, major drivers of environmental change including climate change (Steinfeld 2006). These changes are often localized, such as cutting down or burning forests to create croplands. The impacts of such changes are often local as well, such as increased erosion of topsoil, loss of soil nutrients, and reducing water quality when siltation and agricultural runoff enter waterways. However, local changes can have regional and national impacts that contribute to problems such as toxic dead zones in rivers and oceans, desertification, and global climate change. During the twentieth century, agricultural production came to increasingly rely on mechanization and chemical inputs including fertilizers, insecticides, and pesticides, as well as scientific techniques to measure soil fertility, acidity, and aid in making adjustments to the nutrition and care of livestock. These developments led to significant increases in crop yields but also resulted in a number of unintended consequences such as pests developing resistance to pesticides and herbicides and negative impacts on land, water, and habitat and biodiversity. In response to the negative unintended consequences of intensification and industrialization of agriculture as well as concerns about reductions in productivity, a number of efforts are underway to amplify the positive benefits of agricultural production while minimizing its negative impacts.

A global food system optimized around the goal of sustainability could help boost soil fertility and reduce erosion, improve local water quality, reduce runoff, and aid in efforts to mitigate and adapt to climate change by providing buffer zones, sinks to remove greenhouse gases (GHG) from the atmosphere, and energy from current biological sources in order to reduce fossil fuel GHG emissions. The concept of sustainable development provides a solution to the signs of crisis increasingly apparent in various sectors, including food and agricultural production. In 1987, the World Commission on Environment and Development released its report designed to formulate "a global agenda for change" (WCED 1987: ix). In the report, the WCED articulated the most commonly used definition of sustainable development: "Humanity has the ability to make development sustainable – to ensure that it meets the needs of the present without compromising the ability of future generations to meet their own needs" (ibid.: 8). The importance and significance of sustainable development were affirmed in the Agenda 21 program, approved by 179 nations at the 1992 United Nations Conference on Environment and Development in Rio de Janeiro, Brazil (UN 1992). In the intervening time, the importance of sustainable development has been confirmed by a great deal of policy, scholarly, development, and economic activities in a range of sectors – including water, energy, business; in many of these sectors, people are identifying sustainable goals and targets (Ingram and Ingram 2002; *Canada Gazette* 2006; USDA 2007b; NASAA 2008; NOP 2008; Matthew and Hammill 2009).

Improving agricultural sustainability has been recognized as a key component of sustainable development. The WCED recognized that "agricultural production can only be sustained on a long term basis if the land, water, and forests on which it is based are not degraded" (WCED 1987: 133). The understanding that agricultural production must be made sustainable to meet obligations to future generations and to accomplish its goals of providing food in both the short-, near- and long-term is central to the WCED's concept of sustainable agriculture, and explains the definition's broad appeal to scholars, policymakers, and activists. The conceptualization of sustainable agriculture articulated by the WCED, and expanded on by others, explicitly links concerns about sustainable food to sustainability in other areas. To be sustainable, food policies "must take into account all the policies that bear upon the threefold challenge of shifting production to where it is most needed, of securing the livelihoods of rural poor, and of conserving resources" (WCED 1987: 130). Other definitions of sustainable agriculture have enhanced the ideas set out by the WCED.

Sustainable agriculture has been conceptualized and codified under a number of different formulations including no-till agriculture, low-input agriculture, and organic agriculture, many of which share the spirit of sustainable agriculture. For example, FAO finds that the concept of sustainable agriculture refers to a range of techniques and practices intended to "meet the dual goals of increased productivity and reduced environmental impact. They do this through diversification and selection of inputs and management practices that foster positive ecological relationships and biological processes within the entire agro-ecosystem" (FAO 2003a: 304). According to the International Federation of Organic Agriculture Movements (IFOAM 2008), organic agriculture is based on four ethical principles that are designed to inspire action: the principle of health, the principle of ecology, the principle of fairness, and the principle of care. These principles "apply to agriculture in the broadest sense, including the way people tend soils, water, plants and animals in order to produce, prepare and distribute food and other goods. They concern the way people interact with living landscapes, relate to one another and shape the legacy of future generations" (ibid.). In the United States, organic agriculture is defined as "an ecological production management system that promotes and enhances biodiversity, biological cycles and soil biological activity. It is based on minimal use of off-farm inputs and on management practices that restore, maintain and enhance ecological harmony" (USDA 2007b). While there are differences between definitions of sustainable agriculture and the producers of sustainable agriculture, each of these formulations embraces the notion of sustainable agriculture as a set of practices that can both provide for human needs now and in the future while also nourishing and protecting the earth's living systems.

Recognition of the need to improve the sustainability of the global food system have come from a range of sectors and tend to focus on the need to develop appropriate social, political, and technological systems to enable the sustainable intensification of agriculture. After examining trends in global food system, the WCED concluded that "the agricultural resources and the technology needed to feed growing populations are available. Much has been achieved over the past few decades. Agriculture does not lack resources; it lacks policies to ensure that the food is produced where it is needed and in a manner that sustains the livelihoods of the rural poor" (WCED 1987: 118). Per Pinstrup-Andersen argues that, "at this time, the key question confronting us is not whether natural resources are sufficient to feed future generations, but whether appropriate policies and technologies are introduced. Continued degradation of natural resources may bring us to a situation where our current productive capacity will not be sufficient to meet the demand for food" (Pinstrup-Andersen 2002: 1). Jack Wilkinson comments, "We've got enough land, we've got enough resources and we've got enough farmers. We just don't have enough good agricultural policy or the political will to get on a path towards sustainable development" (IFAP 2008). These statements make clear not only the need to make agricultural and food production systems sustainable, but that developing sustainable global food systems will involve confronting the social, political, and technological limiting factors that often constrain discussions and prevent consideration of alternatives.

Sustainable food security also requires full consideration of the likely intended and unintended consequences of sustainability efforts. The global promotion of biofuels provides an excellent example of such unintended consequences. The substitution of fuels made from current biological sources could prove to be important components of strategies to reduce the greenhouse gas emissions of agriculture and food production while also promoting vibrant rural economies and reducing dependence on fossil fuel energy sources. However, such a substitution must be done in ways that are fully aware of total impacts. A key determinant of a biofuel's utility as a fossil fuel substitute is the crop or plants used as its basis and the manner in which fuel is produced. There is evidence that biofuels derived from crops such as switchgrass or forms of algae can lead to substantial reductions in GHG emission compared to fossil fuels (Schmer et al.

2008). However, in many cases recent studies have found that, especially with biofuels made from crops such as corn, the total impact of GHG emissions from biofuels can be higher than GHG emissions from fossil fuels (Begley 2008). Under certain conditions, efforts to promote biofuels could actually lead to greater environmental impacts from agricultural practices as subsidies combine with higher prices to encourage farmers to plant as many acres as possible in biofuel crops, thus increasing impacts on land resources. Biofuel production could also lead to increased impacts on water quality if farmers dramatically increase production of fertilizer-intensive crops such as corn (Donner and Kucharik 2008). Thus we see that failing to fully consider the consequences of environmental sustainability adaptations can amplify rather than ameliorate threats and vulnerabilities to human health, security, and well-being (FAO 2003a).

For decades, sustainable agricultural techniques were seen as impractical and incompatible with the need to intensify agricultural production to meet global food demands. Only in the last decade or so – driven by consumer demands for sustainably produced foods and increasing recognition of agriculture's role in climate change – have sustainable methods begun to be viewed as viable in accomplishing agricultural goals. Like other changes to the food system, such as genetic modification, the utility of sustainable methods remain controversial. In both cases, these sets of agricultural practices have struggled to achieve legitimacy with skeptical critics. In the case of GM foods, limited scientific understanding of the technology has increased the emotional resonance of "science gone astray" and images of "killer tomatoes." Sustainable agriculture, on the other hand, has struggled to be taken seriously as an alternative to conventional agriculture, particularly as critics questioned its ability to meet market needs at prices competitive with conventional agriculture.

Genetic modification is often seen as the antithesis of sustainable agriculture (in the United States for example, foods that are certified organic by the National Organic Standards Program cannot be produced using genetic modification) but GMO technology could make contributions to achieving sustainable intensification of agriculture and food production. Commenting on the eve of a release of a 2009 report by the Royal Society on the importance of considering GM techniques as part of the answer to food security questions, Professor Sir John Beddington, the chief scientific advisor to HM government, remarked, "a range of solutions will be needed if a world population set to pass 8 billion by 2030 is to be fed equitably and sustainably. Improved protection of crops from pests and diseases in the field and during storage will be critical to reducing crop losses and has a major contribution to make" (*The Times*, October 20, 2009). Paul Collier (2009) writes, "The debate over genetically modified crops and food has been contaminated by political and aesthetic prejudices: hostility to US corporations, fear of big science and romanticism about local, organic production . . . genetic modification is analogous to nuclear power: nobody loves it, but climate change has made its adoption imperative." Per Pinstrup-Andersen (2009) also embraces the notion that, while the health and environmental risks of new technologies must be assessed, "such risks should be compared to the health and environmental risks of not releasing a technology. Status quo is not kind to millions of starving children and failure to act now will further deteriorate the environment and make food very expensive for future generations." As these comments suggest, a growing sense of crisis impelled by trends such as rising food prices, persistent inequalities between rich and poor, and concerns about the expected impacts of global climate change are motivating efforts to adopt new technologies like GMOs (Schmidhuber and Tubiello 2007; Beddington 2009).

Many scholars and policymakers have endorsed the notion that under the proper conditions, crops and methods developed using genetic modification have a range of benefits. According to FAO (2003), the benefits from GM crops could include higher crop and livestock yields, lower pesticide and fertilizer applications, less demanding production techniques, higher product quality, better storage and easier processing, and enhanced methods to monitor the health of plants and animals. Reviews by groups such as FAO (2003a), the Royal Society (2009) and the National Research Council (NRC 2010) recognize that there are significant questions about genetically modified foods that need to be addressed. Concerns include: market concentration in the seed industry; intellectual property rights; and biological security concerns about a range of topics including, but not limited to, transfer of modified genes into microbes or pest species, transfer of allergens, mutation of genes, transfer of traits such as sterility, and impacts on animal welfare and biodiversity. Moreover, considerable barriers exist among consumers and environmental activists. As writers such as Shiva (2009), Patel (2009), and Rodale (2010) point out, developing compelling political, scientific, technological, and ethical answers to questions related to genetic modification is an ongoing concern. However, if such concerns can be adequately addressed, genetic modification could provide an important set of methods in developing crops with traits like drought tolerance, salt tolerance, and lower water usage. Under certain conditions, these more resilient crops could make important contributions to a more sustainable agricultural system that could mitigate and adapt to changes in the global environment while also meeting rising demand for food supplies (Pinstrup-Andersen 2002; FAO 2003a; The Royal Society 2009; NRC 2010; Tester and Langridge 2010).

One of the great challenges of envisioning a sustainable food system is that it must be reconciled with the increasingly globalized, networked structure of our world. Some aspects of the development of a network of global food systems remain stark reminders of the need to consider the full environmental impact of actions in the food system. For example, cod caught in the waters off Norway is shipped to China for processing and then shipped back to Norway for sale and consumption, while Great Britain both imports and exports 15,000 tons of waffles each year and both sends Australia and receives from it 20 tons of bottled water each year (*New York Times*, April 26, 2008). The impact of such trade flows, which often only seem profitable by failing to consider the externalities that accrue from the costs of transportation, could be dramatically altered by efforts such as the European Union's 2008 announcement that it would begin requiring all freight-carrying flights to participate in emissions-trading programs by 2012 (ibid.). While global change processes may make the effort to develop a sustainable global food system more difficult in some ways, advances in technology and communication could also open new pathways through strategic decoupling from global networks and the creation of sustainable local food systems. Changes in technology, demographics, and desires to improve food safety and reduce the energy intensiveness and environmental impacts of agricultural and food production systems could coalesce in the development of more robust local food systems.

A particularly fruitful area for the development of local food systems is in urban areas. Although an increasing number of people live in urban areas, most food production continues to be based in rural areas. Already, there is a great deal of evidence that urban poor in many parts of the world use a variety of informal systems to access food supplies, including use of reciprocal trade agreements or short-distance migrations for hunting of animals for bush meat. Initial studies of the impact of urban agricultural efforts in countries such as Namibia, Togo, Zimbabwe, Botswana, and Cuba have demonstrated the many ways urban agricultural systems could help provide key sources of food in more affordable and safer ways (Mougeot 2005). Even in more developed countries, urban agricultural systems have played key roles in improving health and nutrition by increasing agricultural production. A classic example comes from the program of Victory Gardens begun in the United States and Britain during World War II. During this time, some 20 million people answered the US government's call to grow food for local consumption to aid the war effort. By some estimates, Victory Gardens provided up to 40 percent of the food consumed in the United States between 1944 and 1946 (Thone 1943; Hanna and Oh 2000; Victory Seed Company 2008). One result of recent rising food prices and interest in food sustainability and self-sufficiency has been a renewed interest in urban gardening. In San Francisco, the City Hall Lawn was replaced with an organic vegetable garden in 2008 (*Wall Street Journal*, August 8, 2008). In the spring of 2009, US First Lady Michelle Obama worked with Washington, DC schoolchildren to plant a vegetable garden on a 1,100-square-foot plot of the White House's South Lawn, a garden which is the first at the White House since Eleanor Roosevelt's World War II victory garden (*The New York Times*, March 19, 2009). There are also possibilities for the development of intensive, sustainable urban agricultural systems. For instance, Dickson Despommier, a professor of environmental sciences and microbiology at Columbia University, has worked with his students to develop designs for vertical farms housed in skyscrapers, powered by renewable energy sources (Chamberlain 2007; Vertical Farm Project 2008).

While the need to improve the sustainability of the global food system is great, meeting this challenge requires addressing a wide range of scientific, technical, political, economic, and ethical challenges. Neither global trends nor the pace of scientific and technological innovation suggest that the complications of the sustainable intensification of agriculture will become less complex in the future. Publics, activists, and policymakers that are struggling with the implications of climate change and technologies like genetic modification are also being confronted (or are soon to be confronted) by nutraceuticals, or foods that provide health and medical benefits, as well as foods developed, enhanced, or protected using nanotechnology. The challenge of creating a sustainable global food system that can provide all people with sufficient, safe, and nutritious food is by no means simple. Such efforts must be mindful of human needs, sensitive to current and future ecological conditions, and must navigate complex global political, economic, and social systems. However, the ways human societies meet the challenge of growing a sustainable global food system network will be a significant factor in responding to the challenge of climate change and addressing persistent sources of human insecurity.

6

Optimizing Food Safety: Threats to Health and Food Security from Disease, Contamination, and Biological Weapons

The food system, designed to move perishable goods rapidly from producers to consumers, connects many different peoples and places. While the global food system largely provides safe and healthful food, it can also be a means for transmitting threats to human health. Ensuring the health and safety of the food system presents a major challenge to a variety of actors around the world, from producers to consumers and from nations to international organizations. Contamination of food supplies by infectious diseases or chemical hazards can have significant health impacts; each year millions of people become ill or die after consuming contaminated food. Illness and contamination of crops, livestock, and food supplies can also have a significant impact on the cost and availability of food and the health of agricultural and food production systems. The global network of food systems, which transfers products rapidly and under controlled environmental conditions, could also serve as a vector for the transmission of biological threats by criminals or terrorists or in cases of biological warfare.

Concerns about food safety, like many other challenges to global health and security, have become more complex as a result of globalization processes. As discussed in chapter 2, the establishment of interconnected food systems that link many people and places began long ago as desire for spices, foods, and goods encouraged the establishment of trade routes. In recent decades, however, advances in transportation and communication have enhanced the speed and scale of global interactions. Like many global systems, from the air transit system to post and cargo systems, the food system has been transformed by globalization. For instance, the food chains that connect producers and consumers have grown longer as global food production allows consumers in developed countries year-round access to fresh fruits and vegetables. Moreover, global food chains have allowed for great gains in human well-being as consumers in developing countries have, for the most part, gained access to cheaper staple crops such as corn, wheat, and rice.

However, the globalization of the food system, along with the intensification and increased centralization of agriculture and food industries, has created conditions favorable to the spread of contaminants and known diseases as well as the emergence of new forms of diseases. The increasing speed and scale of connections between nodes in the global food network means that when problems do develop, they are often widespread and impact large numbers of people. As Wendell Berry writes, "in a highly centralized and industrialized food supply system there can be no small disaster. Whether it be a production 'error' or corn blight, the disaster is not foreseen until it exists; it is not recognized until it is widespread" (Berry 1996: 223). High profile experiences with food supply contamination demonstrate Berry's concern that, as the global food system has become more closely interconnected, disruptions can rapidly impact large numbers of people across broad geographical areas.

As will be discussed in this chapter, there are several ways that food can be impacted by health threats or contamination: crops or animals can be sickened by viruses, fungi or other threats (such as wheat stem rust or potato blight); food can carry a disease from sick animals to human consumers (such as bovine spongiform encephalopathy or Mad Cow Disease); food may be accidentally contaminated (such as accidental *E. coli* infections in spinach and ice cream); humans can infect a food supply by moving into marginal areas or eating marginal foods (such as the believed evolution of the SARS virus from bats to civets to humans); or food can be intentionally contaminated with diseases or toxins (such as the 1984 contamination of salad bars in The Dalles, Oregon). The scope of these threats is defined by our global food system; these threats have potentially massive impacts in part because they can be so rapidly and efficiently diffused via global networks. For example, in 2008 milk and infant formula in the People's Republic of China was contaminated with melamine and impacted at least 300,000 people in China and led at least 25 countries to impose bans on dairy products from China. Factors such as environmental change (discussed in the previous chapter) or malnutrition (discussed in chapter 4) exacerbate these problems – environmental degradation from climate change, for instance, may increasingly cause humans to seek food sources in marginal areas, thus bringing them into contact with new species and new diseases; or widespread malnutrition may weaken a population's resistances to disease, thus making them more vulnerable to the impacts of food-borne illness.

This chapter focuses on potential disruptions – accidental and intentional – of the food system, bearing in mind at the same time the many benefits a network of global food systems has for human populations. The chapter opens with a review of the impact of globalization on food contamination and global health. The second section considers the set of threats to food safety from accidental contamination of food supplies (a term used to refer to a set of threats arising from contamination due to negligence, poor quality control, or social processes such as travel). In contrast, the third section examines the potential for actors who seek to intentionally cause harm to target food systems or use food systems to transmit threats to health and food safety. The final section outlines the ways food safety interacts with other aspects of food security and also suggests steps that can be taken to ensure that food safety is a core element of integrated food security efforts.

Food safety and global health

Concerns about the safety of the food supply have attracted media coverage and political attention based on recent food safety incidents such as: the contamination of fresh spinach by *E. coli O157:H7* in 2006, pet food with melamine in 2007, dairy products with melamine in 2008, and peanut butter with salmonella in 2009. Ensuring food safety in the global food system involves several different areas of concerns, including: threats to crops and animals from fungi, weeds and viruses, foodborne illness, chemical hazards, concerns about possible impacts from technologies such as genetic modification, and possibilities that actors with nefarious intent could contaminate food systems in deliberate attempts to cause harm to people and animals and cause disruptions with potentially far-reaching political, social, and economic impacts. Efforts by states and nonstate groups to enhance food safety, at both national and global levels, recognize that access to sufficient and nutritious food is a key component for good health and well-being as well as a basic human right. Ensuring food is free from accidental and intentional contamination is essential to human security's goal of ensuring freedom from fear and want, and safety from chronic and pervasive sources of threat and vulnerability.

During the twentieth century, it was hoped that advances in medicine, technology, and public health would significantly reduce, and perhaps even eradicate, health threats to human security. Efforts to improve human health and fight disease have resulted in significant improvements in global health: vaccinations dramatically reduced incidences of polio, the development of antibiotics provided an important tool in treating many bacteriological infections, and a decade-long international effort was successful at eradicating smallpox as a naturally occurring disease (Armelagos 1998). To many in the global health community, it seemed as if humanity stood on the verge of a golden age where science and medicine – along with improvements in sanitation, infrastructure, and technology – would lead to the treatment and cure of persistent health threats from sources such as infectious disease. The dawn of the twenty-first century, however, has seen continued threats to human security from global health challenges. A number of factors – including the development of virulent new strains of wheat stem rust in the late 1990s, the 2003 outbreak of severe acute respiratory syndrome (SARS), and the more recent attention to the 2009 global influenza A (H1N1) pandemic – have raised awareness of the need to promote global public health security (Garrett 2005; Karesh and Cook 2005; Osterholm 2005; WHO 2007d).

The World Health Organization defines global public health security as "the activities required, both proactive and reactive, to minimize vulnerability to acute public health events that endanger the collective health of populations living across geographical regions and international boundaries" (WHO 2007d: xi). This idea of global public health security corresponds closely to what Christopher Chyba (2002) identifies as biological security or "the protection of people and agriculture against disease threats, whether from biological weapons or natural outbreaks." Both of these concepts capture the emerging reality that improving global health involves dealing with a range of challenges, including naturally occurring disease, accidental contamination of food and water systems, severe weather events, industrial accidents, environmental change, and the potential use of diseases intentionally harnessed to serve nefarious ends (WHO 2007d).

Addressing threats to global health is an integral and critical part of maximizing human security. UNDP (1994) identified health security as one of the seven main categories of threats to human security. The Commission on Human Security found that "good health is both essential and instrumental to achieving human security. It is essential because the very heart of human security is protecting lives" (Commission on Human Security 2003: 96). Understanding health threats as a component of human security is also useful as many threats to global health can be most effectively addressed through preventative measures. In developing countries, efforts to improve the distribution of cheap, reliable bed nets demonstrate that, despite advances in treatment of malaria, the most effective interventions are simple ones that reduce the spread of disease among human populations by separating humans from the mosquitoes that spread malaria. In developed countries, recognitions of the health costs of the obesity epidemic and related diseases such as diabetes have prompted a renewed interest in promoting good health during a person's lifespan through education, diet, and exercise rather than waiting for the manifestation of costly and difficult-to-treat conditions. Human security efforts to improve health and well-being and national security efforts to ensure stable public health are increasingly finding a commonality of purpose: ensuring national security by improving global public health (NIC 2000; Brower and Chalk 2003).

A human security approach also emphasizes addressing distributional aspects of global health challenges. Globalization has led to increasing levels of connectivity, but the impacts of this connectivity are not equally distributed. Timothy W. Luke writes "globalization has meant real material progress for many of the world's people. Yet, these improvements are not being shared equally" (Luke 2001b:

6). Increasing numbers of people in both developed and developing countries face health threats related to their diet and lifestyle such as obesity, heart disease, and diabetes. Concurrently, others face health threats from infectious disease, poor sanitation, inadequate nutrition, and lack of clean water. Efforts to improve global health must take into account these basic inequalities. In recent years, there has been a growing focus on the way that developments in science and technology may make possible great improvements in human health and well-being. Many of these solutions rely on high technology approaches such as genetically re-engineering the genome of mosquitoes to make them unable to serve as a vector for the spread of malaria parasites or the development of new generations of genetically modified crops that could be used to distribute vaccines. Despite the focus on the promise and potential of high technology solutions to improve global health, "improvements in overall health measures for most of humanity will not come from twenty-first century medicine, but rather from nineteenth century public health practices" (ibid.: 15). While new technologies may offer promise and potential, efforts to develop and implement them should not distract from the many real gains to health that can be achieved through strategies such as improvements in basic nutrition, vitamin intake, and the development of water treatment and sanitation systems (Garrett 1994, 2007; Luke 2001b).

A major source of global threats to health and food safety comes from infectious diseases. Infectious diseases are caused by pathogenic microorganisms (including bacteria, viruses, parasites or fungi) that are spread through transmission from an infected host to another organism along four pathways: (1) direct contact with an infected organism; (2) airborne transmission when microorganisms attach to dust particles or when they are contained in aerosols; (3) contact with a contaminated common vehicle, such as food, water, or blood; and (4) by vector-borne spread such as an insect (McNamara 2007). Infectious diseases are a major global cause of death. Each year millions of people succumb to diseases like HIV/AIDS, malaria, and tuberculosis; the everyday health and well-being of many people is also impacted by infectious diseases. Revisions to data in 2007 showed that, while rates of global HIV prevalence are leveling off and rates of new HIV infections are falling, there are still between an estimated 30.6 and 36.1 million people living with HIV and between 1.9 and 2.4 million annual deaths from AIDS (UNAIDS 2007). Malaria also remains a persistent threat to human health. "Approximately, 40% of the world's population, mostly those living in the world's poorest countries, are [sic] at risk of malaria. Every year, more than 500 million people become severely ill with malaria" (WHO 2007a). Deadly in its own right, tuberculosis (TB) has made the news in recent years due to an increase in rates of infection among individuals with compromised immune systems. WHO estimates that in 2005 there were 8.8 million new cases of TB, 7.4 million of these cases occurring in sub-Saharan Africa and Asia. In the same year, 1.6 million people died of TB, including 195,000 who were also infected with HIV (WHO 2007b, 2008).

Infectious diseases can have significant and widespread impacts on individuals, communities, and societies. A 2003 study by the Institute of Medicine found that "the ability of infectious agents to destabilize populations, economies, and governments is fast becoming a sad fact of life. The prevention and control of infectious diseases are fundamental to individual, national, and global health and security" (Smolinski et al. 2003). Moreover, ill health is directly correlated to poverty and other forms of disenfranchisement. WHO reports that "ongoing ill-health is one of the main reasons why the poor stay poor. Infections lead to poverty, and poverty leads to infections" (WHO 2002b: 12). Negative disease impacts also include weakening the workforce and the economic foundation of a state, undermining confidence in a state's ability to protect and provide for its population, as well as negatively impacting peoples' social and cultural lives (Brower and Chalk 2003). The impact of infectious diseases and ill health are magnified by interactive effects from hunger and poor nutrition. In addition to problems directly linked to a lack of proper nutrition, "malnutrition magnifies the effect of every disease, including measles and malaria" (World Hunger Education Service 2006). Numerous factors are responsible for the spread and impact of infectious disease; the nature of threats from infectious disease has been accelerated by development of an increasingly interconnected world and globalization processes that have increased flows of people and goods and reduced the time required to travel from one part of the world to the next (NIC 2000; Garrett 2001; Brower and Chalk 2003; Smolinski et al. 2003).

The potentially devastating and widespread impact of infectious diseases can be seen in historical examples. For instance, an outbreak of bubonic plague that struck Europe between 1346 and 1350 is estimated to have caused mortality in approximately one-third of the total population of Europe (McNeill 1998). The 1918 Spanish influenza pandemic sickened approximately 20 to 40 percent of the global population and is estimated to have killed more than 500,000 people in the United States and 20 million people globally (Crosby 1990; United States Department of Health and Human Services 2004). The eradication of smallpox as a naturally occurring disease is often cited as one of the greatest triumphs of medicine in the twentieth century, for good reason. In the century prior to its eradication, smallpox claimed hundreds of millions of lives and by some estimates killed half a billion people (Tucker 2001). In addition to causing mortality, diseases can impose a range of impacts on people such as permanent health impairments and reduced productivity which can aggregate into considerable social, economic, and political impacts on states. The relationship between humans and diseases has not been static and even the nature of what is considered a disease has altered over time. As historian William McNeill comments, "nearsightedness and a dull sense of smell, which we regard as compatible with good health, would probably have been classed as crippling diseases by our hunting ancestors . . . a person who can no longer perform expected tasks because of bodily disorder will always seem diseases to his fellows" (McNeill 1998: 27). Global health threats remain a major challenge to human well-being and security, yet it is useful to recall that our era is not alone in facing a shifting landscape of health challenges (Omran 1971; Armelagos 1998).

In the twenty-first century, threats to human security from infectious disease include the reappearance of diseases many believed eradicated, as well as the emergence of new forms of infectious disease. In recent decades, diseases once thought treatable and controllable, such as tuberculosis or cholera, have re-emerged in more virulent forms that are resistant to established treatment regimens.

Newly emerging diseases, such as West-Nile virus, SARS, and new influenza strains such as H1N1 are reminders that the disease landscape is continually evolving; as WHO (2007d) notes, for the last forty years there has been at least one new disease identified every year, and forty alone in the last decade. The 2003 outbreak of SARS provided a real world example of the rapid pace with which infectious diseases can emerge and spread. The US Centers for Disease Control and Prevention (CDC 2005) has described the rapid spread of SARS between the first reports of the disease in Asia in February 2003 and its appearance in two dozen countries on three continents before it was contained. This emergence and re-emergence of infectious disease is most troubling when contextualized in an increasingly interconnected world (Garrett 1994; Smolinski et al. 2003; Brower and Chalk 2003; Jones et al. 2008).

Though disease has always had the ability to destabilize localized populations and economies, the speed and scale of interactions of widely dispersed human populations increases disease's resulting disorder. Concerns about amplified threats from disease are also augmented because the number of people living in cities, long recognized as environments conducive to the development and spread of disease, is growing (UNFPA 2007). Although more and more people are living in urban and peri-urban areas, many people, especially poor people, continue to live in rural environments and their lifestyles and settlement patterns are also a significant factor in shaping the global health landscape. According to the World Bank, 75 percent of poor people in developing countries live in rural areas, and these people are increasingly forced onto degraded or marginal land in an effort to survive (World Bank 2007). In these marginal spaces, many rural poor seek food sources from wild animal populations. These interactions between humans and wild animal species are an important factor in the emergence of new infectious diseases. Over 60 percent of identified infectious diseases, including influenza, plague, and salmonella, can affect both humans and animals. The food system is a key connector between animals and people as many zoonotic diseases transfer to humans through processes involved in the killing, processing, and consumption of animals (Karesh and Cook 2005).

Environmental and climate change represent another major factor which could have significant impacts on health and food safety in the twenty-first century. The expected impacts of climate change will likely change the landscape of health threats facing human populations. Climate change could impact global health by altering the range of pathogens and hosts that carry diseases as well as contributing to disease by increasing the frequency, intensity, and duration of extreme weather events (NRC 2001; Brower and Chalk 2003; IPCC 2007). One sign of the growing recognition of links between climate change and health was the World Health Organization's decision to focus on the impacts of climate change on human health as the theme for World Health Day 2008. On the occasion of World Health Day 2008, UN Secretary General Ban Ki-moon acknowledged the linkages between climate change, food, and health in his official remarks: "Climate change endangers the quality and availability of water and food, our fundamental determinants of nutrition and health. It is causing more frequent and more severe storms, heat wave, droughts and floods and worsening the quality of our air. The result is an upsurge in human suffering caused by injury, disease, malnutrition, and health" (Ban 2008). Another source of health threats comes from heat waves, especially among the elderly and people with respiratory conditions such as asthma (Chan 2008). Already, the impacts of climate change are linked to increasing severity of weather patterns such as the heat wave that struck Europe in 2003 and claimed the lives of 35,000 people (WHO 2007d). Finally, as discussed in chapter 3, impacts on global health may also come through mechanisms such as reduced agricultural productivity which could have a range of impacts on health and food security.

Global change processes, including shifting patterns of human habitation, have created new pathways, edge zones, and intermingling population compositions that create fertile ground for the emergence and spread of infectious diseases. The rapid pace of modern transportation means that diseases that emerge in one location can rapidly move into others. In such an urbanized and interconnected world, it is unlikely that spatial distance, such as the barriers between sparsely populated rural areas and dense urban populations, or geographic barriers, such as mountain ranges or oceans, will provide much protection from infectious disease. The global food system is a considerable component of global trade flows, and is a significant link between the world's people and places. Addressing threats to global health and food security is a necessary component of efforts to maximize human health and well-being. As the next section describes, a significant threat to food security comes from natural or accidental contamination of food supplies.

Food safety threats from accidental contamination

Whether localized or global, food contamination is a major source of ill health and death worldwide. WHO estimates that approximately two million children die each year from diarrheal illnesses caused by contaminated food and water (WHO and WTO 2002). Within the United States, CDC estimates that approximately one out of every four Americans will develop a foodborne illness each year (or 76 million cases per year), and that these cases result in 325,000 hospitalizations and 5,000 deaths (Mead 1999). Marion Nestle writes that "such numbers undoubtedly *underestimate* the extent of the problem" (Nestle 2003: 27, emphasis in the original). Though many of these events are local ones, increasing attention is being paid to food contamination that is national or even international in scope. As the global food system is built around increasing international connectivity, global food networks can be vectors for the transmission of health threats. As a result, contamination of food supplies can sicken large numbers of people over a vast geographic area in a relatively short period of time. For example, an outbreak of salmonella in 1985 linked to post-pasteurization contamination of milk from a US dairy sickened 170,000 people (Ryan et al. 1987), and in 1994 an ice cream pre-mix that was contaminated with salmonella caused illness in over 220,000 people in 41 states (Hennessy et al. 1996).

Even in the absence of direct impacts on human populations, contamination of food systems can cause tremendous economic, political and social harm. In 2003, for example, one-third of global meat exports (6 million tons) were affected by an animal disease outbreak, causing an estimated $10 billion in losses (FAO 2004).

Avian influenza A (H5N1) is only one of a series of livestock disease outbreaks that have caused losses of more than $100 billion over the past fifteen years (Bio Economic Research Associates 2003). Contamination of food supplies by diseases or other substances can cause high levels of wastage and spoilage of foods that lead to an increase in prices and a failure to recoup significant resources invested to bring crops or livestock to market. It is also important to consider the full impact of efforts to reduce threats from such diseases. Efforts to control diseases such as avian influenza A (H5N1) often utilize programs that involve culling of infected birds. Such culling programs can be effective in halting the spread of diseases, but if inadequate compensation measures are in place then farmers may be unwilling to report illnesses among their flocks or choose to dispose of livestock through black or grey markets in order to recoup some of the resources invested in the infected animals. Poorly planned or implemented disease control efforts can thus amplify the very threats they are attempting to control (Karesh and Cook 2005).

A significant amount of foodborne illness results from microorganisms that are transmitted to humans through contaminated food. Many countries' public health systems have recognized an increasing threat to human health and well-being from pathogens such as *Salmonella*, *Campylobacter*, and *Escherichia coli*; and parasites such as *Cryptosporidium* and *Cryptospora* (WHO 2002b; Nestle 2003). As discussed above, foodborne diseases can have widespread impacts on human health and high economic costs. Rising rates of foodborne illness are driven by many factors, most of which are linked to changing patterns of food production and consumption driven by globalization. The World Health Organization finds "changes in farm practices, more extensive food distributions systems, and the increasing preference for meat and poultry in developing countries all have the potential to increase the incidence of foodborne illness" (WHO 2002b: 8). Experts such as nutritionist Marion Nestle (2003) identify additional drivers of food safety concerns. The factors include: competitiveness among food companies to encourage people to consume their products rather than a competitor's products; pressures exerted by food companies on government regulators to make decisions favorable to companies and their products; the invocation of science to support achievement of commercial goals by food companies; and a fundamental clash in the values of actors involved in food safety debates, including industry, government, and consumers. Other sources of foodborne illness come from changes in the ways that people are eating food, such as a growing preference for foods that are fresh, whole, or minimally processed (and are thus seen, perhaps ironically, as more natural and healthful but that are likelier than cooked or processed foods to carry foodborne illness). As Barry Glassner writes, "we're more likely to become sick from what we eat today than we were fifty years ago in large measure because we're eating more raw fruits and vegetables. Our parents and grandparents cooked their veggies and skinned their fruits, thereby eliminating bacteria and viruses" (Glassner 2007: xi). There is also a general trend moving away from meals prepared in homes for immediate consumption and towards consumption of prepared foods with longer time intervals between food preparation and consumption, another tendency that increases rates of foodborne illness (WHO 2002b).

As with global health concerns in general, the rising rates and severity of health and food safety threats reflect the emergence of previously unknown threats. Significant threats to food security are represented by fungi and viruses that impact plants, such as stem rusts which are very contagious diseases that affect cereal crops including wheat, oats, and barley. Eradicating stem rust, caused by the fungus *Puccinia graminis*, was a major focus during the Green Revolution. While threats from stem rust were thought to have been eradicated, the emergence of a dangerous new strain in Uganda in 1998 (identified as Ug99) potentially threatens wheat crops throughout Africa, the Middle East, and West Asia. The fear is that it could reduce wheat yields and cause widespread social and economic harm – up to $10 billion annually if the fungus were to reach so far as the United States (Pennisi 2010). With regard to human health, *Escherichia coli* (abbreviated as *E. coli*) are a large and diverse group of bacteria. While most strains of *E. coli* are harmless, some strains cause illness. Of particular interest are those strains of *E. coli* that cause disease by producing what is called a Shiga toxin. The best known of these strains is *E. coli* O157:H7 which was first identified as a pathogen in 1982 and has caused illness and death (especially among children) through contamination of foods such as ground beef, unpasteurized apple cider, milk, lettuce, alfalfa sprouts, and even drinking water in several countries (WHO 2002b). Other newly emerging food safety threats include more virulent or antibiotic resistant forms of *Salmonella typhimurium* (Ryan et al. 1987; Hennessy et al. 1996; WHO 2002b) and exotic diseases such as bovine spongiform encephalopathy, also known as "Mad Cow Disease."

BSE emerged as a subject of concern in Great Britain in the 1990s. By 1999 it had infected 175,000 cattle and prompted the destruction of more than 4 million infected cattle (Nestle 2003). In cattle, BSE is a fatal, neurodegenerative disease; it is believed that the disease may be transmitted to human beings who eat infected carcasses (FDA 2005). In humans, BSE is known as variant *Creutzfeldt-Jakob disease* (vCJD or nvCJD). As of December 2009, vCJD had been identified as the definite or probable cause of death in 166 people in Britain and at least 37 people in other countries, including the United States and Canada (NCJDSU 2009). In addition to causing human fatalities, BSE has had major impacts on the beef production of countries where cases have been discovered. In the United Kingdom, it has cost an estimated $7 billion in losses (Nestle 2003). In the United States, beef exports declined from $3.8 billion in 2003 (prior to the discovery of the first infected cow in the US) to $1.4 billion in 2005 (*USA Today*, August 3, 2006).

Contamination of food supplies by chemicals is another source of food safety concerns. Chemical contaminants originate from a number of sources, including environmental contamination from mercury and lead, marine toxins, and even naturally occurring chemicals in plants, such as glycoalkaloids in potatoes (WHO 2002b). The danger of chemical contamination of food supplies was demonstrated by high profile cases of contaminated pet food in 2007. A variety of pet food brands produced by Menu Foods was contaminated by wheat gluten containing melamine, a coal byproduct used to make plastics that producers added to wheat gluten to increase its weight and increase the appearance of its protein content in nutritional tests (FDA 2008). Melamine contamination in pet food sickened or killed an unknown number of pets (counts range from 14 to several thousand) and led to the recall of 60 million cans and packets of dog and cat foods, which is to date the largest recall of consumer products in the United States (Nestle 2008: 1). Menu Foods estimates that the total costs of the contamination to its pet food brands, including the costs of recalling impacted product lines, damage to its image and market share, and settling civil claims with owners of affected pets, to reach more than $53 million (*MSNBC*, April 1, 2008). Similarly, melamine also appeared in the 2008 Chinese milk scandal where milk, infant formula, and other food materials and components were adulterated with melamine, impacting an estimated 300,000 people and causing almost 52,000 hospitalizations and three confirmed deaths. As with the pet food scandal, melamine appeared to have been added to milk powder in order to cause it to appear to have higher protein content. Impact widened beyond China to at least 25 countries that banned Chinese milk, eggs, and derivative products. In China, where the widespread contamination of infant formulas was dramatically covered by the media and brought public calls for greater regulation, two people were executed and 19 imprisoned for their role in the scandal (*BBC News*, November 30, 2009).

Beyond efforts to ensure that food supplies are not unintentionally contaminated by biological or chemical contaminates, efforts to ensure food safety must also take into account that some actors might intentionally introduce contaminants into food systems. For reasons such as crime, terrorism, or warfare, actors with nefarious intent might turn to the food system as a means to distribute a biological agent to a desired target population.

Food safety threats from intentional contamination

Modern food systems are designed to rapidly move goods to people on a vast scale, thus making them an ideal target for disruption or for use as a delivery system for a biological agent. In recent years, concerns about biological weapons threats have received a great deal of policy and media attention, especially in the post-September 11 period and in the lead-up to the 2003 war in Iraq. In addition to concerns about terrorism, the threat of biological weapons provided an important, although unsubstantiated, component of the case made by the United States for a preemptive war against Iraq (White House 2003). Awareness of the possibility of such intentional use of biological agents to cause harm was increased by the Amerithrax anthrax incidents in the fall of 2001. Beginning one week after the September 11 attacks, the Amerithrax incidents involved anthrax spores spread through the mail system by letters containing anthrax spores. Between September and November 2001, letters were sent to media organizations in New York and Florida as well as the offices of two Democratic Senators, Tom Daschle of South Dakota and Patrick Leahy of Vermont. The incidents, believed to be the work of a US scientist who committed suicide prior to being prosecuted, resulted in anthrax infections in at least 22 individuals, with eleven of these cases presenting as life-threatening inhalation anthrax, and caused the deaths of five people (FBI 2009). The Amerithrax attacks, with their direct impacts on the US government and major media outlets, brought to the fore a discussion of the potential use of biological agents. Following the incident, a significant amount of attention was given to the vulnerability of citizens, livestock, and food supplies to intentional attacks using biological weapons (CDC 2001a, 2001b; FDA 2002; Flynn 2004)

Biological agents have been employed as weapons in numerous conflicts, but rarely have they had significant impacts on the outcomes of conflicts. Some of the earliest documented cases come from the fourteenth and fifteenth centuries, but modern use of biological weapons dates to World Wars I and II, and related technologies experienced a period of rapid development during the Cold War (Guillemin 2005; Lewis n. d.). The Biological and Toxin Weapons Convention (BTWC), which entered into force in March 1975, outlawed the development and use of biological weapons and led to the closing of state-based research in offensive biological weapons (BTWC 1972). However, the defection of a key scientist from the former Soviet Union in the 1990s revealed that significant research programs into biological weapons continued to exist even though the USSR had signed the BTWC (Alibek 1999). Disclosures such as these demonstrate the difficulty involved in monitoring the development of biological weapons.

There is some disagreement about the degree of difficulty involved in creating and successfully employing a weaponized biological agent. Ken Alibek, a former top official in the Soviet Union's biological weapons program, states that biological weapons are "cheap, easy to make and easy to use" (Alibek 1999). In contrast, Raymond Zilinskas, a former UN weapons inspector and director of the Monterey Institute of International Studies' Chemical Biological Weapons Nonproliferation Program, suggests that there are a number of difficulties involved in creating and successfully employing a biological agent (Zilinskas 2000). Some of the discussion about the degree of difficulty involved in creating biological weapons depends on how one defines "success." In the narrowest sense, being successful means creating a biological agent that can cause harm, while a broader interpretation of success, especially with regards to the successful integration of a biological weapon into a military apparatus, includes the employment of such an agent to accomplish a desired goal while also ensuring the protection of military forces and untargeted civilian populations (Lederberg 1999; Zilinskas 2000).

As of 2010, most instances of terrorist or criminal activity using biological weapons have only caused mortality and morbidity in relatively low numbers of people. Two examples will demonstrate this point. First, in September and October 1984, an outbreak of salmonella occurred in The Dalles, Oregon. The contaminant sickened 751 people in what was later revealed to be a deliberate effort by a local religious cult to influence the outcome of a local election by deliberately contaminating ten salad bars in local restaurants. Investigators examining the outbreak had great difficulty determining the cause of the outbreak, and only did so after one of the perpetrators revealed the cult's involvement and motives for the incident (Torok et al. 1997; Christopher et al. 1997). Second, the Japanese Aum Shinrikyo cult attempted unsuccessfully to develop and distribute biological weapons prior to launching their 1995 attack using the nerve agent sarin in the Tokyo subways. Despite significant resources and expertise, the cult encountered difficulties in finding the right strain of anthrax to use as biological weapons and in developing effective aerosol means to distribute the weapon they developed (Kaplan 1996). These two examples demonstrate some of the difficulties involved in the successful development and employment of biological agents, but also reveal high degrees of creativity and flexibility in the use of agents to achieve desired purposes (Tucker 2000). Going forward, one source of concern is that developments in biological science and technology may facilitate the process of selecting, weaponizing, and employing a biological agent to cause harm (CIA 2003).

Some of the difficulties in successfully employing biological weapons relate to the technical challenges of distributing a weapon using an aerosol release. Environmental factors such as wind, sunlight, and precipitation can hamper the effectiveness of an aerosol distribution of a biological weapon. These challenges have led to thoughts that alternative means to transmit a biological weapon, such as using the food system, could provide greater predictability for transmission to humans as well as potential for attacks that target the food system itself. While much attention from the threat of biological weapons has focused on their potential impact on humans, such weapons could also be used on food systems (including crops and livestock as well as threats to nonfood crops and materials such as timber or cotton). As modern food distribution systems are designed to rapidly move large numbers of goods to large numbers of people under highly controlled environmental and temperature conditions, some researchers worry that they could be an ideal target for disruption or for use as a delivery vehicle for some sort of weaponized biological agent (GAO 2003; Chalk 2004; Wein and Liu 2005).

Awareness of the potential vulnerability of the food systems focuses attention on the fact that biological weapons, like naturally occurring diseases, can also impact nonhuman target populations. Despite its seemingly harmless nature compared to other biological weapons scenarios, anti-crop terrorism or warfare could have devastating impacts. In developed countries, loss of significant amounts of crops could have widespread economic and social impacts. In developing countries, attacks on staple crops could create famines and attendant problems such as reduced immune resistance that could ultimately be as destructive as a direct attack on human populations using a biological weapon. Anti-crop attacks might also be used for more distal purposes, such as an effort to discredit a political or economic competitor. This principle was demonstrated by the Revolutionary

Palestinian Commando and the Revolutionary Palestinian Council which used salmonella and mercury to contaminate Israeli produce in the late 1970s in an effort to discredit Israeli agriculture (Khan et al. 2001). On a strategic level, food system attacks might be ideal for situations preceding other military activity such as an invasion by a foreign power, commencement of a civil war, or for situations where combatants seek to distract or cripple an opponent rather than directly confront them (Whitby and Rogers 1997; Rogers et al. 1999).

Despite a great deal of public and policy attention to nefarious biological threats in recent years, many more people are impacted on a daily basis by chronic infectious disease threats and problems like malnutrition and lack of clean water. Efforts to address global health threats must thus address natural infectious diseases as well as preparing for potential nefarious uses of biological agents. Popular media coverage of weaponized biological agents and their potential use tends to focus on the gruesome aspects of their use, but specialists urge that we be mindful that "the revulsion evoked by these weapons does not push us to take actions with unacceptable adverse effects on competing interests, including the promotion of legitimate research, civil liberties and public health" (Stern 2002: 123). There is also a need to develop more sophisticated understandings of various actors such as terrorist organizations who may seek to utilize biological agents to cause harm. Research into the behavior of terrorist organizations demonstrates that multiple factors, beyond just the ability of a weapon to cause harm or death, determine the sorts of weapons and tactics are seen as desirable to be deployed by groups and individuals in efforts to accomplish political aims (Horgan 2005; Bloom 2007). The World Health Organization (2007d) also emphasizes the need to consider potential health impacts from deliberate contamination incidents as part of the much broader range of challenges facing the global public health community. Global health and security communities should not let the possibility of nefarious infectious disease threats impede efforts to make real progress on more pervasive threats to global health and human security.

Addressing threats to health and food safety

While this chapter focuses on contamination of food supplies, it is worth stressing that the global food system largely provides safe and nutritious foods. However, there is general agreement that globalization and global change have resulted in amplification of food safety threats. Despite efforts to improve food safety, foodborne illness remains a significant source of sickness and death and it is worth examining the systems that have developed to promote safety and security in the food system. As with analysis of any network, examining the trends, outliers, and anomalies can reveal important information about the ways it is functioning well and help identify areas where there is room for improvement.

With regards to improving food safety in the United States, the recognition of more complex challenges to health and food safety has resulted in some revisions to established food safety systems. The current food safety system in the United States is heavily influenced by the history of its development. Prior to the twentieth century, food safety was not seen as a responsibility of the US federal government. Reporting by journalists such as Upton Sinclair (2003) on the practices of slaughterhouses and meatpacking operations prompted public concern and resulted in the passing in 1906 of the Pure Food and Drugs Act and the Meat Inspection Act. By passing these acts, Congress accepted that food safety was an appropriate area for federal oversight and made the US Department of Agriculture, because of its established staff of veterinary specialists, responsible for inspecting animals and keeping sick animals out of the food system. In subsequent decades, the Pure Food and Drugs Act was revised and amended and USDA underwent several reorganizations. While it retained responsibility for the inspection of meat and poultry, the management of other food products gradually shifted away from USDA. In 1930, the Food and Drug Administration was created within USDA but was eventually transferred out of USDA and into the Department of Health and Human Services (Institute of Medicine 1998; Nestle 2003).

US federal oversight of food safety continued to evolve, though it often lacked a grand vision of a comprehensive and coordinated strategy to ensure food safety. By 2001, the system had grown in complexity until, as described in a report to Congress by the US Government Accountability Office (GAO; prior to 2004, GAO was called the General Accounting Office), the federal food safety system included up to 35 different laws and involved 12 different agencies (GAO 2001). The result of the gradual evolution of responsibility for food safety is that oversight responsibility is dispersed among different agencies, often without logical divisions. As Marion Nestle writes, "the consequences of this system are famously absurd . . . The USDA, for example, oversees production of hot dogs in pastry dough, the FDA regulates hot dogs in rolls. The USDA regulates corn dogs, the FDA regulates bagel dogs. The USDA regulates pepperoni pizza; the FDA regulates cheese pizza" (Nestle 2003: 55–7).

A number of studies have discussed the flaws in this system and outlined the need for a streamlined system that could better protect the interests of consumers and ease the burden of regulation on food producers. A 2001 study by GAO concluded that "the current food safety system is a patchwork structure that hampers efforts to adequately address existing and emerging food safety risks" (GAO 2001). While piecemeal reforms to food safety oversight continued to be made, calls to rectify the food safety situation in the US often stress the need for a single independent agency focused solely on the goals of food safety along the lines of the UK's Food Standards Agency. A 1998 report from the Institute of Medicine found that the fragmentation of oversight for food safety resulted in a system that was not well equipped to meet emerging challenges (IOM 1998). Following a review of a number of recommendations to improve food safety from government agencies and independent bodies, the GAO stressed the need to create "a single food safety agency to administer a uniform, risk based inspection system" (GAO 2001: 16). By 2008, the web of federal agencies with responsibilities for food safety had grown to 15 agencies, administering at least 30 laws related to food safety (GAO 2008). However, as of 2010, US governmental reform efforts remained focused on improving the FDA rather than moving to the unified food system recommended by many experts and the GAO.

The importance of improving coordination of food safety efforts has also gained attention at the international level. In May 2000, the

53rd World Health Assembly adopted a resolution calling for WHO and its members to recognize food safety as an essential component of global public health. Among other requests, Resolution WHA53.15 asks that WHO: "give greater emphasis to food safety . . . and to work towards integrating food safety as one of WHO's essential public health functions, with the goal of developing sustainable, integrated food-safety systems for the reduction of health risk along the entire food chain, from the primary producer to the consumer" (WHO 2000b). Ensuring food safety was recognized as involving a range of issues that operate at many levels of analysis, from the national level to the subnational level, from the global level to the individual level, and that if they are to be successful, food safety efforts must reduce health risks "along the entire food chain, from the primary producer to the consumer" (WHO 2002b). In response to this resolution, WHO has given increased attention to the promotion of food safety as an integral part of its mission to ensure "the attainment by all people of the highest possible level of health" (ibid.: 10). The WHO's Global Strategy for Food Safety includes seven dimensions of activity: strengthening surveillance systems of foodborne diseases; improving risk assessments; developing methods for assessing the safety of the products of new technologies; enhancing the scientific and public health role of WHO international forums; enhancing risk communication and advocacy; improving international and national cooperation; and strengthening capacity building in developing countries (ibid.). These seven approaches are not meant to be exclusive areas of activity, and WHO recognizes interdependencies among the approaches, as well as the importance of integrating their efforts with the activities of FAO and the Codex Alimentarius Commission.

FAO works through a variety of programs, including its Food Quality and Standards division, which are concerned with the improvement of the quality and safety of food at the international, regional, and national levels. It operates through the promotion of national food safety frameworks that take into account relevant international requirements and provide technical advice, capacity building, and scientific assistance (FAO 2008). The Codex Alimentarius (or food code) Commission is an international body that was created in 1963 by the WHO and FAO to develop food standards aimed at protecting the health of consumers, ensuring fair trade practices in the food trade, and promoting coordination of all food standards work undertaken by international governmental and nongovernmental organizations. These international efforts to promote food safety operate primarily by developing capacity and standardization among national-level food safety programs and also seek to tie food safety efforts into larger programs designed to improve global health.

A key element of conceptualizations of human security is that all people must be empowered to address the disruptions in their daily lives and the threats to their health and well-being. This chapter has focused on discussing the evolving nature of threats to food safety, with a specific focus on the way that contamination of food systems, either unintentional or intentional, constitutes a significant source of threat and vulnerability to food security. The chapter has paid particular attention to the fact that efforts to protect human health from foodborne illness do not exist in isolation and are an important component of broader efforts to improve global health and well-being. Recognizing this interdependence between health and food safety is essential to developing meaningful strategies to address threats to global health. Meeting food safety and global health needs will involve state and nonstate diplomatic, security, health, and development organizations working together to achieve goals that none are able to achieve independently.

Addressing global health challenges must also be done in ways that are mindful of human security goals to protect and empower individuals and communities and ensure freedom from fear and want. Such efforts must also ensure that discussions about the goals to be met, the methods to be used, and the strategies to evaluate success allow for the participation of involved individuals and communities. One of the essential functions of efforts to address health threats to human security is that such efforts bring discussions about how to reduce threat and vulnerability into forums where individuals and communities can be involved in defining problems, prioritizing efforts, and developing solutions. Efforts to improve food safety may also require more detailed examinations of the extent to which network connectivity enhances food security and food safety. As discussed in chapter 5, strategic decoupling from global food networks could provide ways, in certain places and for certain types of foods, to both enhance food security and support the development of sustainable livelihoods. The promise of public health in the twentieth century was a world free from disease and ill health. While the lessons of past decades may have dimmed hopes that health challenges and infectious disease will ever be part of humanity's past, the magnitude of impacts on human livelihoods and well-being from global health threats like foodborne illness make it clear that improving the health of people around the world is a necessary component of efforts to ensure food security.

Conclusion: Sustainable Food Security

The objective of this book was to consider how processes of global change and the emergence of a more networked world shape efforts to provide people with the food they need to live healthy lives. In the increasingly globalized network of agricultural and food production systems I have described, fewer people produce for themselves the food they require but are instead dependent on the emerging global food system. This means that food security issues such as malnutrition, global environmental change, and food safety, each explored in depth in this book, must be understood as multi-causal and multidisciplinary challenges. Understanding the interactive nature of these food security challenges identifies important solution sets and reveals the need for better coordination between often disparate efforts to address core factors that contribute to food insecurity.

As the discussions in previous chapters reveal, solutions to food insecurity must come through strategies that are sustainable both for human societies and for the environment on which they rely. These two goals have long been seen in opposition to one another, as solutions to food insecurity often relied on simply increasing global food supplies. Instead, understanding the complex causes of food insecurity opens up a range of solutions that encompass far more actions than expanding agricultural productivity. While addressing food security does require sustainably intensifying agricultural production in order to meet demands from growing global populations, food security also means confronting social, ethical, economic, and political questions about how we grow, produce, and consume food. In this way, many questions about food security are intimately intertwined with larger questions about the consequences of consumption and the need to carefully consider what material requirements truly enable people to lead secure, dignified, and sustainable lives (Luke 1997, 1999; Princen 2005, 2010; Dauvergne 2008).

Too often, discussions of food security begin in response to national, regional, or global crises, rather than identifying the policies and methods needed to build a just, equitable, and sustainable global food system. In times of crisis, solutions must be crafted in short time frames, before political, economic, and public attention shifts elsewhere. Short-term solutions developed to meet crises – from local droughts to global price increases – tend to lead only to more short-term solutions which may seem to address the needs of immediate crisis situations but often cause problems further down the line. As global, national, and human security become increasingly dependent on finding ethical and equitable ways to address issues like food security, it is vital that considerations of world food problems take holistic rather than piecemeal perspectives.

This book presents two sets of standards that have great utility in guiding these kinds of holistic efforts to ensure food security. First, from human security, we can take four essential characteristics of solutions: they must be universal and relevant to all people everywhere; they must be interdependent; they must embrace understandings that human security is easier to ensure through early prevention rather than later intervention; and they must be people centered and reach solutions by empowering individuals and communities (UNDP 1994; Commission on Human Security 2003). Human security does not seek to replace international or national security as areas of concern, but rather to supplement them by bringing attention to a range of factors – from food insecurity to ill health to loss of livelihoods – whose impacts are most often felt in the lives of individuals and communities. In the decades since the end of the Cold War, the defense, diplomatic, and developmental sectors have increasingly come to see their missions as interactive and complementary. As US Secretary of Defense Robert Gates writes, “In the decades to come, the most lethal threats to the United States’ safety and security . . . are likely to emanate from states that cannot adequately govern themselves or secure their own territory” (Gates 2010: 2). Militaries facing protracted asymmetrical conflicts find that development and diplomacy that enable real and enduring human security gains are key components of successful war-fighting strategies (Ministry of Defense 2010; United States Department of Defense

2010). Development agencies and nongovernmental organizations also increasingly recognize the need to ensure security in order to make progress on humanitarian, health or conservation goals (Rutherford 2008; Hammill et al. 2009). Frameworks that enable understanding of environment and natural resources issues, which are often discussed for their role in causing, funding and contributing to conflicts, can also present opportunities for cooperation and peacebuilding (Matthew, Brown and Jensen 2009). In an age where the dimensions of security challenges are defined by failing states, instability, and transnational threat systems, human security represents an important component of understanding the changing security landscape.

The second guiding concept for this book is sustainability, a set of concerns about the ability of human and natural systems to provide the basic necessities needed so life can flourish. Sustainable development is commonly defined as the ability to meet vital human needs in the present without compromising the ability of future generations to meet their own vital needs (WCED 1987). The significance of sustainable development was affirmed in the Agenda 21 program, approved by 179 nations at the 1992 United Nations Conference on Environment and Development in Rio de Janeiro, Brazil (UN 1992). As the world approaches the 20th anniversary of the Rio Declaration (and the 40th anniversary of the 1972 Stockholm Declaration of the United Nations Conference on the Human Environment), the intervening time has only enhanced the importance of sustainable development as a set of concerns that lie at a critical nexus of economic, environmental, political, social, and technological systems. From sustainable development comes a core understanding that, while solutions in the near term must be responsive to present needs, they must not degrade the health of natural systems and their resulting ability to provide for human needs in the long term. Solutions that are not mindful of these standards of sustainability will be suboptimal and could lead to greater human insecurity in the future. Unsustainable solutions may also incur opportunity costs by missing chances to enhance efforts to address human insecurity across a range of threat categories.

In response to the many and varied ways processes of global

change have impacted multiple aspects of human life, two powerful visions of the future have developed. One vision, promoted by cornucopian thinkers, shows a world where globalization, technology, and human ingenuity will lead to a better world where the benefits of increased interconnectedness are available to all people. In contrast, a competing vision championed by neo-Malthusian thinkers imagines a future where the sources of threat and vulnerability, amplified by processes of global change, eventually overwhelm societies and lead to widespread social and ecological collapse. These two compelling visions, of a better world or a coming anarchy, turn on whether the capacity of societies to mitigate and adapt to processes of global change will be sufficient to address the economic, ethical, political, social, and technological challenges they face.

Through explorations of core challenges to food security in the twenty-first century, this book contributes to this debate which, at core, revolves around a set of questions on the governance of complex transnational challenges in an increasingly globalized and networked world. At this moment, a critical challenge for politics and international relations is to gain a more complete understanding of the ways we can maximize the opportunities that networks provide to enhance human health, livelihoods, and well-being, while also finding ways to reduce the sources of insecurity they amplify. Answering these questions raises a number of further questions that link the present study to major lines of inquiry in political science and international relations. These include questions about the role of state and nonstate actors in global governance processes (Wapner 1996, 2002); the rise and governance of information technology networks (Deibert 1997; Flynn 2007); the increasingly important role of informal economic systems (Schlosser 2003; Naim 2005); concerns about the proliferation of nuclear technology and nuclear weapons (Falkenrath et al. 1998); and the security and ethical implications of advanced biological technologies (Lederberg 1999; Zilinskas 2000; Tucker 2000; CIA 2003). While these multiple lines of inquiry are well established in political science and international relations, the field has yet to fully engage with food security issues as they relate to human security and sustainability. Processes of global change have made the need for this engagement even more essential.

The world is at a critical moment where globalization and global environmental change have raised key questions about how and to what extent the world can govern networks and harness them to make progress on goals such as ensuring food security, promoting justice and equality, and protecting human rights. In-depth examinations of networks such as the global food system help us identify areas in which actions need to be, and can be, taken to effectively improve security and well-being. An investigation such as this one prompts us to consider to what extent optimizing networks to maximize the positive aspects of network connectivity and minimize the negative aspects of connectivity will involve actions at multiple levels of political activity including: creating or modifying regulations, policies, and laws at national and subnational levels; action at the international level such as treaties, declarations, and the setting of international standards; or actions in the nonstate and commercial realm involving individuals, businesses, and nongovernmental organizations. The discussions in this book are thus both substantively significant, as issues of food security continue to be persistent sources of human insecurity, and theoretically significant, as questions about food security can provide valuable insight into the challenges of governing in an increasingly globalized and networked world.

While there remain considerable obstacles to ensuring food security, there are many reasons for optimism that the challenges faced by human societies are not beyond our capacity for adaptation and innovation. As the early chapters in this book make clear, many perspectives, knowledge traditions, and actors will need to be involved in growing a secure, ethical, and environmentally sustainable network of global food systems. Chapter 1 reviewed the connection between food security and human, national, and international security. Chapter 2 explored the long history of interactive changes between human and natural systems and discussed the rise of a global food system in recent decades. Chapter 3 assessed five major trends that will have significant impacts on food security. The in-depth discussions in later chapters review the ways that ensuring food security involves complex questions including the multifaceted challenge of malnutrition, managing global environmental change to sustainably intensify food production, and optimizing the global food system to protect crops, animals, and people from health threats.

Chapter 4 considered the challenge of malnutrition and reviewed the ways that reducing food insecurity requires addressing three elements of malnourishment: energy deficiencies, nutrient deficiencies, and problems from overweight and obesity related to excessive energy intake. Recognizing the ways malnourishment continues to operate as three distinct yet interrelated challenges is vitally important to locating the causes and possible solutions to malnutrition. Understanding that many people are not receiving the proper nutrition they need on a daily basis from either inadequate or improper diets makes clear the complexity of the challenge of ensuring nutrition. This challenge is especially critical given significant increases in the global number of chronically hungry people over the past few years. Chronic undernutrition, one of our oldest security and development challenges, remains a critical problem confronting human societies in the twenty-first century.

However, the chapter explores how food insecurity is more than just chronic hunger resulting from energy deficiencies. Malnutrition is a universal concern that impacts people everywhere. While many people may still face grave human insecurity from undernutrition, many more have their livelihoods and well-being reduced by micronutrient deficiency, and others have their health and well-being degraded by overweight and obesity. Understanding the nature of challenges to ensuring proper nutrition makes it clear that, in multiple ways, the global food system must be optimized if it is to meet the challenge of food security. Optimizing nutrition means far more than simply increasing food production or improving food distribution. Instead, solutions to malnutrition will involve developing global food systems that can sustainably provide all people with the food they need to lead active and healthy lives. This process will involve confronting the multiple individual/household level factors that lead to malnutrition as well as larger structural problems like poverty, agricultural subsidies, and lack of infrastructure and health care. Solutions designed to reduce malnutrition must thus address factors at both individual/household and structural levels.

Chapter 5 reviewed the ways food security requires managing

global environmental change to confront the environmental impacts of food and agricultural production systems, as well as considering the impacts environmental change, such as climate change, will have on food and agricultural production systems. Throughout history, unsustainable agricultural and food production practices have had significant environmental and social impacts. In recent decades the magnitude and dispersion of the aggregate effects of these impacts have become clearer. Growing understanding of global environmental change has problematized simplistic models that see agriculture and environment as existing in circular feedback. Greater understanding of the global impacts of localized environmental changes – including impacts that agricultural and food production systems have on land and soil, water, biodiversity and habitat loss, and the global climate system – further emphasize the importance of developing sustainable agricultural and food production systems.

Sustainably intensifying food production requires the maintenance of land and water systems and encourages the use of food production methods and technologies that will maintain agricultural productivity while also reducing environmental impact. Developing sustainable agricultural systems requires confronting limiting ecological factors in food production, but also necessitates discussions about changing diets and consumer preferences, such as a growing global desire for meat and fish that is difficult to meet sustainably. A further set of considerations for nutrition and sustainability lies in reducing misuse and loss of productivity through food and agricultural waste (Blair and Sobal 2006; Stuart 2009). Additionally, it is also worth examining ways to strategically decouple local, regional, and national food systems from global networks. Such decoupling could increase food safety and could be particularly advantageous for communities if it simultaneously augmented health and proper nutrition (by increasing the availability of key food sources for health and proper nutrition such as fresh fruits and vegetables) and linked into sustainable development efforts to create agricultural systems that mitigate and adapt to global climate change (by, for instance, creating agro-ecological buffer zones and limiting the production of food crops that have high climate and environmental impact from transportation costs).

Finally, chapter 6 addressed the ways food security requires ensuring that crops, animals, and foods are free from threats to health. Ensuring the health of crops and animals and the safety of food supplies are integral to improving global health. Processes of global change have increased connections between people and places, dramatically reducing the time needed for diseases to emerge and become problems of global significance. Along with increased connectivity, processes of global change have consolidated food systems, resulting in benefits such as lower prices and greater availability of foods. At the same time, however, this consolidation means that when problems arise, either through accidental or intentional contamination of food systems, they can be widespread and have significant human security impacts, particularly as health and economic costs.

The relationship of food safety concerns to the global food network suggests two sorts of solutions. The first is to improve standardization, regulation, and harmonization among local, regional, national, and international food safety systems. Considerable advances have been made in recent years to improve national and international food safety systems, but policymakers must keep pace with the increasing speed and scale of global food networks. The second set of solutions is to improve food security through strategic decoupling from global food systems. Food safety concerns, which have been heightened to a large part by the lengthening and acceleration of global food chains, could be lessened by considering ways to strategically decouple local, regional, and national food systems from global networks. Done improperly, such decoupling could lead to great harm to food security and well-being. If accomplished with consideration for both ethical and environmental needs, decoupling could enhance health and the sustainability of community food systems by increasing the availability of fresh fruits and vegetables through urban agriculture, farmers' markets and community-supported agricultural programs.

While this book is not intended to provide specific policy prescriptions, there are connections at many levels between policy and food. Perhaps the most important policy implication of the discussions in this volume is its illustration of the value of considering policies related to food security from a broad human security perspective that takes into account both the sudden and chronic sources of food insecurity. Adopting a human security perspective suggests that policymaking must reach across the academic and bureaucratic divisions that characterize many discussions of food and agriculture in order to protect and empower individuals and communities to create conditions for people to have the capacity and freedom to define and participate in pursuing options to improve their human security. Opening discussions to multiple perspectives and traditions is vital to ensuring they are participatory and effective. Too often, as Ulrich Beck writes, "the structuring of the future is taking place indirectly and unrecognizably in research laboratories and executive suites, not in the parliament or in political parties. Everyone else . . . more or less lives off the crumbs of information that fall from the planning tables of technological sub-politics" (Beck 1992: 223). In the case of food security, decisions that shape the global food system often occur in scientific, business, academic, and governmental sub-political forums such as complex farm and energy bills. One of the essential functions of efforts to address food security threats is elevating discussions reducing threat and vulnerability in the food system from sub-political arenas into political forums where individuals and communities can define problems, prioritize efforts, increase transparency, and develop solutions. The elevation of such questions into forums for open discussions is increasingly vital in a globalizing world where questions about the location of political authority are becoming relevant across a wide range of policy domains.

A further policymaking implication is that addressing challenges to food security will involve efforts at a range of activity levels. This book has discussed a number of ways that individual and household choices about food have significant impacts on food security. One aim of policy solutions should be to educate people to better understand the implications of their food choices. For instance, the growing prominence of (and in some places the requirement for) displays of nutritional information about foods allows people to make informed consumption decisions. Another example is the publicizing of concepts such as the ecological and climate "footprint," which help people roughly estimate the environmental impacts of food choices (Global Footprint Network 2006). While these educational efforts can improve understanding of the relationship of individual choices to food security, such tools can also lead to oversimplification of the environmental impacts of food if they do not take into account differing impacts from production and transportation methods.

One way to address the shortcomings of such efforts is to increase the sophistication of environmental impact information. Increasing the quality of information provided about the origins, production methods, and nutritional value of foods will better inform food choices. The labeling of organic foods provides an example of how additional information about origins and production methods can enhance the value of food. Examples of such enhancements can be found in the "Our Footprint" labeling on Timberland Company products, which provides information about the social and environmental impacts of products and packaging materials; the "location of origin" information displayed on produce and other products at stores such as Whole Foods, which tells consumers about food origins and production methods; and environmental impact labeling introduced by Home Depot, which provides environmental information about products such as light bulbs that use less electricity and natural pesticides that have reduced impacts on land, water, and energy resources (Timberland 2006; *New York Times*, April 17, 2007). Labeling is not an easy fix, as often efforts highlight the great difficulty faced in operationalizing concepts such as sustainability, especially in the context of food. However, they do represent important tools to provide more information to consumers and encourage companies to increase their transparency and corporate social responsibility.

Increasing consumer information helps to provide the details people need to know to make informed choices about foods that support their health and well-being. Individual and household food choices are driven by a range of factors, including tradition, culture, family behaviors, advertising, and economics. In the case of consumer labeling, many companies have found that the increased costs of labeling products, which involves tracing the origins of all components in products, are compensated for by benefits provided by increased efficiency and the willingness of consumers to pay higher prices for goods they feel are in line with their social or environmental values. While important, efforts to improve individual and household consumption behaviors do have limitations and they are only one part of developing ethical and environmentally friendly food systems (Luke 1997; Price 1999).

National policy actions can enhance or inhibit development of fairer and more environmentally sustainable food systems. For instance, national governments can provide better information and incentives to help farmers transition away from less sustainable practices. In the United States, farmers must wait three years after using chemical pesticides and fertilizers on fields before products grown in those fields can be labeled as organic, even if they are grown according to methods required by organic labeling. The risks of undertaking such a transition could be lessened by programs to support crop prices during transition periods. In addition, such strategies, if used effectively, can promote values such as rural landscape conservation and preservation of ecological features such as woodlots and wetlands which have little or no market value to farmers.

Many national conversations about food occur around complex pieces of legislation such as farm and energy bills. These ultimately may not be the best instruments to use in shaping a food system that is responsive to needs to ensure human security and promote environmental sustainability. Such legislative processes are also shaped by policy and bureaucratic history and may not adequately confront the questions of health, security, and welfare that food security encompasses in the twenty-first century. For example, efforts by a number of consumer and environmental groups during the negotiation of the 2007/2008 US Farm Bill to expand discussion towards a more comprehensive Food Bill that considered a broad range of food and environment issues were of limited success. In regard to national policies, taking a human security perspective means addressing the pressing priorities of multiple constituencies including farmers and agribusiness interests, but also families, communities, businesses and healthcare providers. In general, human security (especially when used to consider the global impact of national policies) and sustainability provide important lenses to evaluate policy decisions.

International food security activities are important along three primary dimensions. First, international organizations such as the FAO, the World Bank, the World Food Program and the Codex Alimentarius Commission help set standards and harmonize national systems. As with domestic definitions of products labeled as "organic," the lack of harmonized standards can inhibit international trade and undermine the value of labeling if standards are not uniform. These organizations also serve a vital need by providing information about food and agricultural production systems trends. A second important role of international activities is that they build capacity in key areas such as agricultural research, food aid, and food safety systems in developing countries. A third and final area of activity is the provision of emergency relief and disaster assistance. Collectively, actions at the international level will have the most positive impacts where they can provide practice and policy integration for concerns such as trade, aid, security, and food safety.

States, whether independently or together, are not the only institutions that can and should address food security issues. Processes of global change have empowered a number of new kinds of social movements and activist organizations that are active in a range of sectors from human rights to environmental conservation to banning anti-personnel landmines (Rosenau 1990; Wapner 1996; Rutherford, Brem, and Matthew 2003; Matthew, McDonald and Rutherford 2004). These nonstate actors can play an important role in food security efforts. Groups such as Heifer International provide livestock, seed crops, and education in sustainable agriculture to help individuals and families develop sustainable food sources and livelihoods (Heifer International 2008). A variety of nonstate efforts, such as the Slow Food Movement (2010), also seek to address and counteract what they see as the negative impacts of fast food culture by encouraging greater understanding of the cultural significance and environmental impacts of food consumption. While the activities of nongovernmental organizations are unlikely to ever replace the important roles of states and international bodies, through their agility, responsiveness, and ability to set priorities based on organizational vision and donor preferences, they can play important roles in developing an ethical and environmentally sustainable global food system.

Food security, like many international security issues, is not a goal that states can accomplish on their own. Achieving the goals of food security will require the actions and involvement of individuals and households, as well as actors in public, private, and nonprofit sectors. Too often, decisions that affect the human security of individuals and communities are made in nonpolitical forums; an important policy goal should be to find participatory and transparent ways to address human security needs. The present study has demonstrated that global change has had a significant impact on the global food system. Given these impacts, policies and strategies must also evolve and innovate if they are to provide human security for all people through nutrition, health, safety, and sustainability.

Efforts to promote good health and nutrition often recite the reminder "you are what you eat" as a means to encourage healthful food choices and behaviors. One of the core insights that emerges out of this book is the recognition that our world is also shaped by the choices we make related to food and food systems. More and more, the earth is what we eat. This project has embraced Timothy W. Luke's (2001b) notion that understanding global issues requires looking not just at nature or society, but at the sites where the natural and social converge. Much of the work in environmental history and politics has focused on questions related to the challenge of, as Wes Jackson writes, "becoming native to this place" (Jackson 1996: 2). As Roderick Nash writes, Henry David Thoreau saw that by bringing together both civilization and wilderness, it would be possible to create a new kind of relationship with the land that would be beneficial to humans and not entirely destructive to nature. Prior to Thoreau,

> most Americans had revered the rural, agrarian condition as a release from both wilderness and from high civilization . . . Thoreau on the other hand . . . rejoiced in extremes and, by keeping a foot in each, believed he could extract the best of both worlds . . . wildness and refinement were not fatal extremes but equally beneficent influences (Nash 1982: 94–5).

Wendell Berry expressed a similar sentiment about the value of not seeing humans and nature as separate:

> It is a rule, apparently, that whatever is divided must compete. We have been wrong to believe that competition invariably results in the triumph of the best. Divided, body and soul, man and woman, producer and consumer, nature and technology, city and country are thrown into competition with one another. And none of these competitions is ever resolved in the triumph of one competitor, but only in the exhaustion of both (Berry 1996: 223).

What is needed, these writers suggest, are relationships between nature and society that enhance the security, health, vitality, and well-being of all the planet's inhabitants. While the challenges of sustainable development are considerable, there is growing recognition that finding ways to sustainably meet human needs is a core challenge of our time. Writers such as Thoreau, Berry, Snyder and Williams (Williams 1973) remind us that the relationships human societies negotiate (and constantly renegotiate) with natural systems are not only significant in their own right, but are also deeply interconnected with a range of pressing global challenges from poverty to ill health, from global inequality to gender disparity, from migration and displacement to conflict and civil violence.

While the challenge of making human societies sustainable is considerable, there are a number of guideposts to point the way. Aldo Leopold suggests we should "examine each question in terms of what is ethically and esthetically right, as well as what is economically expedient. A thing is right when it tends to preserve the integrity, stability and beauty of the biotic community. It is wrong when it tends otherwise" (Leopold 1949: 224–5). Paul Wapner writes that it is important to recognize the changing relationships between humans and nature in the new millennium: "As the divide between humans and nature disappears, we must realize that environmentalism as a nature movement is anachronistic. In its stead, we must develop a genuinely environmental movement. This means focusing attention on the world around us – as it is given and as it can be transformed" (Wapner 2010: 219). To address world food problems, Raj Patel endorses notions of food sovereignty that articulate the rights of individuals and communities to define their own food policies:

> Food sovereignty is a vision that aims to redress the abuse of the powerless by the powerful, wherever in the food system that abuse may happen. It is very far from a call to return to some bucolic past bound by tradition. By laying particular emphasis on the rights of women farmers, for instance, food sovereignty goes for the jugular in many rural societies, opening the door to profound social change (Patel 2008: 302).

These guiding sentiments demonstrate that while ensuring food security is a critical component of human, national, and global security, it must also integrate a diverse array of perspectives from ethics to technology, from economics to aesthetics, and from the rights of consumers to the rights of women.

Ensuring food security requires improvements and harmonization in increasingly global food and agricultural production systems. Efforts to enhance food security should be mindful of the four essential characteristics of human security as defined by UNDP (1994): it is a universal concern, its components are interdependent, it is easier to ensure through early prevention rather than later intervention, and it is people-centered. Ideas of sustainable agriculture embrace holistic notions that food and agricultural production must learn how to enhance the health and vitality of human and nonhuman communities (IFOAM 2008). To date, great amounts of energy, ingenuity, and effort have been dedicated in global efforts to ensure food security. The challenge ahead lies in enhancing these efforts through our increasingly global networks in order to address the interactive sets of threats and vulnerabilities that impact the security, livelihoods, and well-being of states and people.

References

Alibek, Ken, with Handelman, Stephen (1999). *Biohazard: The Chilling True Story of the Largest Covert Biological Weapons Program in the World – Told from the Inside by the Man Who Ran It.* New York: Delta.

Alston, Julian M., Taylor, Michael J., and Pardey, Philip G. (eds) (2001). *Agricultural Science Policy: Changing Global Agendas.* Baltimore, MD: Johns Hopkins University Press.

Annan, Kofi (2006). "Annan Stresses Climate Threat at UNFCCC Conference." www.unep.org/Documents.Multilingual/Default.asp?DocumentID=495&ArticleID=5424&l=en (February 22, 2008).

Appadurai, Arjun (1988). "How to Make a National Cuisine: Cookbooks in Contemporary India." *Comparative Studies in Society and History* 30.1 (January): 3–24.

Armelagos, George J. (1998). "The Viral Superhighway." *The Sciences* (January/February): 24–9.

Ash, Caroline, Jasny, Barbara, Malakoff, David, and Sugen, Andrew (2010). "Feeding the Future." *Science* 327(5967): 797.

Ban Ki-moon (2008). "The New Face of Hunger." *Washington Post.* March 12; A19.

Barabási, Albert-László (2003). *Linked: How Everything Is Connected to Everything Else and What It Means for Business, Science, and Everyday Life.* New York: Plume.

Barnett, Jon, Matthew, Richard A., and O'Brien, Karen L. (2009). "Global Environmental Change and Human Security: An Introduction," in Richard A. Matthew, Jon Barnett, Bryan McDonald and Karen L. O'Brien (eds) *Global Environmental Change and Human Security.* Cambridge: MIT Press, 3–32.

Barnett, Thomas P. M. (2004). *The Pentagon's New Map: War and Peace in the Twenty-First Century.* New York: G. P. Putnam's Sons.

Barnett, Thomas P. M. (2009). *Great Powers: America and the World After Bush.* New York: G. P. Putnam's Sons.

Barney, Darin (2004). *The Network Society.* Cambridge: Polity Press.

Barrett, Christopher B. (2010). "Measuring Food Insecurity." *Science* 327(5967): 825–8.

Barrett, Christopher, and Maxwell, Daniel G. (2005). *Food Aid After Fifty Years: Recasting its Role*. London: Routledge.

Beck, Ulrich (1992). *Risk Society: Towards a New Modernity*. London: Sage.

Beck, Ulrich (2000). *What Is Globalization?* Cambridge: Polity Press.

Beddington, John (2009). "Professor Sir John Beddington's Speech at SDUK 09." www.govnet.co.uk/news/govnet/professor-sir-john-beddingtons-speech-at-sduk-09 (December 24, 2009).

Begley, Sharon (2008). "Sounds good, but . . . : We can't afford to make any more mistakes in how to 'save the planet.' Start by ditching corn ethanol." *Newsweek* (April 14). www.newsweek.com/id/130628 (April 18, 2008).

Bentley, Jerry H. (1993). *Old World Encounters: Cross-Cultural Contacts and Exchanges in Pre-Modern Times*. Oxford: Oxford University Press.

Berry, Wendell (1996). *The Unsettling of America: Culture & Agriculture*, 3rd ed. San Francisco: Sierra Club Books.

Bio Economic Research Associates (2003). "SARS Shows Weakness in Biosecurity; Strategies To Address Root Causes Recommended." www.bio-era.net/news/add_news_4.html (December 28, 2009).

Blackstock, Jason J. (2009). "The Utility and Implications of Real Geoengineering Concepts." Paper presented at the 2009 Annual Meeting of the American Political Science Association, Toronto, ON, Canada, September 3–6, 2009.

Blair, Dorothy, and Sobal, Jeffery (2006). "Luxus Consumption: Wasting Food Resources through Overeating." *Agriculture and Human Values* 23: 63–74.

Bloom, Mia (2007). *Dying to Kill: The Allure of Suicide Terror*. New York: Columbia University Press.

Boyer, R., and Drache, D. (eds) (1996). *States Against Markets*. London: Routledge.

Brauch, Hans Gunter, et al. (eds) (2009). *Facing Global Environmental Change: Environmental, Human, Energy, Food, Health and Water Security Concepts*. Peace Research and European Security Studies Press.

Brower, Jennifer, and Chalk, Peter (2003). *The Global Threat of New and Reemerging Infectious Disease: Reconciling US National Security and Public Health Policy*. Arlington, Virginia: RAND.

Brown, Lester R. (1970). *Seeds of Change*. New York: Praeger Publishers.

Brown, Lester R. (1977). "Redefining National Security. Worldwatch Paper No 14." Washington, DC: Worldwatch Institute.

Brown, Lester R. (2004). *Outgrowing the Earth: The Food Security Challenge in an Age of Falling Water Tables and Rising Temperatures*. New York: W.W. Norton.

Brown, Lester R. (2009). *Plan B 4.0: Mobilizing to Save Civilization*. New York: W. W. Norton.

BTWC (Biological and Toxin Weapons Convention) (1972). "Convention on the Prohibition of the Development, Production and Stockpiling of Bacteriological (Biological) and Toxin Weapons and on Their Destruction." www.opbw.org/ (December 28, 2009).

Buchanan, Mark (2002). *Small Worlds and the Groundbreaking Theory of Networks*. New York: W. W. Norton.

Bush, George H. W. (1991). "National Security Strategy of the United States." www.fas.org/man/docs/918015-nss.htm (December 28, 2009).

Butts, Kent Hughes (1999). "The Case for DOD Involvement in Environmental Security," in Daniel Deudney and Richard A. Matthew (eds), *Contested Grounds: Security and Conflict in the New Environmental Politics*. Albany, NY: SUNY Press, 109–26.

Caldeira, Ken (2009). "Geoengineering to Shade the Earth," in Worldwatch Institute, *State of the World 2009: Into a Warming World*. New York: W. W. Norton, 96–8.

California Farm Bureau Federation (2007). "Arrests follow tip in case of almond thefts." www.cfbf.com/agalert/AgAlertStory.cfm?ID=718&ck=50C3D7614917B24303EE6A220679DAB3 (December 28, 2009).

Campbell, Kurt M. (ed.) (2008). *Climatic Cataclysm: The Foreign Policy and National Security Implications of Climate Change*. Washington, DC: Brookings Institution Press.

Canada Gazette (2006). "Organic Products Regulations." http://canadagazette.gc.ca/partII/2006/20061221-x6/html/extra-e.html (December 28, 2009).

Carson, Rachel (1962). *Silent Spring*. Boston: Houghton Mifflin.

Castells, M. (1996). *The Rise of the Network Society*. Oxford: Blackwell.

CDC (US Centers for Disease Control and Prevention) (2001a). "Recognition of Illness Associated with the Intentional Release of a Biological Agent." *Morbidity & Mortality Weekly Report* 50: 893–7.

CDC (US Centers for Disease Control and Prevention) (2001b). "Update: Investigation of Anthrax Associated with Intentional Exposure and Interim Public Health Guidelines." *Morbidity & Mortality Weekly Report* 50: 889–93.

CDC (US Centers for Disease Control and Prevention) (2005). "Basic Information about SARS." www.cdc.gov/ncidod/sars/factsheet.htm (December 28, 2009).

CDC (US Centers for Disease Control and Prevention) (2008). *Public Health Preparedness: Mobilizing State by State.* http://emergency.cdc.gov/publications/feb08phprep/ (December 28, 2009).

CDC (US Centers for Disease Control and Prevention) (2009a). "Overweight and Obesity." www.cdc.gov/obesity/index.html (December 28, 2009).

CDC (US Centers for Disease Control and Prevention) (2009b). "2009 H1N1 Flu" www.cdc.gov/H1N1FLU/ (December 28, 2009).

Chalk, Peter (2004). *Hitting America's Soft Underbelly: The Potential Threat of Deliberate Biological Attacks Against the US Agricultural and Food Industry.* Santa Monica, CA: RAND.

Chamberlain, Lisa (2007). "Skyfarming." *New York Magazine.* http://nymag.com/news/features/30020/ (February 22, 2008).

Chan, Margaret (2008). "The impact of climate change on human health: Statement by WHO Director-General Dr Margaret Chan." www.who.int/mediacentre/news/statements/2008/s05/en/index.html (April 18, 2008).

Chang, Te-Tzu (2007). "Rice," in Kenneth F. Kiple and Kriemhild Conee Ornelas (eds), *The Cambridge World History of Food.* Cambridge: Cambridge University Press, pp. 132–48.

Christian, David (2004). *Maps of Time: An Introduction to Big History.* Berkeley: UC Press.

Christian, David (2008). *This Fleeting World: A Short History of Humanity.* Great Barrington, MA: Berkshire Publishing Group.

Christopher, George W., Pavlin, Julie A., Eitzen, Edward M., Jr., Cieslak, Theodore J. (1997). "Biological Warfare: A Historical Perspective." *Journal of the American Medical Association* 278: 412–16.

Christopher, Warren (1996). "American Diplomacy and the Global Environmental Challenges of the 21st Century." Address at Stanford University, 9 April 1996: www.usgcrp.gov/usgcrp/documents/CWarren.html (April 29, 2008).

Chyba, Christopher (2002). "Toward Biological Security." *Foreign Affairs* 81(3) (May/June): 122–36.

CIA (Central Intelligence Agency) (2003). "The Darker Bioweapons Future." www.fas.org/irp/cia/product/bw1103.pdf (February 22, 2008).

Clapp, Jennifer (2005). "The Political Economy of Food Aid in an Era of Agricultural Biotechnology." *Global Governance* 11(4): 467–85.

Clapp, Jennifer, and Fuchs, Doris (eds) (2009). *Corporate Power in Global Agrifood Governance*. Cambridge, MA: MIT Press.

Clay, Edward (2002). "Food Security: Concepts and Measurement." Paper for FAO Expert Consultation on Trade and Food Security: Conceptualising the Linkages. Rome, July 11–12, 2002. www.rlc.fao.org/iniciativa/cursos/Curso%202005/3prog/1_1_3.pdf (April 30, 2010).

Clay, Jason (2004). *World Agriculture and the Environment*. Washington: Island Press.

Clinton, Hillary Rodham (2009). "Remarks at Food Security Event Co-Hosted with UN Secretary-General Ban Ki-Moon During the UN General Assembly." www.state.gov/secretary/rm/2009a/09/129673.htm (December 12, 2009).

CNA Corporation (2007). *National Security and the Threat of Climate Change*. Arlington: CNA.

Collier, Paul (2007). *The Bottom Billion: Why the Poorest Countries are Failing and What Can be Done About It*. New York: Oxford University Press.

Collier, Paul (2009). "Put Aside Prejudices," in "Room for Debate: Can Biotech Food Cure World Hunger?" *The New York Times*, October 26. http://roomfordebate.blogs.nytimes.com/2009/10/26/can-biotech-food-cure-world-hunger/ (April 30, 2010).

Commission on Human Security (2003). *Human Security Now*. New York.

Conca, Ken (2005). *Governing Water: Contentious Transnational Politics and Global Institution Building*. Cambridge, MA: MIT Press.

Conca, Ken, and Dabelko, Geoffrey D. (eds) (2002). *Environmental Peacemaking*. Baltimore: Johns Hopkins University Press.

Conca, Ken, and Dabelko, Geoffrey D. (2010). Green Planet Blues: *Four Decades of Global Environmental Politics*, 4th ed. Boulder, CO: Westview Press.

Convention on Biological Diversity (1992). "The Convention on Biological Diversity." www.cbd.int/ (April 28, 2008).

Crosby, Alfred (1986). *Ecological Imperialism: The Biological*

Expansion of Europe 900–1900. New York: Cambridge University Press.

Crosby, Alfred (1990). *America's Forgotten Pandemic: The Influenza of 1918*. Cambridge: Cambridge University Press.

CRS (Congressional Research Service) (2004). "Energy Use in Agriculture: Background and Issues." www.ncseonline.org/NLE/CRSreports/04nov/RL32677.pdf (April 19, 2008).

Curtin, Philip (1984). *Cross-Cultural Trade in World History*. Cambridge: Cambridge University Press.

Dabelko, Geoffrey D. (2008). "An Uncommon Peace: Environment, Development and the Global Security Agenda." *Environment* 50(3): 32–45.

Dalby, Simon (2009). *Security and Environmental Change*. Cambridge: Polity Press.

Dannreuther, Roland (2007). *International Security: The Contemporary Agenda*. Cambridge: Polity Press.

Dauvergne, Peter (2008). *The Shadows of Consumption: Consequences for the Global Environment*. Cambridge, MA: MIT Press.

Davis, Mike (2001). *Late Victorian Holocausts: El Niňo Famines and the Making of the Third World*. New York: Verso.

DEFRA (Department for Environment, Food and Rural Affairs) (2006). Food Security and the UK: An Evidence and Analysis Paper. https://statistics.defra.gov.uk/esg/reports/foodsecurity/ (December 27, 2009).

Deibert, Ronald J. (1997). *Parchment, Printing, and Hypermedia: Communication in World Order Transformation*. New York: Columbia University Press.

Deudney, Daniel (1990). "The Case Against Linking Environmental Degradation and Security." *Millennium Journal of International Studies* 19(3): 461–76.

Deudney, Daniel, and Grove, Jairus V. (2009). "Geoengineering and World Order: Past and Future." Paper presented at the 2009 Annual Meeting of the American Political Science Association, Toronto, ON, Canada, September 3–6, 2009.

Deudney, Daniel, and Matthew, Richard A. (eds) (1999). *Contested Grounds: Security and Conflict in the New Environmental Politics*. Albany, NY: SUNY Press.

Devereux, Stephen, and Maxwell, Simon (eds) (2001). *Food Security in Sub-Saharan Africa*. London: ITDG.

Diamond, Jared (1999). *Guns, Germs and Steel: The Fates of Human Societies*. New York: W. W. Norton.

Diamond, Jared (2005). *Collapse: How Societies Choose to Fail or Succeed.* New York: Viking.

Diehl, Paul F. (2008). *Peace Operations.* Cambridge: Polity Press.

Dimento, Joseph F. C., et al. (2007). "A Primer on Global Climate Change and Its Likely Impacts," in Joseph F. C. Dimento and Pamela Doughman (eds), *Climate Change: What It Means for Us, Our Children, and Our Grandchildren.* Cambridge, MA: MIT Press, pp. 13–44.

Diriba, Getachew (2007). "Reversing Food Insecurity: Linking Global Commitments to Local Recovery Needs." *The Journal of Humanitarian Assistance.* http://jha.ac/2007/10/28/reversing-food-insecurity-linking-global-commitments-to-local-recovery-needs/ (April 30, 2010).

Doak, Colleen, Adair, Linda S., Monteiro, Carlos, and Popkin, Barry (2000). "Overweight and Underweight Coexist within Households in Brazil, China, and Russia." *The Journal of Nutrition* 130(12): 2965–71.

Doak, Colleen, Adair, Linda S., Bentley, M., Monteiro, Carlos, and Popkin, Barry (2005). "The Dual Burden Household and Nutrition Transition Paradox." *International Journal of Obesity* 29(1): 129–36.

Donner, Simon D., and Kucharik, Christopher J. (2008). "Corn-Based Ethanol Production Compromises Goal of Reducing Nitrogen Export by the Mississippi River." *Proceedings of the National Academy of Sciences* 105(11): 4513–18.

Doyle, Michael (1995). "Liberalism and World Politics Revisited," in Charles W. Kegely (ed.), *Controversies in International Relations Theory: Realism, Liberalism and the Neoliberal Challenge.* New York: St. Martins.

Drèze, J., and Sen, A. (1989). *Hunger and Public Action.* Oxford: Clarendon Press.

Easterbrook, Gregg (2007). "Global Warming: Who Loses – And Who Wins?" *The Atlantic* (April). www.theatlantic.com/doc/200704/global-warming (April 19, 2008).

Easterling, W., et al. (2007). "Food, fibre and forest products," in M. L. Parry, O. F. Canziani, J. P. Palutikof, P. J. van der Linden and C. E. Hanson (eds), *Climate Change 2007: Impacts, Adaptation and Vulnerability. Contribution of Working Group II to the Fourth Assessment Report of the Intergovernmental Panel on Climate Change.* New York, NY: Cambridge University Press, pp. 273–313.

Ehrlich, Paul (1968). *The Population Bomb*. New York: Ballantine Books.

Ehrlich, Paul, and Ehrlich, Anne (1990). *The Population Explosion*. New York: Simon and Schuster.

Ellis, Linden J., and Turner, Jennifer L. (2007). "Surf and Turf: Environmental and Food Safety Concerns of China's Aquaculture and Animal Husbandry." *China Environment Series* 9: 19–42.

Evenson, R. E., and Gollin, D. (2003). "Assessing the Impact of the Green Revolution, 1960 to 2000." *Science* 300(5620): 758–62.

Fagan, Brian (1999). *Floods, Famines, and Emperors: El Nino and the Fate of Civilizations*. New York: Basic Books.

Falkenrath, Richard A., Newman, Robert D., and Thayer, Bradley A. (1998). *America's Achilles Heel: Nuclear, Biological, and Chemical Terrorism and Covert Attack*. Cambridge, MA: MIT Press.

FAO (Food and Agriculture Organization of the United Nations) (1983). *World Food Security: A Reappraisal of the Concepts and Approaches. Director General's Report*. Rome: FAO.

FAO (Food and Agriculture Organization of the United Nations) (2009). *The State of Food Insecurity in the World 2009: Economic Crises – Impacts and Lessons Learned*. Rome: FAO.

FAO (Food and Agriculture Organization of the United Nations) (2003a). *World Agriculture: Towards 2015/2030*. London: Earthscan.

FAO (Food and Agriculture Organization of the United Nations) (2003b). *Trade Reforms and Food Security: Conceptualizing the Linkages*. Rome: FAO.

FAO (Food and Agriculture Organization of the United Nations) (2004). "Animal disease outbreaks hit global meat exports: One-third of global meat exports affected – losses could be high." www.fao.org/newsroom/en/news/2004/37967/index.html (February 22, 2008).

FAO (Food and Agriculture Organization of the United Nations) (2006). *The State of Food Insecurity in the World 2006*. www.fao.org/docrep/009/a0750e/a0750e00.htm (April 28, 2008).

FAO (Food and Agriculture Organization of the United Nations) (2007). "FAO Food Outlook: November 2007." www.fao.org/docrep/010/ah876e/ah876e00.htm (April 28, 2008).

FAO (Food and Agriculture Organization of the United Nations) (2008). "Nutrition and Consumer Protection." www.fao.org/ag/agn/ (April 19, 2008).

FAO (Food and Agriculture Organization of the United Nations) (2009). *The State of Food Insecurity in the World: Economic Crises – Impacts and Lessons Learned.* www.fao.org/publications/sofi/en/ (December 27, 2009).

FBI (Federal Bureau of Investigation) (2009). "Amerithrax Investigation." www.fbi.gov/anthrax/amerithraxlinks.htm (December 1, 2009).

FDA (US Food and Drug Administration) (2002). "Public Health Security and Bioterrorism Preparedness and Response Act of 2002 (the Bioterrorism Act)." www.fda.gov/oc/bioterrorism/bioact.html (April 19, 2008).

FDA (US Food and Drug Administration) (2005). "Commonly Asked Questions about BSE in Products Regulated by FDA's Center for Food Safety and Applied Nutrition (CFSAN)." www.cfsan.fda.gov/~comm/bsefaq.html (September 14, 2005).

FDA (US Food and Drug Administration) (2008). "Charges Filed in Contaminated Pet Food Scheme." www.fda.gov/consumer/updates/pet_food021908.html (April 18, 2008).

Federico, Giovanni (2005). *Feeding the World: An Economic History of Agriculture, 1800–2000.* Princeton, NJ: Princeton University Press.

Fernandez-Armesto, F. (2002). *Near a Thousand Tables: A History of Food.* New York: Free Press.

Finkelstein, Eric A., Trogdon, Justin G., Cohen, Joel W., and Dietz, William (2009). "Annual Medical Spending Attributable to Obesity: Payer- and Service-specific estimates." *Health Affairs* 28(5): 822–31.

Floyd, Rita (2008). "The Environmental Security debate and its Significance for Climate Change." *International Spectator* 43(3): 51–65.

Flynn, Stephen (2004). *America the Vulnerable: How Government is Failing to Protect Us from Terrorism.* New York: HarperCollins.

Flynn, Stephen (2007). *The Edge of Disaster: Rebuilding a Resilient Nation.* New York: Random House.

Fogel, Robert (2004). *The Escape from Hunger and Premature Death, 1700–2100: Europe, America, and the Third World.* New York: Cambridge University Press.

Friedman, Thomas (1999). *The Lexus and the Olive Tree: Understanding Globalization.* New York: Anchor Books.

Fukuyama, Francis (1992). *The End of History and the Last Man.* New York: Avon.

Gadgil, Madhav, and Guha, Ramachandra (1996). *This Fissured Land: An Ecological History of India*. Berkeley: UC Press.

GAO (General Accounting Office) (2001). "Food Safety and Security: Fundamental Changes Needed to Ensure Safe Food." Washington: GAO.

GAO (General Accounting Office) (2003). "Bioterrorism: A Threat to Agriculture and the Food Supply." Washington: GAO.

GAO (Government Accountability Office) (2008). "Federal Oversight of Food Safety: FDA's Food Protection Plan Proposes Positive First Steps, but Capacity to Carry Them Out is Critical." Washington: GAO.

Garnsey, Peter (1999). *Food and Society in Classical Antiquity*. Cambridge: Cambridge University Press.

Garret, Laurie (1994). *The Coming Plague: Newly Emerging Disease in a World Out of Balance*. New York: Penguin Books.

Garrett, Laurie (2001). *Betrayal of Trust: The Collapse of Global Public Health*. New York: Hyperion.

Garrett, Laurie (2005). "The Next Pandemic?" *Foreign Affairs* 84(4): 3–23.

Garrett, Laurie (2007). "The Challenge of Global Health." *Foreign Affairs* 86(1): 14–38.

Gates, Bill (2007). "The Tech Revolution Has Just Begun." PC Magazine. (December 19, 2007). www.pcmag.com/article2/0,2704,2238181,00.asp (April 29, 2008).

Gates, Robert M. (2010). "Helping Others Defend Themselves: The Future of US Security Assistance." *Foreign Affairs* 89(3): 2–6.

Gereffi, Gary, Humphrey, John, and Sturgeon, Timothy (2005). "The Governance of Global Value Chains." *Review of International Political Economy* 12(1): 78–104.

Gereffi, Gary, and Korzeniewicz, Miguel (eds) (1994). *Commodity Chains and Global Capitalism*. Westport, CT: Praeger.

Giddens, Anthony (1990). *The Consequences of Modernity*. Cambridge: Polity Press.

Giddens, Anthony (2009). *The Politics of Climate Change*. Cambridge: Polity Press.

Glassner, Barry (2007). *The Gospel of Food: Everything You Think You Know about Food is Wrong*. New York: HarperCollins.

Gleick, Peter H. (1991). "Environment and Security: The Clear Connections." *Bulletin of the Atomic Scientists* 47(3): 16–21.

Gleick, Peter H. (1993). *Water in Crisis: A Guide to the World's Fresh Water Resources*. New York: Oxford University Press.

Global Footprint Network (2006). "Ecological Footprint: Overview." www.footprintnetwork.org/gfn_sub.php?content=footprint_overview (April 27, 2008).

Godfray, H. et al. (2010). "Food Security: The Challenge of Feeding 9 Billion People." *Science* 327(5967): 812–18.

Goldstone, Jack A. (2010). "The New Population Bomb: The Four Megatrends that Will Change the World." *Foreign Affairs* 89(1): 31–43.

Gore, Albert (1992). *Earth in the Balance: Ecology and the Human Spirit*. Boston, MA: Houghton Mifflin.

Gore, Albert (1999). "Remarks as Prepared for Delivery by Vice President Al Gore." World Economic Forum, Davos, Switzerland. January 29, 1999. http://clinton2.nara.gov/WH/EOP/OVP/speeches/davos.html (April 28, 2008).

Gottlieb, Robert (1993). *Forcing the Spring: The Transformation of the American Environmental Movement*. Washington, DC: Island Press.

Gottweis, Herbert (1998). *Governing Molecules: The Discursive Politics of Genetic Engineering in Europe and the United States*. Cambridge, MA: MIT Press.

Grace, Eric (1997). *Biotechnology Unzipped: Promises and Realities*. Washington: John Henry Press.

Guehenno, J. M. (1995). *The End of the Nation-State*. Minneapolis: The University of Minnesota Press.

Guillemin, Jeanne (2005). *Biological Weapons: From the Invention of State Sponsored Programs to Contemporary Bioterrorism*. New York: Columbia University Press.

Gunderson C., and Gruber, J. (2001). "The Dynamic Determinants of Food Insecurity," in Margaret Andrews and Mark Prell (eds), *Second Food Security Measurement and Research Conference, Volume II: Papers*. FANRR-11-2, pp. 92–110.

Haddad, Lawrence et al. (1995). "More than Food is Needed to Achieve Good Nutrition by 2020." Washington, DC: IFPRI.

Haddad, Lawrence, and Smith, Lisa (1999). "Explaining Child Nutrition in Developing Countries: A Cross-Country Analysis." Washington, DC: IFPRI.

Halweil, Brian (2006). "Fish Harvest Stable but Threatened," in *Vital Signs 2006–2007*. New York: W. W. Norton, pp. 26–7.

Halweil, Brian, and Nierenberg, Danielle (2008). "Meat and Seafood: The Global Diet's Most Costly Ingredients," in Worldwatch

Institute, *State of the World 2008: Innovations for a Sustainable Economy*. New York: W. W. Norton, pp. 61–74.

Hammill, Anne, Crawford, Alec, Craig, Robert, Malpas, Robert, and Matthew, Richard (2009). *Conflict-Sensitive Conservation: Practitioners' Manual*. Winnipeg: International Institute for Sustainable Development.

Hanna, Autumn K., and Oh, Pikai (2000). "Rethinking Urban Poverty: A Look at Community Gardens." *Bulletin of Science, Technology & Society* 20(3): 207–16.

Hansen, John Mark (1991). *Gaining Access: Congress and the Farm Lobby, 1919–1981*. Chicago: University of Chicago Press.

Hartmann, Betsy (2009). "Rethinking the Role of Population in Human Security," in Richard A. Matthew, Jon Barnett, Bryan McDonald and Karen L. O'Brien (eds), *Global Environmental Change and Human Security*. Cambridge: MIT Press, pp. 193–214.

Hartmann, Betsy, Subramaniam, Banu, and Zerner, Charles (2005). *Making Threats: Biofears and Environmental Anxieties*. Lanham, MD: Rowman and Littlefield.

Harvey, David (1989). *The Condition of Postmodernity*. Oxford: Blackwell.

Hawken, Paul, Lovins, Amory, and Lovins, Hunter (1999). *Natural Capitalism: Creating the Next Industrial Revolution*. Boston: Little, Brown.

Hazell, Peter (2002). *Green Revolution: Curse or Blessing?* Washington, DC: IFPRI.

Heifer International (2008). www.heifer.org/ (April 28, 2008).

Held, David, McGrew, Anthony, Goldblatt, David, and Perraton, Jonathan (1999). *Global Transformations: Politics, Economics and Culture*. Stanford: Stanford University Press.

Hennessy, T. W., et al. (1996). "A National Outbreak of *Salmonella enteritidis* Infections from Ice Cream." *New England Journal of Medicine* 334: 1281–6.

Hirst, P. (1997). "The Global Economy: Myths and Realities." *International Affairs* 73(3): 409–25.

Hirst, P., and Thompson, G. (1996). *Globalization in Question: The International Economy and the Possibilities of Governance*. Cambridge: Polity Press.

Homer-Dixon, Thomas (1991). "On the Threshold: Environmental Changes as Causes of Acute Conflict." *International Security* 16(2) (Fall): 76–116.

Homer-Dixon, Thomas (1994). "Environmental Scarcities and Violent Conflict: Evidence from Cases," *International Security* 19(1) (Summer): 5–40.

Homer-Dixon, Thomas (1999). *Environmental Scarcity and Violence.* Princeton, NJ: Princeton University Press.

Homer-Dixon, Thomas (2000). *The Ingenuity Gap.* New York: Alfred A. Knopf.

Homer-Dixon, Thomas (2006). *The Upside of Down: Catastrophe, Creativity and the Renewal of Civilization.* Washington: Island Press.

Homer-Dixon, Thomas (2009). "Uncertainty, Fat Tails, and Time Lags: Why We Must Start Planning Now to Geoengineer Earth Soon." Paper presented at the 2009 Annual Meeting of the American Political Science Association, Toronto, ON, Canada, September 3–6, 2009.

Homer-Dixon, Thomas, and Blitt, Jessica (1998). *Ecoviolence: Links among Environment, Population, and Security.* New York: Rowman and Littlefield.

Horgan, John (2005). *The Psychology of Terrorism.* London: Routledge.

Human Security Centre (2005). *Human Security Report 2005: War and Peace in the 21st Century.* New York: Oxford University Press.

IFAP (International Federation of Agricultural Producers) (2008). Press release: "IFAP Calls for Support of Farmers at the CSD." www.ifap.org/en/newsroom/documents/IFAP_CSD16.pdf (April 28, 2008).

IFOAM (International Federation of Organic Agriculture Movements) (2008). "The Principle of Organic Agriculture." www.ifoam.org/about_ifoam/principles/index.html (April 25, 2008).

Ingram, Mrill, and Ingram, Helen (2002). "Creating Credible Edibles: The Alternative Agriculture Movement and Passage of US Federal Organic Standards." Paper presented at Social Movements and Public Policy Workshop, Laguna Beach, CA, January 11–12.

IOM (Institute of Medicine) (1998). *Ensuring Safe Food: From Production to Consumption.* Washington, DC: National Academies Press.

IPCC (Intergovernmental Panel on Climate Change) (2007). *Fourth Assessment Report. Climate Change 2007: Synthesis Report.* www.ipcc.ch/publications_and_data/ar4/syr/en/contents.html (April 30, 2010).

Jackson, Wes (1996). *Becoming Native to this Place.* Washington, DC: Counterpoint.

Jones, Kate, et al. (2008). "Global Trends on Emerging Infectious Diseases." *Nature* 451(21): 990–3.

Kakonen, Hurki (ed.) (1994). *Green Security or Militarized Environment.* Aldershot: Dartmouth.

Kaplan, David (1996). *The Cult at the End of the World: The Terrifying Story of the Aum Doomsday Cult, from the Subways of Tokyo to the Nuclear Arsenals of Russia.* New York: Crown.

Kaplan, Robert (1994). "The Coming Anarchy." *The Atlantic Monthly* (February). www.theatlantic.com/doc/199402/anarchy (April 25, 2008).

Kaplan, Robert (2000). *The Coming Anarchy: Shattering the Dreams of the Post Cold War.* New York: Random House.

Karasch, Mary (2007). "Manioc," in Kenneth F. Kiple and Kriemhild Conee Ornelas (eds), *The Cambridge World History of Food.* Cambridge: Cambridge University Press, pp. 181–6.

Karesh, William B., and Cook, Robert A. (2005). "The Human–Animal Link." *Foreign Affairs* 84(4): 38–50.

Khan, A. S., Swerdlow, D. L., and Juranek, D. D. (2001). "Precautions against Biological and Chemical Terrorism Directed at Food and Water Supplies." *Public Health Reports* 116: 3–14.

Khan, Marya (2006). "The Dual Burden of Overweight and Underweight in Developing Countries." *Population Reference Bureau.* www.prb.org/Articles/2006/TheDualBurdenofOverweightandUnderweightinDevelopingCountries.aspx (April 19, 2008).

Kiple, Kenneth F. (2007). *A Movable Feast: Ten Millennia of Food Globalization.* Cambridge: Cambridge University Press.

Kiple, Kenneth F., and Ornelas, Kriemhild C. (eds) (2000). *The Cambridge World History of Food.* Cambridge, UK: Cambridge University Press.

Kissinger Report (1974). *Implications of Worldwide Population Growth for US Security and Overseas Interests. National Security Study Memorandum: NSSM 200.* Washington, DC: The White House.

Klare, Michael (2001). *Resource Wars: The New Landscape of Global Conflict.* New York: Metropolitan Books.

Kolavic, S. A., et al. (1997). "An Outbreak of *Shigella dysenteria* Type 2 Among Laboratory Workers Due to Intentional Food Contamination." *Journal of the American Medical Association* 278: 396–8.

Krepinevich, Andrew F. (2009). *7 Deadly Scenarios: A Military Futurist Explores War in the 21st Century*. New York: Bantam Books.

Krugman, Paul (2008). "Grains Gone Wild." *The New York Times*. www.nytimes.com/2008/04/07/opinion/07krugman.html (April 17, 2008).

Kugelman, Michael (2009). "Going Gaga over Grain: Pakistan and the International Farms Race." http://newsecuritybeat.blogspot.com/2009/09/going-gaga-over-grain-pakistan-and.html (December 27, 2009).

Lambrecht, Bill (2001). *Dinner at the New Gene Café: How Genetic Engineering is Changing What We Eat, How We Live, and the Global Politics of Food*. New York: Thomas Dunne Books.

L'Aquila (2009). "'L'Aquila' Joint Statement on Global Food Security." www.g8italia2009.it/static/G8_Allegato/LAquila_Joint_Statement_on_Global_Food_Security[1],0.pdf (December 27, 2009).

Lederberg, Joshua (ed.) (1999). *Biological Weapons: Limiting the Threat*. Cambridge, MA: MIT Press.

Leopold, Aldo (1949). *A Sand County Almanac and Sketches Here and There*. New York: Oxford University Press.

Lester, Toby (1996). "Beyond 'The Coming Anarchy.'" *The Atlantic Monthly* (August). www.theatlantic.com/issues/96aug/proport/kapsid.htm (April 25, 2008).

Levitt, Steven, and Dubner, Stephen (2009). *SuperFreakonomics: Global Cooling, Patriotic Prostitutes, and Why Suicide Bombers Should Buy Life Insurance*. New York: William Morrow.

Lewis, Susan K. (2001). "The History of Biowarfare." www.pbs.org/wgbh/nova/bioterror/history.html (January 24, 2006).

Lomborg, B. (2001). *The Skeptical Environmentalist: Measuring the Real State of the World*. Cambridge: Cambridge University Press.

Lonergan, S. C. (ed.) (1999). *Environmental Change, Adaptation, and Security*. Boston: Kluwer Academic Publishers.

Luke, Timothy W. (1989). *Screens of Power: Ideology, Domination and Resistance in Informational Society*. Urbana: University of Illinois Press.

Luke, Timothy W. (1997). *Ecocritique: Contesting the Politics of Nature, Economy, and Culture*. Minneapolis: University of Minnesota Press.

Luke, Timothy W. (1999). *Capitalism, Democracy and Ecology: Departing from Marx*. Urbana: University of Illinois Press.

Luke, Timothy W. (2000). "The 'Net' Effects of E-Publicanism." Paper presented at the Annual Meeting of the International Studies Association, March 15–18, 2000.

Luke, Timothy W. (2001a). "International or Interenvironmental Relations: What Happens to Nations and Niches in Global Ecosystems?" Paper presented at the 42nd annual meeting of the International Studies Association, February 20–24.

Luke, Timothy W. (2001b). "World Health and the Environment: Globalization's Ambiguities." Paper presented at the Third Annual Staff Development Conference, University of Wisconsin System Institute of Global Studies, Lake Geneva, Wisconsin, October 28–30, 2001.

Luke, Timothy W. (2009). "An Emergent Mangle of Practice: Local Adaptation, Regional Planning, and National Management of Global Climate Change as Vernacular Geo-Engineering." Paper presented at the 2009 Annual Meeting of the American Political Science Association, Toronto, ON, Canada, September 3–6, 2009.

Lurquin, Paul (2001). *The Green Phoenix: A History of Genetically Modified Plants*. New York: Columbia University Press.

MacMillan, J., and Linklater, A. (1995). *Boundaries in Question*. London: Frances Pinter.

Malthus, Thomas (1826). *An Essay on the Principle of Population: A View of its Past and Present Effects on Human Happiness; With an Inquiry into Our Prospects Respecting the Future Removal or Mitigation of the Evils which It Occasions*, 6th ed. London: John Murray. www.econlib.org/library/Malthus/malPlong.html (February 29, 2008).

Matthew, Richard A. (2002). *Dichotomy of Power: Nation Versus State in World Politics*. Lanham: Lexington Books/Rowman and Littlefield.

Matthew, Richard A. (2007). "Climate Change and Human Security," in Joseph F. C. Dimento and Pamela Doughman (eds), *Climate Change: What It Means for Us, Our Children, and Our Grandchildren*. Cambridge, MA: MIT Press, pp. 161–80.

Matthew, Richard A. (2008). "Security in an Age of Converging Crises." Paper presented to Osher Lifelong Learning Institute, Irvine, CA, April 17, 2008. Concept explored more fully in Richard A. Matthew (forthcoming), *Two Solitudes: Environment and Security*. Cambridge, MA: MIT Press.

Matthew, Richard A., Barnett, Jon, McDonald, Bryan, and O'Brien,

Karen (eds) (2009). *Global Environmental Change and Human Security*. Cambridge, MA: MIT Press.

Matthew, Richard A., Brown, Oli, and Jensen, David (2009). *From Conflict to Peacebuilding: The Role of Natural Resources and the Environment*. Nairobi: United Nations Environment Programme.

Matthew, Richard, Halle, Mark, and Switzer, Jason (2002). *Conserving the Peace: Resources, Livelihoods and Security*. Geneva: IISD.

Matthew, Richard A. and Hammill, Anne (2009). "Sustainable Development and Climate Change." *International Affairs* 85(6): 1117–28.

Matthew, Richard A., and McDonald, Bryan L. (2006). "Cities under Siege: Urban Planning and the Threat of Infectious Disease." *Journal of the American Planning Association (JAPA)* 72.1 (Winter 2006): 109–17.

Matthew, Richard A., and McDonald, Bryan L. (2009). "Environmental Security: Academic and Policy Debates in North America," in Hans Gunter Brauch et al. (eds), *Facing Global Environmental Change: Environmental, Human, Energy, Food, Health and Water Security Concepts*. Peace Research and European Security Studies Press, pp. 791–802.

Matthew, Richard A., McDonald, Bryan, and Rutherford, Kenneth (eds) (2004). *Landmines and Human Security: International Politics and War's Hidden Legacy*. Albany: SUNY Press.

Matthew, Richard A., and Shambaugh, George E. (1998). "Sex, Drugs and Heavy Metal: Transnational Threats and National Vulnerabilities." *Security Dialogue* 29(2): 163–75.

Matthew, Richard A., and Shambaugh, George E. (2005). "The Limits of Terrorism: A Network Perspective." *International Studies Review* 7(4): 617–27.

Matthews, Jessica (1989). "Redefining Security." *Foreign Affairs* 68(2): 162–77.

Matthews, Jessica (1997). "Power Shift." *Foreign Affairs* 76(1): 50–66.

McCorriston, Joy (2007). "Wheat," in Kenneth F. Kiple and Kriemhild Conee Ornelas (eds), *The Cambridge World History of Food*. Cambridge: Cambridge University Press, pp. 158–74.

McHughen, Alan (2000). *Pandora's Picnic Basket: The Potential and Hazards of Genetically Modified Foods*. Oxford: Oxford University Press.

McNamara, Peter J. (2007). "Infectious disease." www.accessscience.com (February 22, 2008).

McNeill, J. R. (2000). *Something New Under the Sun: An Environmental History of the Twentieth-Century World.* New York: W. W. Norton.

McNeill, William H. (1998). *Plagues and Peoples.* New York: Anchor Books.

McNeill, William H. (2008). "Globalization: Long Term Process or New Era in Human Affairs?" *New Global Studies* 2(1). www.bepress.com/ngs/vol2/iss1/art4 (April 30, 2010).

Mead, Paul (1999). "Food Related Illness and Death in the United States." *Emerging Infectious Diseases* 5: 607–25.

Meadows, D. H., Meadows, D. L., Randers, J., and Behrens, W. W. III (1972). *Limits to Growth: A Report for the Club of Rome's Project on the Predicament of Mankind.* New York: Universe Books.

Melucci, Alberto (1996). *Challenging Codes: Collective Action in the Information Age.* Cambridge: Cambridge University Press.

Messer, Ellen (2007). "Maize," in Kenneth F. Kiple and Kriemhild Conee Ornelas (eds), *The Cambridge World History of Food.* Cambridge: Cambridge University Press, pp. 97–111.

Messer, Ellen, Cohen, Marc J., and Marchione, Thomas (2001). "Conflict: A Cause and Effect of Hunger." *Environmental Change and Security Project Report,* pp. 1–38 http://ecsp.si.edu/PDF/ECSP7-featurearticles-1.pdf (April 4, 2008).

Met Office (2009). "Four degrees and beyond." www.metoffice.gov.uk/climatechange/news/latest/four-degrees.html (December 10, 2009).

Meyers, Norman (1989). "Environment and Security." *Foreign Policy* 74(2): 23–41.

Micronutrient Initiative (2009). *Investing in the Future: A United Call to Action on Vitamin and Mineral Deficiencies.* www.micronutrient.org/english/View.asp?x=614 (April 30, 2010).

Ministry of Defense (2010). *Defense Plan 2010–2014.* www.mod.uk/NR/rdonlyres/AB3A3278-2820-40EF-AA15-9BDA7D0A5318/0/Defence_Plan_2010_2014.pdf (April 30, 2010).

Mintz, Sidney (1985). *Sweetness and Power: The Place of Sugar in Modern History.* New York: Penguin.

Mission: Readiness (2010). *Too Fat to Fight: Retired Military Leaders Want Junk Food Out of America's Schools.* http://cdn.missionreadiness.org/MR_Too_Fat_to_Fight-1.pdf (April 30, 2010).

Montgomery, David R. (2007). "Soil erosion and agricultural sustainability." *Proceedings of the National Academy of Sciences* 104(33): 13268–72.

Mougeot, Luc J. A. (2005). *Agropolis: The Social, Political and Environmental Dimensions of Urban Agriculture*. London: Earthscan.

Naím, Moisés (2005). *Illicit: How Smugglers, Traffickers, and Copycats are Hijacking the Global Economy*. New York: Doubleday.

NASAA (National Association for Sustainable Agriculture, Australia) (2008). www.nasaa.com.au/ (April 25, 2008).

Nash, Roderick (1982). *Wilderness and the American Mind*, 3rd ed. New Haven, CT: Yale University Press.

NASS (National Agricultural Statistics Service) (2007). "Acreage" http://usda.mannlib.cornell.edu/usda/current/Acre/Acre-06-29-2007.pdf (April 19, 2008).

NCJDSU (The National Creutzfeldt-Jakob Disease Surveillance Unit) (2009). www.cjd.ed.ac.uk/ (December 14, 2009).

Nestle, Marion (2003). *Safe Food: Bacteria, Biotechnology, and Bioterrorism*. Berkeley: University of California Press.

Nestle, Marion (2008). *Pet Food Politics: The Chihuahua in the Coal Mine*. Berkeley: University of California Press.

NIC (National Intelligence Council) (2000). *National Intelligence Estimate: The Global Infectious Disease Threat and Its Implications for the United States*. www.dni.gov/nic/special_globalinfectious.html (February 22, 2008).

NIC (National Intelligence Council) (2008). *Global Trends 2025: A Transformed World*. Washington, DC: National Intelligence Council.

Nierenberg, Danielle (2003). "Meat Production and Consumption Growing," in *Vital Signs 2003*. New York: W. W. Norton, pp. 30–2.

Nierenberg, Danielle (2006). "Meat Consumption and Output Up," in *Vital Signs 2006–2007*. New York: W. W. Norton, pp. 24–5.

NIH (National Institute of Health) (1998). "Clinical Guidelines on the Identification, Evaluation, and Treatment of Overweight and Obesity in Adults: The Evidence Report." Prepared by the NHLBI Obesity Education Initiative Expert Panel on the Identification, Evaluation, and Treatment of Overweight and Obesity in Adults. www.nhlbi.nih.gov/guidelines/obesity/ob_gdlns.pdf (April 19, 2008).

Nobel Foundation (2007). "The Nobel Peace Prize for 2007." http://nobelprize.org/nobel_prizes/peace/laureates/2007/press.html (April 18, 2008).

NOP (National Organic Program) (2008). "Organic Labeling and Marketing Information." www.ams.usda.gov/AMSv1.0/getfile?dDocName=STELDEV3004446&acct=nopgeninfo (April 25, 2008).

Nord, Mark, and Brent, C. Philip (2002). "Food Insecurity in Higher Income Households." E-FAN-02-016, USDA, Economic Research Service. www.ers.usda.gov/publications/efan02016 (March 12, 2008).

NRC (National Research Council) (1984). *Genetic Engineering of Plants: Agricultural Research Opportunities and Concerns.* Washington, DC: National Academy Press.

NRC (National Research Council) (1987). *Agricultural Biotechnology Strategies for National Competitiveness.* Washington, DC: National Academies Press.

NRC (National Research Council) (2001). *Under the Weather: Climate, Ecosystems, and Infectious Disease.* Washington, DC: National Academies Press.

NRC (National Research Council) (2002). *Environmental Effects of Transgenic Foods.* Washington, DC: National Academies Press.

NRC (National Research Council) (2010). *Impact of Genetically Engineered Crops on Farm Sustainability in the United States.* Washington, DC: National Academies Press.

Ohmae, K. (1995). *The End of the Nation State.* New York: Free Press.

Omran, Abdel (1971). "The Epidemiologic Transition: A Theory of the Epidemiology of Population Change." *Milbank Memorial Fund Quarterly* 29: 509–38.

Osborne, Anne (1994). "The Local Politics of Land Reclamation in the Lower Yangzi Highlands." *Late Imperial China* 15(1) (June): 1–46.

Osterholm, Michael T. (2005). "Preparing for the Next Pandemic." *Foreign Affairs* 84(4): 24–37.

Paris, Roland (2001). "Human Security: Paradigm Shift or Hot Air?" *International Security* 26(2): 87–102.

Patel, Raj (2008). *Stuffed and Starved: The Hidden Battle for the World Food System.* New York: Melville House.

Patel, Raj (2009). "When Cheap Water and Oil Disappear," in "Room for Debate: Can Biotech Food Cure World Hunger?" *The New York Times*, October 26. http://roomfordebate.blogs.nytimes.com/2009/10/26/can-biotech-food-cure-world-hunger/ (April 30, 2010).

Pelletier, David, Deneke, K., Kidane, Y., Haile, B., and Negussie, F. (1995). "The Food-First Bias and Nutrition Policy: Lessons from Ethiopia." *Food Policy* 20(4): 279–98.

Pelletier, Nathan, et al. (2009). "Not All Salmon Are Created Equal: Life Cycle Assessment (LCA) of Global Salmon Farming Systems." *Environ. Sci. Technol* 43(23): 8730–6.

Peluso, Nancy Lee and Watts, Michael (eds) (2001). *Violent Environments*. Ithaca: Cornell University Press.

Pennisi, Elizabeth (2010). "Armed and Dangerous." *Science* 327(5967): 804–5.

Pew Initiative on Food and Biotechnology (2003). "Resources Fact Sheet: Genetically Modified Crops in the United States." http://pewagbiotech.org/resources/factsheet/display.php3?FactsheetID=2 (June 30, 2004).

Pinstrup-Andersen, Per (2002). "Towards a Sustainable Global Food System: What Will it Take?" Keynote presentation for the Annual John Pesek Colloquium in Sustainable Agriculture, Iowa State University, March 26–27, 2002.

Pinstrup-Andersen, Per (2007). "Agricultural Research and Policy for Better Health and Nutrition in Developing Countries: A Food Systems Approach." *Agricultural Economics* 37: 187–98.

Pinstrup-Andersen, Per (2009). "A Green Revolution Done Right," in "Room for Debate: Can Biotech Food Cure World Hunger?" *The New York Times*, October 26. http://roomfordebate.blogs.nytimes.com/2009/10/26/can-biotech-food-cure-world-hunger/ (April 30, 2010).

Pollan, Michael (1998). "Playing God in the Garden," *New York Times Magazine*. www.nytimes.com/1998/10/25/magazine/playing-god-in-the-garden.html?pagewanted=1 (April 30, 2010).

Pollan, Michael (2001). *The Botany of Desire: A Plant's-Eye View of the World*. New York: Random House.

Pollan, Michael (2006). *The Omnivore's Dilemma: A Natural History of Four Meals*. New York: Penguin Press.

Pollan, Michael (2009a). *In Defense of Food: An Easter's Manifesto*. New York: The Penguin Press.

Pollan, Michael (2009b). *Food Rules: An Eater's Manual*. New York: Penguin Books.

Pomeranz, Kenneth (2000). *The Great Divergence: China, Europe, and the Making of the Modern World Economy*. Princeton: Princeton University Press.

Ponting, Clive (1991). *A Green History of the World*. London: Sinclair-Stevenson.

Pottier, Johan (1999). *Anthropology of Food: The Social Dynamics of Food Security*. Cambridge: Polity Press.

Price, Jennifer (1999). *Flight Maps: Adventures with Nature in Modern America*. New York: Basic Books.

Princen, Thomas (2005). *The Logic of Sufficiency*. Cambridge, MA: MIT Press.

Princen, Thomas (2010). *Treading Softly: Paths to Ecological Order*. Cambridge, MA: MIT Press.

Regis, Ed (1997). "The Doomslayer." *Wired* 5.02. www.wired.com/wired/archive/5.02/ffsimon_pr.html (April 25, 2008).

Robinson, Paul (2008). *Dictionary of International Security*. Cambridge: Polity Press.

Rodale, Maria (2010). *Organic Manifesto: How Organic Farming Can Heal our Planet, Feed the World and Keep us Safe*. New York: Rodale.

Rodier, Guenael, Greenspan, Allison L., Hughes, James M., and Heymann, David L. (2007). "Global Public Health Security." *Emerging Infectious Diseases* 13(10): 1447–52.

Rogers, Paul, Whitby, Simon, and Dano, Malcolm (1999). "Biological Warfare against Crops." *Scientific American* (June): 70–5.

Rome, Adam (2001). *The Bulldozer in the Countryside: Suburban Sprawl and the Rise of American Environmentalism*. New York: Cambridge University Press.

Rome Declaration (1996). "The Rome Declaration on World Food Security and the World Food Summit Plan of Action." www.fao.org/documents/show_cdr.asp?url_file=/docrep/003/w3613e/w3613e00.htm (February 29, 2008).

Roosevelt, Franklin D. (1941). "Annual Message to Congress," from John T. Woolley and Gerhard Peters, *The American Presidency Project*, www.presidency.ucsb.edu/ws/?pid=16092.

Rosenau, James N. (1990). *Turbulence in World Politics: A Theory of Change and Continuity*. Princeton: Princeton University Press.

Rothman, Hal (1997). *The Greening of Nation? Environmentalism in the US since 1945*. Fort Worth, TX: Harcourt Brace.

Royal Society, The (2009). *Reaping the Benefits: Science and the Sustainable Intensification of Global Agriculture*. http://royalsociety.org/reapingthebenefits/ (December 27, 2009).

Ruggie, J. G. (1993). "Territoriality and Beyond." *International Organization* 47(1): 139–74.

Ruigrok, W., and van Tulder, R. (1995). *The Logic of International Restructuring*. London: Routledge.

Runge, C. Ford, et al. (2003). *Ending Hunger in Our Lifetime: Food Security and Globalization*. Baltimore: The Johns Hopkins University Press.

Rutherford, Kenneth R. (2008). *Humanitarianism under Fire: The US and UN Intervention in Somalia*. Sterling, VA: Kumarian Press.

Rutherford, Kenneth R., Brem, Stefan, and Matthew, Richard A. (eds) (2003). *Reframing the Agenda: The Impact of NGO and Middle Power Cooperation in International Security Policy*. New York: Praeger Publishers.

Ryan, C. A., et al. (1987). "Massive Outbreak of Antimicrobial-Resistant *Salmonellosis* Traced to Pasteurized Milk." *Journal of the American Medical Association* 258: 3269–74.

Scherr, Sara J., and Sthapit, Sajal (2009). "Mitigating Climate Change through Food and Land Use. *Worldwatch Report* 179." Washington, DC: Worldwatch Institute.

Schlosser, Eric (2002). *Fast Food Nation: The Dark Side of the All-American Meal*. New York: Harper Perennial.

Schlosser, Eric (2003). *Reefer Madness: Sex, Drugs, and Cheap Labor in the American Black Market*. New York: Houghton Mifflin.

Schmer, M. R., Vogel, K. P., Mitchell, R. B., and Perrin, R. K. (2008). "Net Energy of Cellulosic Ethanol from Switchgrass." *Proceedings of the National Academy of Sciences* 105(2): 464–9.

Schmidhuber, Josef, and Tubiello, Francesco (2007). "Global Food Security under Climate Change." *Proceedings of the National Academy of Sciences* 104(50): 19703–8.

Scholte, J. A. (1993). *International Relations of Social Change*. Buckingham: Open University Press.

Scott, James (1998). *Seeing Like a State: How Certain Schemes to Improve the Human Condition Have Failed*. New Haven: Yale University Press.

Sen, Amartya (1982). *Poverty and Famines: An Essay on Entitlement and Deprivation*. Oxford: Clarendon Press.

Sen, Amartya (1999). *Development as Freedom*. Oxford: Oxford University Press.

Shaw, John (2007). *World Food Security: A History since 1945*. New York: Palgrave Macmillan.

Shiva, Vandana (1993). *Monocultures of the Mind: Perspectives on Biodiversity and Biotechnology.* London: Zed Books.

Shiva, Vandana (2000). *Stolen Harvest: The Hijacking of the Global Food Supply.* Cambridge, MA: South End Press.

Shiva, Vandana (2009). "The Failure of Gene-Altered Crops," in "Room for Debate: Can Biotech Food Cure World Hunger?" *The New York Times*, October 26. http://roomfordebate.blogs.nytimes.com/2009/10/26/can-biotech-food-cure-world-hunger/ (April 30, 2010).

Simon, Julian (1981). *The Ultimate Resource.* Princeton: Princeton University Press.

Simon, Julian (1996). *Ultimate Resource 2.* Princeton: Princeton University Press.

Simon, Julian L., and Kahn, Herman (eds) (1984). *The Resourceful Earth – A Response to Global 2000.* New York: Blackwell.

Sinclair, Upton (2003). *The Jungle: The Uncensored Original Edition.* Tucson, AZ: See Sharp Press.

Slaughter, Anne-Marie (2004). *A New World Order.* Princeton: Princeton University Press.

Slow Food Movement (2010). www.slowfood.com/ (April 25, 2010).

Smil, Vaclav (2000). *Feeding the World: A Challenge for the Twenty-First Century.* Cambridge, MA: MIT Press.

Smil, Vaclav (2001). *Enriching the Earth: Fritz Haber, Carl Bosch, and the Transformation of World Food Production.* Cambridge, MA: MIT Press.

Smil, Vaclav (2008). *Global Catastrophes and Trends: The Next Fifty Years.* Cambridge, MA: MIT Press.

Smith, Lisa C., Alderman, Harold, and Aduayom, Dede (2005). "Food Insecurity in Sub-Saharan Africa: New Estimates from Household Expenditures Surveys." Washington, DC: IFPRI.

Smolinski, Mark S., Hamburg, Margaret A., and Lederberg, Joshua (eds) (2003). *Microbial Threats to Health: Emergence, Detection, and Response.* Washington, DC: National Academies Press.

Steinfeld, Henning (2006). *Livestock's Long Shadow: Environmental Issues and Options.* www.fao.org/docrep/010/a0701e/a0701e00.HTM (December 27, 2009).

Stern Review (2007). *The Economics of Climate Change.* Cambridge: Cambridge University Press.

Stern, Jessica (2002). "Dreaded Risks and the Control of Biological Weapons." *International Security* 27(3): 89–123.

Stern, Nicholas (2009). *The Global Deal: Climate Change and the Creation of a New Era of Progress and Prosperity*. New York: PublicAffairs.

Stokstad, Erik (2010). "Could Less Meat Mean More Food?" *Science* 327(5967): 810–11.

Stuart, Tristram (2009). *Waste: Uncovering the Global Food Scandal*. New York: W. W. Norton.

TED Prize (2010). "Congratulations Jamie Oliver – 2010 TED Prize Winner." www.tedprize.org/jamie-oliver/ (April 30, 2010).

Tester, Mark, and Langridge, Peter (2010). "Breeding Technologies to Increase Crop Production in a Changing World." *Science* 327(5967): 818–22.

Thone, Frank (1943). "Victory Gardens." *Science News Letter* (March 20): 186–8.

Timberland (2006). "Timberland Sets New Standard for Product Transparency and Increases Efforts to Minimize Environmental Impact." www.timberland.com/corp/index.jsp?eid=8500007242&page=pressrelease (April 27, 2008).

Torok, T. J., et al. (1997). "A Large Community Outbreak of Salmonellosis Caused by Intentional Contamination of Restaurant Salad Bars." *Journal of the American Medical Association* 278(5): 389–95.

Tucker, Jonathan B. (ed.) (2000). *Toxic Terror: Assessing Terrorist Use of Chemical and Biological Weapons*. Cambridge, MA: MIT Press.

Tucker, Jonathan B. (2001). *Scourge: The Once and Future Threat of Smallpox*. New York: Grove Press.

Ullman, Richard (1983). "Redefining Security." *International Security* 8(1): 129–53.

UN (United Nations) (1948). "Universal Declaration of Human Rights." www.un.org/Overview/rights.html (February 29, 2008).

UN (United Nations) (1966). "Covenant on Economic, Social and Cultural Rights." www.unhchr.ch/html/menu3/b/a_cescr.htm (February 29, 2008).

UN (United Nations) (1975). *Report of the World Food Conference*. New York: United Nations.

UN (United Nations) (1992). "Agenda 21." www.un.org/esa/sustdev/documents/agenda21/english/agenda21toc.htm (February 29, 2008).

UN (United Nations) (2008a). "UN Millennium Development Goals." www.un.org/millenniumgoals/ (April 19, 2008).

UN (United Nations) (2008b). *World Urbanization Prospects: The 2007 Revision*. www.un.org/esa/population/unpop.htm (February 27, 2008).

UN Daily News (March 15, 2006). "Security Council hails first convening of Somalia's transitional legislature." Issue DH/4604: 5. www.un.org/news/dh/pdf/english/2006/15032006.pdf (April 28, 2008).

UN Habitat (2007). *Global Report on Urban Settlements 2007: Enhancing Urban Safety and Security*. London: Earthscan.

UN Water (2007). "Coping with Water Scarcity: Challenge of the Twenty-First Century." www.unwater.org/wwd07/downloads/documents/escarcity.pdf (April 18, 2008).

UNAIDS (United Nations Programme on HIV/AIDS and World Health Organization) (2007). "AIDS epidemic update: December 2007." www.unaids.org/en/KnowledgeCentre/HIVData/EpiUpdate/EpiUpdArchive/2007default.asp (February 22, 2008).

UNDP (United Nations Development Programme) (1994). *Human Development Report 1994*. New York: Oxford University Press.

UNDP (United Nations Development Programme) (1999). "The World at Six Billion." www.un.org/esa/population/publications/sixbillion/sixbillion.htm (December 27, 2009).

UNDP (United Nations Development Programme) (2003). *Human Development Report 2003*. New York: Oxford University Press.

UNEP (United Nations Environment Programme) (1992a). "Convention on Biological Diversity." www.cbd.int/convention/convention.shtml (April 19, 2008).

UNEP (United Nations Environment Programme) (1992b). "Rio Declaration on Environment and Development." www.unep.org/Documents.Multilingual/Default.asp?DocumentID=78&ArticleID=1163 (April 19, 2008).

UNEP (United Nations Environment Programme) (2002). *Global Environmental Outlook 3: Past, Present and Future Perspectives*. London: Earthscan.

UNEP (United Nations Environment Programme) (2006). *The State of the Marine Environment: Trends and Processes*. www.gpa.unep.org/documents/global_soe_webversion_english.pdf (December 27, 2009).

UNEP (United Nations Environment Programme) (2008). *Global Environment Outlook 4: Environment for Development*. www.unep.org/geo/geo4/media/ (April 28, 2008).

UNFPA (United Nations Population Fund) (2007). *State of World*

Population 2007: Unleashing the Potential of Urban Growth. www.unfpa.org/swp/2007/presskit/pdf/sowp2007_eng.pdf (April 28, 2008).

UNFPA (United Nations Population Fund) (2009). *State of World Population 2009: Facing a Changing World – Women, Population and the Environment.* www.unfpa.org/swp/2009/en/pdf/EN_SOWP09.pdf (December 27, 2009).

UNHCR (Office of the United Nations High Commissioner for Refugees) (2009). "World Refugee Day 2009." www.unhcr.org/pages/49c3646c46d.html (August 14, 2009).

UNICEF (2004). "Vitamin & Mineral Deficiency: A Global Progress Report." www.micronutrient.org/reports/reports/Full_e.pdf (February 29, 2008).

United States Department of Defense (2010). *Quadrennial Defense Review Report.* Washington, DC: United States Department of Defense.

United States Department of Health and Human Services (2004). "Pandemics and Pandemic Scares in the Twentieth Century." www.hhs.gov/nvpo/pandemics/flu3.htm#9 (February 22, 2008).

United States Joint Forces Command (2010). *The Joint Operating Environment: 2010.* Suffolk, VA: United State Joint Forces Command.

USDA (United States Department of Agriculture) (2007a). "Household Food Security in the United States, 2006." www.ers.usda.gov/publications/err49/ (April 19, 2008).

USDA (United States Department of Agriculture) (2007b). "Organic Production/Organic Food: Information Access Tools." www.nal.usda.gov/afsic/pubs/ofp/ofp.shtml (April 25, 2008).

USDA (United States Department of Agriculture) (2009). Household Food Security in the United States, 2008. www.ers.usda.gov/Publications/ERR83/ERR83.pdf (December 15, 2009).

Vertical Farm Project (2008). www.verticalfarm.com/ (February 22, 2008).

Victory Seed Company (2008). "The Victory Garden." www.victoryseeds.com/TheVictoryGarden/page3.html (April 18, 2008).

Wapner, Paul (1996). *Environmental Activism and World Civic Politics.* Albany: State University of New York Press.

Wapner, Paul (2002). "Defending Accountability in NGOs." *Chicago Journal of International Law* 3(1): 197–205.

Wapner, Paul (2010). *Living through the End of Nature: The Future of American Environmentalism.* Cambridge, MA: MIT Press.

Watts, Duncan J. (1999). *Small Worlds: The Dynamics of Networks between Order and Randomness.* Princeton: Princeton University Press.

Watts, Duncan J. (2003). *Six Degrees: The Science of a Connected Age.* New York: W. W. Norton.

WCED (World Commission on Environment and Development) (1987). *Our Common Future: The World Commission on Environment and Development.* New York: Oxford University Press.

Webb, P., and Weinberger, K. (eds) (2001). *Women Farmers: Enhancing Rights, Recognition and Productivity.* Frankfurt, Germany: Lang Verlag.

Wein, Larry, and Liu, Yifan (2005). "Analyzing a Bioterror Attack on the Food Supply: The Case of Botulinum Toxin in Milk." *Proceedings of the National Academy of Sciences* 102(28): 9737–8.

Weinthal, Erika (2002). *State Making and Environmental Cooperation: Linking Domestic and International Politics in Central Asia.* Cambridge, MA: MIT Press.

Weinthal, Erika (2004). "From Environmental Peacemaking to Environmental Peacekeeping." *Environmental Change and Security Project Report* 10: 19–22.

WFP (World Food Programme) (2008). "Banditry against food trucks forces WFP to cut rations in Darfur," April 17, 2008. www.wfp.org/english/?ModuleID=137&Key=2819 (April 28, 2008).

WGBU (German Advisory Council on Global Change) (2008). *World in Transition: Climate Change as a Security Risk.* London: Earthscan.

Whitby, Simon, and Rogers, Paul (1997). "Anti-Crop Biological Warfare: Implications of the Iraqi and US Programs." *Defense Analysis* 13(3): 303–18.

White House (2003). "US Secretary of State Colin Powell Addresses the UN Security Council." www.whitehouse.gov/news/releases/2003/02/20030205-1.html (March 14, 2006).

WHO (World Health Organization) (2000a). "Obesity: Preventing and Managing the Global Epidemic." *WHO Technical Report Series* 894.

WHO (World Health Organization) (2000b). "Resolution WHA53.15 on Food Safety Adopted by the Fifty-Third World Health Assembly." www.welshfoodalliance.org.uk/hospitalitywales/nyfaweb/fap4fnp/fap_25.htm (April 28, 2008).

WHO (World Health Organization) (2002a). *Scaling up the Response to Infectious Disease, A Way Out of Poverty: Report on Infectious Diseases 2002.* www.who.int/infectious-disease-report/ (February 22, 2008).

WHO (World Health Organization) (2002b). *WHO Global Strategy for Food Safety.*

WHO (World Health Organization) (2003). "Obesity and overweight." www.who.int/dietphysicalactivity/publications/facts/obesity/en/ (April 30, 2010).

WHO (World Health Organization) (2006). "Obesity and overweight." www.who.int/mediacentre/factsheets/fs311/en/index.html (December 26, 2009).

WHO (World Health Organization) (2007a). "Malaria." www.who.int/mediacentre/factsheets/fs094/en/index.html (February 22, 2008).

WHO (World Health Organization) (2007b). "Tuberculosis." www.who.int/mediacentre/factsheets/fs104/en/index.html (February 22, 2008).

WHO (World Health Organization) (2007c). *Working for Health: An Introduction to the World Health Organization.* www.who.int/about/brochure_en.pdf (February 22, 2008).

WHO (World Health Organization) (2007d). *The World Health Report 2007: A Safer Future: Global Public Health Security in the 21st Century.* Geneva: World Health Organization.

WHO (World Health Organization) (2008). "Infectious Diseases." www.who.int/topics/infectious_diseases/en/ (February 22, 2008).

WHO, and WTO (World Trade Organization) (2002). *WTO Agreements and Public Health: A Joint Study by the WHO and the WTO Secretariat.* Geneva, Switzerland: World Health Organization and World Trade Organization.

Will, Pierre-Étienne, and Wong, R. Bin, with Lee, James (1991). *Nourish the People: The State Civilian Granary System in China, 1650–1850.* Ann Arbor: University of Michigan.

Williams, Raymond (1973). *The Country and the City.* Oxford: Oxford University Press.

WMO (World Meteorological Organization) (2009). "2000–2009, The Warmest Decade." www.wmo.int/pages/mediacentre/press_releases?pr_869_en.html (June 11, 2010).

Wolf, Aaron T. (1997). "International Waster Conflict Resolution: Lessons from Comparative Analysis." *International Journal of Water Resources Development* 13(2) (September): 333–65.

Wolf, Aaron T., Kramer, Annika, and Carius, Alexander (2005).

"Managing Water Conflict and Cooperation." *State of the World 2005: Redefining Global Security*: 80–95.

Wong, R. Bin (1997). *China Transformed: Historical Change and the Limits of the European Experience.* Ithaca, NY: Cornell University Press.

World Bank (2006). *Repositioning Nutrition as Central to Development: A Strategy for Large-Scale Action.* Washington, DC: The World Bank.

World Bank (2007). *World Development Report 2008: Agriculture for Development.* Washington, DC: The World Bank.

World Hunger Education Service (2006). "World Hunger Facts 2006." www.worldhunger.org/articles/Learn/world%20hunger%20facts%202002.htm (February 29, 2008).

Worster, Donald (1979). *Dust Bowl: The Southern Plains in the 1930s.* Oxford: Oxford University Press.

Wriston, W. (1992). *The Twilight of Sovereignty.* New York: Charles Scribner and Sons.

Yan, Yunxiang (2000). "Of Hamburger and Social Space: Consuming McDonald's in Beijing," in Deborah Davis (ed.), *The Consumer Revolution in Urban China*, pp. 201–25. Berkeley: University of California.

Zacher, Mark W. (1992). "The Decaying Pillars of the Westphalian Temple: Implications for International Order and Governance," in James N. Rosenau and Ernst-Otto Czempiel (eds), *Governance without Government.* Cambridge: Cambridge University Press, pp. 58–101.

Zacher, Mark W., and Matthew, Richard A. (1995). "Liberal International Theory: Common Threads, Divergent Strands," in Charles W. Kegley (ed.), *Controversies in International Relations Theory: Realism and the Neoliberal Challenge.* New York: St. Martin's Press.

Zacher, Mark W., and Sutton, Brent A. (1995). *Governing Global Networks: International Regimes for Transportation and Communications.* Cambridge, UK: Cambridge University Press.

Zilinskas, Raymond (ed.) (2000). *Biological Warfare: Modern Offense and Defense.* Boulder, CO: Lynne Rienner.

Index

The Normans and the Battle of Hastings

Philip Parker

The History Detective Investigates series:
The Celts
Anglo-Saxons
Tudor Exploration
Tudor Home
Tudor Medicine
Tudor Theatre
Tudor War
The Civil Wars
Victorian Crime
Victorian Factory
Victorian School
Victorian Transport
Local History
The Industrial Revolution
Post-War Britain
The Normans and the Battle of Hastings
Monarchs
Weapons and Armour through the Ages
Castles

First published in 2010 by Wayland

This paperback edition published in 2012

Wayland
338 Euston Road
London NW1 3BH

Wayland Australia
Level 17/207 Kent Street
Sydney, NSW 2000

Editor: David John
Designer: Darren Jordan
Consultant: Andy Robertshaw

British Library Cataloguing in Publication Data:
Parker, Philip.
Normans and the Battle of Hastings. -- (The history detective investigates)
1. Hastings, Battle of, England, 1066--Juvenile literature. 2. Great Britain--History--Norman period, 1066-1154--Juvenile literature.
I. Title II. Series
942'.021-dc22

ISBN: 978-0-7502-6800-4
Printed in China

Wayland is a division of Hachette Children's Books, an Hachette UK company

Picture Acknowledgments: Front cover l © iStockphoto.com; Front cover r © Stuartrtay/Dreamstime.com; 1 and 17t AFP/Getty Images; 2 © iStockphoto; 5t © Taolmor/Dreamstime.com, 5c iStockphoto.com; 6 © Eric Golson/Creative Commons ShareAlike; 7t Getty Images 7b The Bridgeman Art Library; 8b Russell Kaye/Sandra-Lee Phipps, 9b The Bridgeman Art Library; 10t © Horiabogda/Dreamstime.com; 11tl © Rob Roy Creative Commons Attribution ShareAlike, 11tr © Gernot Keller/Creative Commons Attribution ShareAlike; 12 iStockphoto.com; 12t iStockphoto.com 13b The Bridgeman Art Library; 14b © Paul Moore/Dreamstime.com; 15b © Argestes/Dreamstime.com; 16b AFP/Getty Images; 18 © Jurand/Dreamstime.com; 19tr © Magann/Dreamstime.com, 19b GNU Free Documentation License; 20 Getty Images; 22© Michael Hanselmann/GNU Creative Commons Attribution ShareAlike; 23t The Bridgeman Art Library; 24 © Emiddelkoo./Dreamstime.com; 25t GNU/Creative Commons Attribution ShareAlike, 25b Getty Images; 27tr © Bluescript/Dreamstime.com, 27b © Hmproudlov/Dreamstime.com; 28 © Stuartrtay/Dreamstime.com; 29t iStockphoto.com, 29b © Lanceb/Dreamstime.com.

This replica of a Norman helmet shows the long metal tab that protected the wearer's nose.

Contents

Words in **bold** can be found in the glossary on page 30.

The history detective Sherlock Bones will help you to find clues and collect evidence about the Normans and the Battle of Hastings. Wherever you see one of Sherlock's paw-prints, you will find a mystery to solve. The answers can be found on page 31.

Who were the Normans?

The Normans became powerful in northern France more than a thousand years ago. When they invaded England in the year 1066, they dramatically changed the history of our country, bringing their own styles of building, art and warfare. They still influence us today.

The Norman people had not always lived in France. They came originally from Scandinavia (modern-day Denmark, Sweden and Norway) and were part of a group of people known as the Vikings. From about 800 to 1000, the Vikings raided rich towns and monasteries along the coasts of Britain, Ireland and France in search of gold and slaves. The French called them 'Northmen', which later became 'Normans'.

In 911, a group of Vikings led by Hrolf attacked the French town of Rouen. The French king, Charles the Simple, was impressed by Hrolf. He made an agreement with Hrolf's Vikings. In return for lands around Rouen, Hrolf's Viking group would defend France against other Viking bands.

Hrolf was given the title of **count** and was known afterwards as Count Rollo (the French version of his name). In the years that followed, the Normans took more and more land until they controlled most of modern Normandy. They soon turned their backs on the old Viking gods and became Christians. To demonstrate their new faith, they built great stone churches, such as the one at Jumièges, which was the most important in Normandy. Over time, the Normans intermarried with their French neighbours. They began to speak French, too, instead of their old Scandinavian language, which died out.

Detective work

Although it's now a ruin, the famous abbey at Jumièges shows us how important the Normans' Christian faith was to them. Find out more about the abbey's history at http://en.wikipedia.org/wiki/Jumièges_Abbey

The Vikings crossed the North Sea from Scandinavia in warships, terrorising the coasts of France and England. The French king gave them land in northern France in return for protection.

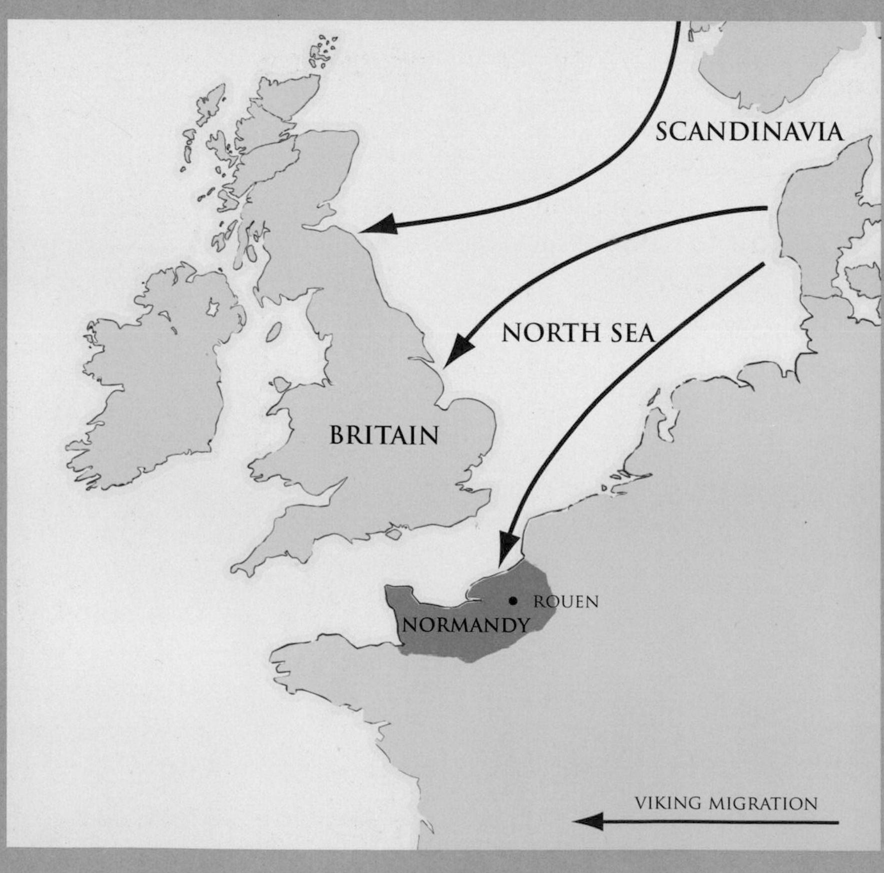

In the ninth century, the 'Northmen' burnt the abbey at Jumièges to the ground, but they had built an even larger one to replace it by 1067.

'If the Normans are disciplined under a just and firm rule, they are men of great valour… But without such rule they tear each other to pieces and destroy themselves, for they hanker after rebellion, cherish sedition, and are ready for any treachery.'

English chronicler Orderic Vitalis, writing in *Ecclesiastical History* (**circa** 1114–41)

By the end of the tenth century, the ruler of Normandy was known as a duke – the highest rank below a king. The lands of a duke are known as a duchy, and Normandy became one of the most powerful duchies in Europe. The Normans became famous for their fighting spirit and strong Christian beliefs. Their armies crossed the Mediterranean Sea and set up Norman kingdoms in Sicily and southern Italy. They also set off on **crusades** to capture the Holy Lands of the Bible from Muslim rulers in the Near East (modern-day Syria, Lebanon and Israel). But it was in their **conquest** of England that they had the biggest impact on history.

Norman knights were armed with a sword, a dagger and sometimes a mace (a type of club).

Apart from his chain mail coat, what other protection does this knight have?

Who was Duke William of Normandy?

In 1035, a seven-year-old boy called William became the duke of Normandy. His father, Robert II, had died while returning from a pilgrimage. William was much too young to rule by himself, so a series of guardians ruled for him until he was 15. Although he was young, William soon became the greatest of all the Normans.

William was an impressive young man. He was healthy, tall and fair, with arms so powerful he could shoot an arrow while riding his horse at full gallop. He also had a strong personality and could attract the support of his people.

But William's power in Normandy was not secure. He faced threats of **rebellion** and invasion. However, by the time he was 19 he was successfully fighting off his enemies. The king of France, Henry I, was so worried about the growing power of Normandy that he twice tried to invade William's lands. Both times William defeated him.

Detective work

When William was born it was not certain that he would follow his father to become the duke of Normandy. This was because William's father and mother were not married. William's mother was said to come from a lowly background. Find out who she was on http://en.wikipedia.org/wiki/Herleva

William was born in this castle at Falaise, near Calvados, in Normandy.

In his struggle against Normandy's enemies, William received help from many **noble** Norman families, such as the Beaumonts and Montgomeries, whose members later went with him to England and became great Anglo-Norman aristocrats. He was also helped by his half-brother, Odo of Bayeux, who became a famous bishop.

This is a scene from the famous Bayeux Tapestry, which records many details of life in Norman times. William (centre) is shown passing judgement on a prisoner.

By about 1060, William's position in Normandy was much stronger. He was a very active and driven man. His main enemies, including King Henry I of France, had died, and the new king of France, Philip I, was just eight years old. William now felt strong enough to begin enlarging Normandy's territory and increasing Norman power.

This penny coin was made after William became king of England, so everyone in the country would see the face of their ruler.

On the coin, William wears a crown. What does he hold in front of his face?

> *'From this time William began with the utmost zeal to protect the churches of God, to uphold the cause of the weak, to impose laws which would not be burdensome, and to make judgements which never deviated from equity and temperance. He especially prohibited slaughter, fire and pillage.'*
>
> William of Poitiers writing in *Gesta Gulielmi*, a book about the life of William of Normandy (c.1071–77)

Why did the Normans want to invade England?

William had become a confident, energetic and successful ruler. Now that he was secure in Normandy, he began to think about the rich lands across the Channel in England.

The king of England, Edward the Confessor, had ruled England since 1042. But Edward had spent more than 20 years living as an **exile** in Normandy after his father, King Aethelred, had been **overthrown** by the Vikings. Edward was also William's first cousin, and the two men knew each other well. William probably visited Edward in London in 1051. Later, William claimed that Edward had promised him the English throne. Many English nobles did not believe this. Whether it was true or not, William became very interested in England.

'Harold swore fealty to him... And... at the crucial point in the oath he... pronounced these words, that as long as he lived he would be the vicar of Duke William... that he would strive to the utmost... to ensure that the English monarchy should be pledged to him after Edward's death.'

William of Poitiers writing in *Gesta Gulielmi*

In the summer of 1064, Harold Godwinson, the earl of Wessex and the most powerful man in England after the king, sailed to Normandy. Nobody is quite sure what the reason for Harold's mission was, but it may have been to ask for the release of his brother, who was being held **hostage** in Normandy. Harold's ship, however, was driven by a storm into the lands of Count Guy of Ponthieu, who arrested Harold.

Harold would have crossed the Channel to Normandy in a longship similar to those of the Vikings.

King Edward the Confessor (centre) is shown in this famous portrait known as the *Wilton Diptych*. It was painted in about 1395.

Duke William, hearing of this, forced Guy to release Harold and invited him to stay at his castle in Normandy as his guest. In return for the favours William showed him, Harold swore an **oath** to the Norman duke. The Normans saw this as **fealty**, a sign that Harold was now William's man and would help William become king of England if called upon to do so. Harold did not see it that way, but this oath gave William an extra reason to claim the English throne if the chance arose.

Harold got to know William well. He fought alongside him in Normandy, and gained first-hand experience of Norman battle tactics. When Harold finally returned home to England, he was not aware that the oath that he had sworn to William would one day come back to haunt him, or that the two of them would become bitter enemies. They would not meet again until they were face to face on the battlefield.

DETECTIVE WORK

Some of what we know about Edward the Confessor comes from a very old book called the *Anglo-Saxon Chronicle*. This book was begun by a famous English king. Find out who it was. Why was he known as 'the Great'?

In the picture below, Harold (centre) is touching a type of box. What do you think it might be?

In this detail of the Bayeux Tapestry, Harold is shown swearing fealty to William.

Who were the Anglo-Saxons?

> *'In their days Hengest and Horsa, invited by Vortigern, king of the Britons... described the worthlessness of the Britons, and the richness of the land. They [the Angles] then sent them greater support. Then came the men from three powers of Germany; the Old Saxons, the Angles, and the Jutes.'*
>
> The *Anglo-Saxon Chronicle*

The people of England at the time of William of Normandy were called Anglo-Saxons. In the fifth century, groups of warlike German tribes known as Jutes, Angles and Saxons started to cross over the North Sea to England. Gradually they pushed the native British people westwards to Wales and Cornwall, and northwards to Scotland. The new arrivals set up their own kingdoms, and by the ninth century, the strongest of these was Wessex, which controlled almost all of England. The Anglo-Saxons had a rich tradition of reciting poetry and stories. They were also skilled in metalwork and making jewellery.

While William was ruling Normandy, England was ruled by King Edward the Confessor. When Edward came to the throne in 1042, he faced many problems controlling the Anglo-Saxon **earls**, who held the real power in large areas of the kingdom.

Corfe Castle in Dorset (above) is the site of an Anglo-Saxon fort. It was rebuilt in stone after the Norman Conquest.

This is a reconstruction of a ceremonial Anglo-Saxon helmet found buried at Sutton Hoo in Suffolk.

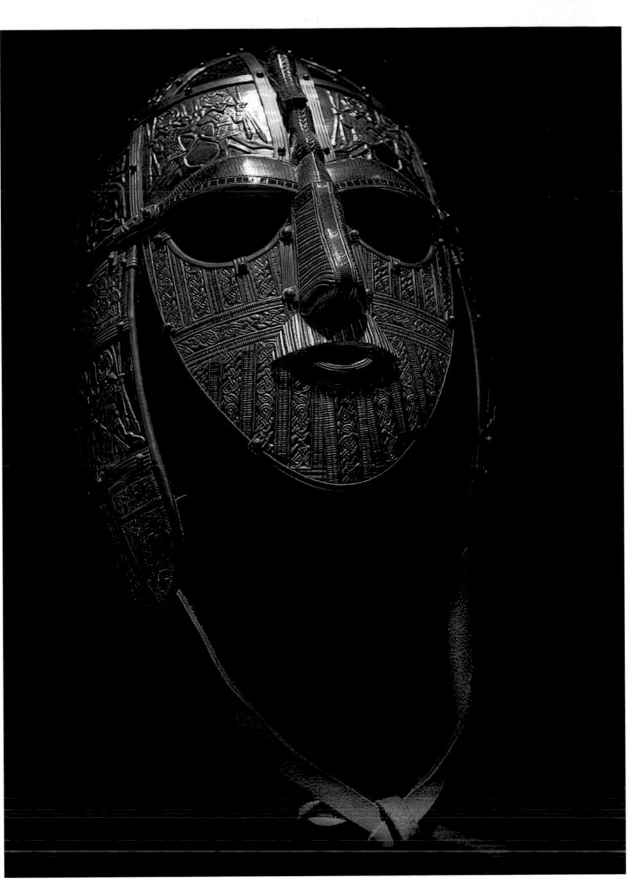

This fine gold clasp would have held an Anglo-Saxon cloak in place.

Edward tried to stop them becoming too strong by giving important jobs in England to Normans, rather than the earls. Edward had strong links to Normandy because he had lived in exile there.

The Normans that lived in England were not popular with the earls, and in 1051 Earl Godwin of Wessex rebelled against the king. Although he was defeated and sent into exile, Godwin returned with an army in 1052 and forced Edward to send away his Norman advisers.

In 1053, Earl Godwin died and his son, Harold Godwinson, became the earl of Wessex. Harold served King Edward the Confessor loyally. It seemed unlikely that Harold would ever become king himself. But when Edward fell seriously ill in 1065, Edward's great-nephew and **heir** to the English throne was only 14 years old. So Harold acted quickly. He married the sister of Earl Edwin of Mercia and Earl Morcar of Northumbria, who were his only serious rivals. When Edward died on 5 January 1066, the council of royal advisers, known as the Witan, chose Harold to be the next king of England. He was crowned the following day at Westminster Abbey, and, with all the earls supporting him, it looked as though he might **reign** for a long time. In fact he reigned for only nine months.

Why do you think Anglo-Saxon nobles were buried with their gold and valuables?

DETECTIVE WORK

One of the most famous Anglo-Saxon stories is about a hero defeating a horrible monster called Grendel who had been attacking an imaginary kingdom. What was the name of the story? This story would have been told aloud to entertain people. Try reciting the story to your family or friends.

What was life like in England in the year 1066?

Over time, England changed a lot from the early years of Anglo-Saxon rule. By 1066 the country was unified under the kings of Wessex, and the threat from Viking invaders was over. But life was still hard for ordinary people.

Most of the people of Anglo-Saxon England lived in small villages and on farms. They were known as *ceorls*. They laboured on the land or they were craftsmen, and they had the right to give their land to their heirs (or to sell it) if they wanted to. As time went on, the *ceorls* had to pay the local lord a share of their produce or do a fixed number of days' work on his estate.

Detective work

Oxford or Winchester are very ancient cities so it seems strange to think of a time when they were new and planned. Find out what other cities in England were built as *burhs* in the time of the Anglo-Saxons on http://www.britainexpress.com/architecture/burhs.htm

There are about 50 Anglo-Saxon churches left in Britain. Some are built with stone reused from Roman buildings.

In 1066, Anglo-Saxon towns were thriving. During the reign of King Alfred the Great (who ruled Wessex from 871 to 899) England faced great danger from Viking invaders. To defend Wessex against the Vikings, Alfred set up a system of *burhs* – towns with fortress walls around them. Landowners had to provide money and men to support these new towns. Some, such as Oxford and Winchester, attracted tradesmen and merchants. As a result, town populations increased. However, they were small by modern standards: Oxford had about 3,000 inhabitants, and London about 12,000.

Anglo-Saxon houses were made of wood with straw roofs. Only churches were built of stone.

Most people in Anglo-Saxon England could not read or write. Only monks or priests could read, and they did so in Latin, not in Anglo-Saxon. King Alfred the Great had encouraged monks to translate some books from Latin into Anglo-Saxon, but libraries with lots of books were found only in **monasteries**.

Anglo-Saxon peasants sometimes cooked inside their huts and sometimes outside. When did they cook inside the hut and why?

The Anglo-Saxon nobles were called ***thegns*** (pronounced 'thanes'). They lived in manor houses surrounded by the lands of the peasants who owed them labour service. Some of the most important *thegns* became powerful earls.

Ordinary people would see an earl only on rare occasions. Their contact with the government was through the *shire-reeve* (or sheriff) who was in charge of the local courts where justice was given.

An Anglo-Saxon peasant knocks down acorns for his boars to eat.

What threats did the Anglo-Saxons face?

Harold Godwinson's reign was brief but action-packed. He had only been king of England for a few months when he received some alarming news. A force of invaders had landed in the north of England, and Harold's own brother, Tostig, the earl of Northumbria, was with them.

The invaders were led by Harald Hardrada, the king of Norway. He believed the English throne should be his. In the summer of 1066, Harold Godwinson's brother Tostig had escaped to Norway when the people of Northumbria rebelled against his harsh rule. With such an important earl as Tostig on his side, Harald Hardrada decided to invade England, and in autumn 1066 set sail for England with 300 ships. They landed at Riccall in Yorkshire. The invaders then defeated the local Anglo-Saxon forces just south of York, at Fulford.

Harold Godwinson reached the area of York with a large army just four days after the Battle of Fulford. Harald Hardrada was caught by surprise and, at Stamford Bridge on 25 September, a bloody battle ended with the total defeat of the Norwegians.

'The closer the army came, the greater it grew, and their glittering weapons sparkled like a field of broken ice.'

Icelandic historian Snorri Sturluson on the approach of Harold Godwinson's army to York (c.1230)

DETECTIVE WORK

Harald Hardrada thought he would get support in northern England because York used to be a stronghold of the Vikings. Find out the Viking name for York. What was the name of the most famous Viking ruler of York?

What were the wooden heads on the Viking ships?

The Norwegians arrived in 300 ships (reconstructed here), but so few survived the battle that they needed only 24 ships to sail home.

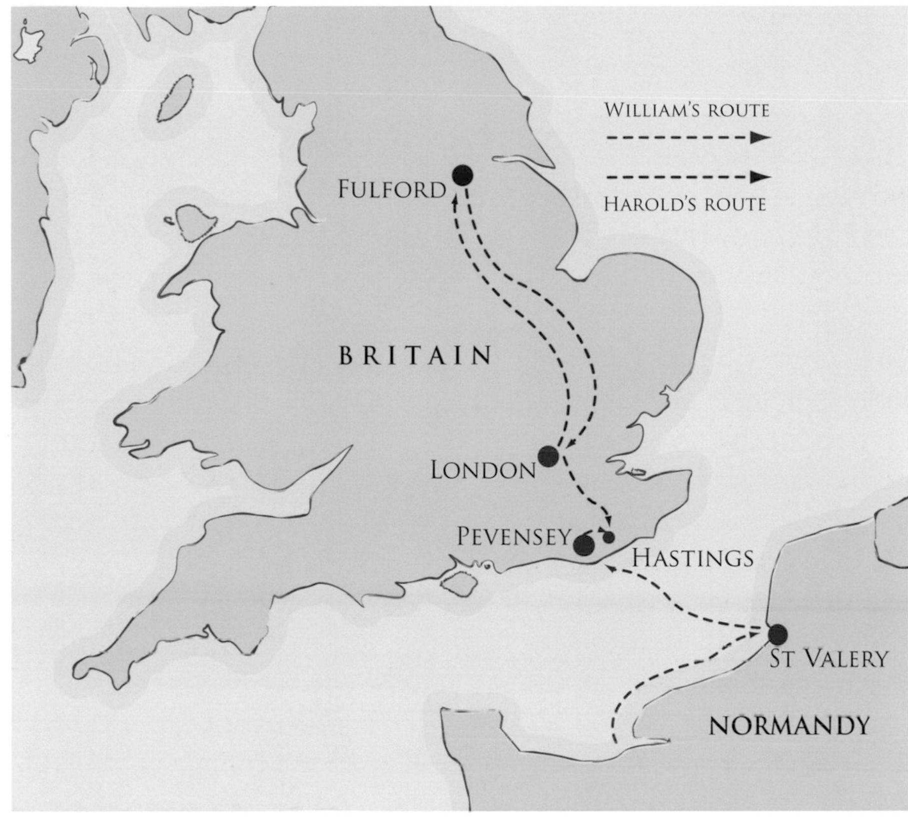

This map shows Harold's race northward to Yorkshire, and then southward to face William.

Both Harald Hardrada and Tostig were killed. But Harold Godwinson was not safe yet. Soon after the battle, he heard even more worrying news – that William of Normandy had set sail from France with a large army.

Harold Godwinson turned his army around and began the long march back south to face this new threat. By 8 October he had reached London, and, after a pause to gather more men, he moved southeast to Hastings, where William had set up his headquarters.

The Norman army had landed at Pevensey in Sussex on 29 September and at once built a wooden castle there. The Normans were not very secure on the English coast. They were far from home and without proper supplies. Although his own army was tired, Harold Godwinson believed that, if he could defeat the Normans quickly, he would be able to drive them out of England.

The Battle of Fulford was mostly fought hand to hand. Few horses were used.

What happened in the Battle of Hastings?

The Battle of Hastings is one of the most important battles in English history. It was a complete victory for the Normans, and marked the end of Anglo-Saxon power in England. But on the day of the battle it was not obvious who would win...

By 13 October, Harold was very close to Hastings. His army was about 8,000 strong and he positioned it to prevent the Normans – whose force was probably about the same size – from breaking out and advancing towards London. At dawn on 14 October, William sent his men forward. The Anglo-Saxons had taken up position on top of a hill called Senlac, and they formed a dense wall by **interlocking** their shields together. This made it difficult for the Normans, who had to struggle up the steep slope, to penetrate the Anglo-Saxon line.

Later that morning, the Normans sent a thick rain of arrows into the Anglo-Saxon ranks, then attacked on foot, but were beaten back. Next, the Norman **cavalry** moved up the hill, but they failed to break the shield wall. Some of William's men began to run away and a rumour spread that William had been killed. Some Anglo-Saxons left the hill to attack the escaping troops, but were surrounded and cut down.

DETECTIVE WORK

In the very last stages of the Battle of Hastings, many Norman knights were killed by the Anglo-Saxons as their horses fell into a deep ditch. Can you find out what it was called? Why do you think William chose Christmas Day to be crowned king?

Why are the archers shooting up into the air instead of aiming at a target?

The battle opens with a dense volley of Norman arrows, followed by a cavalry charge.

William **rallied** his troops and at about midday changed his tactic. He ordered a series of feigned (pretend) retreats, to try to tempt the Anglo-Saxons once more off the hill. This tactic was only partly successful. The main Anglo-Saxon line of shields held firm. William then ordered his archers to shoot another rain of arrows and it seems that one of these may have hit Harold in the eye, wounding him badly. News of this spread and some Anglo-Saxons retreated, allowing the Normans to storm the top of the hill. By this time, Harold had died, along with two of his brothers. Harold's elite force, the *huscarls*, made a brave last stand on Senlac Hill, but most of them were killed.

The two sides fight in a bloody, face-to-face battle.

William stayed for a week around Hastings and then marched on London. Within a few weeks, most of the leading Anglo-Saxon nobles had surrendered, been captured or become loyal to William. On Christmas Day 1066, in Westminster Abbey, William was crowned king of England.

'The king who was the glory of the realm, the darling of the clergy, the strength of his soldiers, the shield of the defenceless… the pearl of princes, was slain by his fierce foe.'

The *Waltham Chronicle* on the death of Harold Godwinson

'The Normans, suddenly wheeling round their horses, checked and encircled them, and slaughtered them to the last man.'

William of Poitiers writing in *Gesta Gulielmi*

The Bayeux Tapestry is said to show the moment Harold (on the right) is hit.

What weapons were used in the battle?

The two sides in the Battle of Hastings were not like modern armies. Apart from the arrows of the Norman archers, shot from a distance away, most of the fighting took place face to face, with heavy swords, axes, lances, shields and daggers. It was noisy, chaotic and very bloody.

On the Anglo-Saxon side, there were not many professional soldiers. Most of them were ordinary farmers. They were given weapons by the big landowners. The number of men the landowners supplied depended on the size of their estates. These soldiers were responsible for defending local areas against raiders, and were known as the *fyrd*. If there was a national emergency, they could serve outside their home counties and more men might be called up, but those would be less well trained and armed.

DETECTIVE WORK

Even though the Normans were fighting uphill, they had two things that gave them a big advantage over Harold's army – cavalry and archers. Why do you think these gave William such an advantage? Imagine the beginning of the battle before the hand-to-hand fighting started.

This is a selection of replica weapons used in the battle. *Fyrd* without swords fought with farmers' tools.

The Anglo-Saxon king's bodyguard, the *huscarls*, were much better trained than the *fyrd*. They wore leather armour with iron rings sewn into it (called chain mail) and pointed steel helmets with long nose-guards. They carried large wooden shields and long battle-axes. A soldier in the *fyrd* normally had worse equipment than this, with only a leather shirt (and no iron rings), a small round shield and a variety of weapons, such as the seax (a long dagger), a spear and a small axe. There were also a few archers in the Anglo-Saxon army, but very little cavalry.

The Norman side probably had better weapons. The Norman knights were more like professional soldiers and many of them had experience of fighting, from Duke William's long wars to become ruler of Normandy. Because they fought on horseback, they could ride at foot soldiers in a devastating **charge**.

Norman knights wore coats of chain mail similar to those of the Anglo-Saxon *huscarls*. Beneath this they wore a protective padded under-coat as a cushion against blows and to prevent the iron rings being driven into the wearer's body by an enemy's sword-thrust. The Norman chain mail was slashed at the front and back to allow its wearer to ride on horseback. Normans, too, wore pointed metal helmets. The Norman knights carried long spears or javelins to thrust at enemies as they charged. They also carried swords. Some of the Normans – including Bishop Odo of Bayeux – are shown in the Bayeux Tapestry carrying a mace or a club. The Normans had far more archers than the Anglo-Saxons and could use these from a distance to strike at the Anglo-Saxon army.

The Anglo-Saxon *fyrd* used small, rounded shields similar to those of the Vikings.

Chain mail took a long time to make. Each ring had to be linked with a hammer.

Do you think arrows could penetrate chain mail?

What does the Bayeux Tapestry tell us about the battle?

The Bayeux Tapestry is an amazing piece of embroidery nearly 70 m (230 ft) long. It uses pictures to tell the story of the Norman Conquest, beginning in 1064. It ends with the defeat of King Harold by William of Normandy at Hastings.

There are 58 separate scenes, and many of them have writing in Latin to explain the action. The tapestry might have been ordered by Bishop Odo of Bayeux, but there is no real evidence for this. No one is quite sure when it was made, or where.

Because the tapestry may have been woven within a few decades of the Battle of Hastings, it gives us a good idea of what people at the time believed had happened in the battle. It does not tell the whole story of 1066, however, because the invasion of Harald Hardrada and the Battle of Stamford Bridge are missed out completely.

In the scene below, what are Harold's men doing with their shields?

This part of the tapestry shows the thick of the fighting.

Bishop Odo of Bayeux is seen here fighting with a mace.

Detective work

In one scene of the tapestry, a comet is shown in the sky. We know this comet appeared in 1066 because it passes the Earth every 76 years. Find out the name of this comet. How old will you be when it next appears in our skies?

'Item: a very long and narrow strip of linen, embroidered with figures and inscription representing the Conquest of England, which is hung round the nave of the church on the Feast of Relics and throughout the Octave.'

From an inventory of the Church of Notre-Dame of Bayeux, 1476 – the first definite mention of the Bayeux Tapestry

Some episodes shown in the tapestry, such as Harold's visit to Normandy in 1064 and the appearance of a comet in the sky in 1066, are also mentioned in other sources of evidence from the time. This means that much of what is shown on the tapestry is probably near the truth. The battle itself is shown in the final eight scenes of the tapestry. Episodes such as the Norman attacks on the Anglo-Saxon shield wall, the false retreat by the Normans and their turning on the Anglo-Saxons and cutting them down, are all pictured, as is the death of Harold and the final escape of the remaining Anglo-Saxons.

As well as showing us what went on in 1066, the Bayeux Tapestry is also a vital source of evidence for the types of clothes the Anglo-Saxons and Normans wore, and the weapons they carried into battle. It even shows us what some buildings (such as Westminster Abbey, which was built in 1065) looked like.

Here the tapestry shows the surviving Anglo-Saxons running away.

What was England like under Norman rule?

Detective work

After William became king of England, he and his descendants continued to rule Normandy for more than 100 years. But in 1204 Normandy was eventually conquered by the French. In the reign of which English king did this happen?

Although he had won the Battle of Hastings, William did not conquer the rest of England so easily. Many parts of the country fought hard against him. To become the true ruler of England, William acted cruelly. From 1067 to 1072 he crushed a series of revolts and gave orders for the remaining Anglo-Saxon nobles to be killed or to have their lands taken from them.

William began building a great number of castles to keep the country under control. Norman nobles were given vast areas of territory, and the king kept for himself a fifth of the total agricultural land of the country. Large numbers of *fiefs* were created. These were estates held by a lord who owed service directly to the king. The lord had **vassals** who owed him service, including workers who lived on his estate. This is called the **feudal system**, and it lasted for centuries in England.

This castle at Bamburgh, Northumberland, has the square keep typical of Norman style.

What do you think 'Domesday' means?

Under the feudal system, peasants held land from the local lord's estate.

> *'After this had the king a large meeting, and very deep consultation with his council, about this land; how it was occupied, and by what sort of men. Then sent he his men over all England into each shire; commissioning them to find out how many hundreds of hides were in the shire, what land the king himself had, and what stock upon the land; or, what dues he ought to have by the year from the shire.'*
>
> *Anglo-Saxon Chronicle* entry for 1085 on the commissioning of the *Domesday Book*

To work out the value of the vast lands he now held, in 1086 William sent agents to travel throughout England and make a record of all the villages and estates in the country. The information was collected together in the *Domesday Book*. This records a rural life that had changed little over the centuries. The population mainly worked on the land, although the lords of the manor were now French-speaking Normans, not Anglo-Saxon *thegns*. The freedom of many of the peasants was reduced. For example, they had to ask the lord's permission for their daughters to get married.

William died in 1087 and was followed by his son, William Rufus. Direct **descendants** of William ruled England until 1154, when a related family, the Plantagenets, took power under Henry I. The royal household became more and more complicated, headed by a chancellor and other officers such as the earl marshal – positions that still exist today.

WARWICSCIRE.

This page of the *Domesday Book* lists estates, manors and villages in the county of Warwickshire.

How did the Normans build great castles and cathedrals?

The Normans were great builders, both in Normandy and, after the conquest, in England. They built massive stone castles and cathedrals that still stand today. Sometimes the building work lasted for decades.

Transporting and working in stone was difficult and expensive. At the **quarry** the stone was taken out by hammering iron wedges into the seam of stone to break off chunks, which were then sawn to the size needed. Most of the Norman buildings in the southeast of England and Normandy were constructed using stone from Normandy. Heavy stone had to be moved by boat, and so quarries near the coast or rivers were best. Once at the building site, materials were moved around on sledges, or, if lighter, in baskets. The lower layers of buildings were made from an inner core of rubble, with an outer face of ashlar – blocks of stone worked to give them a smoother finish. To raise stones to a higher level, a special form of crane operated by a wheel was used.

'So many smiths, carpenters, and other workmen were working so vehemently with bustle and noise that a man could scarcely hear the one next to him speaking.'

William FitzStephen,
in his *Life of Thomas Becket*,
the archbishop of Canterbury
(c.1190)

Apart from the tall tower, what other defences does this castle have?

Rochester Castle in Kent is one of the best preserved Norman castles remaining in England. It was built in the 1120s.

DETECTIVE WORK

Why do you think the lengths of the walls on some Norman castles and cathedrals are different sizes? Why would one wall be slightly longer or shorter if it was measured by a different person?

These delicately carved pillars surround the cloister of the Norman cathedral at Monreale in Sicily.

Building the largest castles and cathedrals would take many years. Before starting, the lines of the building were marked out on the ground. The distances were most often measured by walking and recording the number of feet paced. The construction was supervised by a master **mason**, a skilled craftsman who combined the roles of an **architect**, sculptor and builder. The stones, once placed, were smoothed off using an axe, or, for finer work, a chisel. The master mason would have been in charge of a team of craftsmen, including other masons and carpenters, since the roofs of the buildings were almost always made of a timber frame, finished off with thatch or tiles.

When the buildings were finished, the walls were often coated with plaster or whitewashed. This is how the great White Tower of the Tower of London got its name. Once finished, Norman buildings easily caught fire because of the material used in their roofs – in 1212 the authorities in London banned the use of straw or reeds to try to prevent this. Some Norman buildings were so poorly constructed that they simply fell down.

A Norman drawing shows carpenters and masons hard at work on a new cathedral.

What is left of Norman England today?

Most of the buildings in Norman England would have been made of wood and so have long ago disappeared. Only the most important buildings, such as castles and churches, were built of stone. Many buildings became ruined over time and local people often removed the stone to build their own houses.

Within 20 years of the conquest, the Normans had built about 100 castles in England. The earliest type of castle was the **motte and bailey**. The motte was an artificial mound on which a wooden tower was built – often later replaced by a stone one – while the bailey was the building in which the castle's inhabitants lived. There are still some mottes surviving, such as at Berkhamstead in Hertfordshire. Later the Normans built stone keeps for their castles, with surrounding walls.

DETECTIVE WORK

The word 'motte' comes from a Norman French word meaning mound (similar to *mont* in modern French). Can you find any other words in English that were taken from Norman French words?

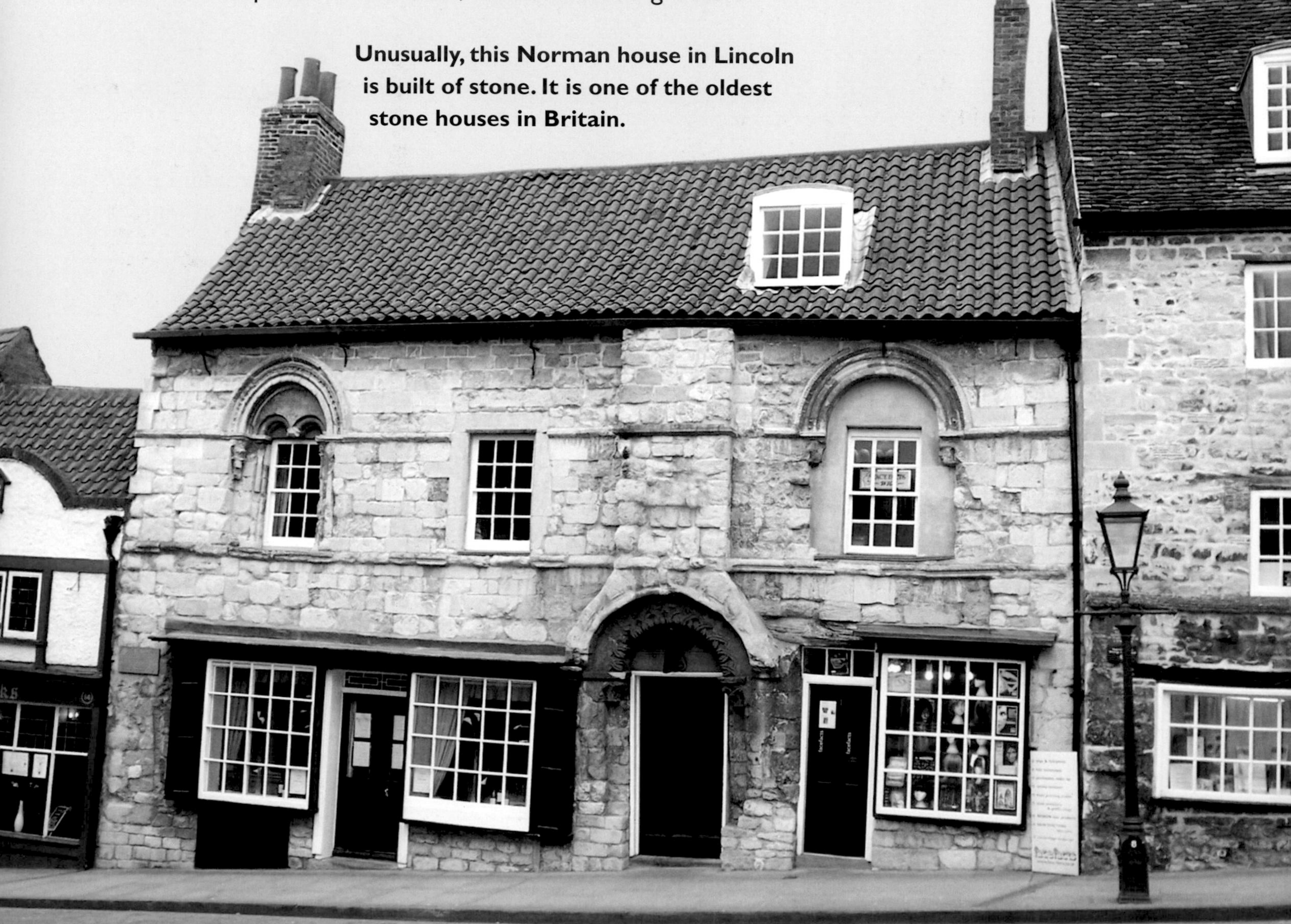

Unusually, this Norman house in Lincoln is built of stone. It is one of the oldest stone houses in Britain.

The tower of Ely Cathedral is 30 m (100 ft) high.

One of the best examples of this stage of Norman castle design is at Richmond in Yorkshire. The largest surviving Norman keeps are at the White Tower (part of the Tower of London) and Colchester Castle.

The Normans also built many stone churches and cathedrals in a style known as **Romanesque**. This was popular in the eleventh century. Romanesque churches had larger windows and doorways than Anglo-Saxon churches, with great arches and columns inside to support the weight of the building. Many of them had a great stone tower. The longest Norman cathedral was at Winchester, where the nave (the central section of the church) was about 180 m (590 ft) long. Other cathedral churches built in Norman times include Durham, St Albans, Norwich, Peterborough, Winchester, Hereford and Chichester.

Many surnames that are common today were originally Norman, such as Archer, Menzies, Graham, Morris and Knight. Some Norman customs survive, too. In the Channel Islands, the queen is still known as the 'duke of Normandy' as the islands are the last part of the old duchy of Normandy to be ruled by the English crown. When a bill is passed in the British Parliament, it is sent to the queen for her Royal Assent, or approval. She indicates her approval by writing '*La Reine le veult*', which is Norman French for 'The Queen wishes it so'.

In the house opposite, what features make it obviously Norman?

The rounded arches of Norman churches allowed them to have wider doors and sturdier structures than Anglo-Saxon buildings.

Your project

The Normans have left many great castles and cathedrals, especially in England and Wales. Often we know the names of the great lords who lived in the castles, or the bishops and archbishops who ordered the cathedrals to be built.

Topic questions

- Are there any castles in your area that were built in Norman times? When were they built and what were the names of the Norman nobles who lived there? (If there are none in your area, choose a Norman castle from somewhere else.)

- Are there any Norman churches in your area? When were they built? Can you find the names of the priests/vicars from that time? Do their names sound English or French?

- Visit a Norman castle or church and draw a plan of the building. Which parts of it are from Norman times and which parts were added later? Is there a part that is Anglo-Saxon?

- Look for your area in the *Domesday Book* on: http://www.nationalarchives.gov.uk/documentsonline/domesday.asp Have any of the place names survived today? How have the names changed?

The Norman tower of St Alban's Cathedral dates from 1077 and was built by a bishop known as Paul of Caen.

The Tower of London was begun by William the Conqueror in about 1078.

Project presentation

- Research your project well. Use the Internet and libraries to find out about the Normans and Anglo-Saxons.
- Tell the story of 1066 and the Norman Conquest from the point of view of either a Norman or an Anglo-Saxon.
- What was it like crossing the English Channel in boats and landing at Pevensey?
- How did it feel to march all the way to York to defeat Harald Hardrada and then back down south again?
- What did you do after the Anglo-Saxons lost the battle?

The Norman cathedral in Rochester, Kent, was built over an older Anglo-Saxon church.

Glossary

architect A person who designs a building.

cavalry Soldiers who fight from horseback.

charge To rush forward suddenly to attack someone.

circa (shortened to c.) Used when dates are only approximately known.

conquest The taking of a kingdom by force.

count A man appointed by a king to rule over an area of land called a county.

crusades A series of expeditions by Christian knights to the Holy Land (modern-day Israel, Lebanon and Syria).

descendants The children, grandchildren and so on, of a person.

earl A powerful noble in Anglo-Saxon times.

exile Living abroad because it is not possible to return home.

fealty A special type of oath, by which a person promises to be loyal to a noble.

feudal system A system of society in which nobles received land from the king in return for military service.

heir A person who will take on the property or title of another person (often a parent) after their death.

hostage A prisoner who will only be released if a condition, such as paying money, is met.

interlock To overlap, for instance, shields, so that there are no gaps.

keep The tower of a castle.

mace A weapon with a metal ball at the end of a short pole.

mason A craftsman who is skilled at working in stone.

monasteries Places where a group of religious men, or monks, live together.

motte and bailey A type of castle with an inner fort (or keep) built on a mound called a motte, and an outer area, called a bailey.

noble A person from a family with a high status.

oath A special promise to behave in a particular way, often made on the Bible.

overthrow To remove someone (such as a king) from power by force.

pilgrimage A journey to a shrine or other sacred place.

quarry A place from which stone is cut.

rally To gather together ready for battle.

rebellion To organise a group to defy a government or authority.

reign The period of a king's or a queen's rule.

revolt To rise up against a figure of authority, such as the king.

Romanesque A style of building with round arches and large columns.

thegn A noble of less importance than an earl in Anglo-Saxon times.

vassal A person who swears fealty and receives land in return.

Answers

Page 5: He also wears a steel helmet and carries a shield.
Page 7: He holds a sceptre, which is a symbol of royalty.
Page 9: It is a reliquary, which is a box containing the bones of a saint. This would have made Harold's oath more sacred and binding.
Page 11: Before the arrival of Christianity, goods and valuables were buried with a person for use in the next life.
Page 13: They often cooked inside the hut in winter to heat it.
Page 14: They were dragons' heads. Sometimes a fire was lit beneath the head so that smoke came from the dragon's mouth to frighten people on the coast.
Page 16: They shot into the air so that the arrows would fall down like rain on the enemy, rather than just hitting the first row.
Page 19: Arrows could penetrate chain mail and even plate armour at the joins between plates.
Page 20: They are making an interlocking shield wall.
Page 22: The name comes from the old English word for 'doom'. 'Domesday' means day of judgement or reckoning. In other words, something that is being accounted for.
Page 24: The castle has an outer, defensive stone wall, known as a curtain wall.
Page 27: The rounded arches over the windows and doorway are typical Norman features.

Further Information

Books to read

The History Detective Investigates: Anglo-Saxons by Neil Tonge (Wayland 2006)
Hastings 1066: The Fall of Saxon England by Christopher Gravett
(Osprey 2000)
The Normans: Warrior Knights and their Castles by Christopher Gravett
(Osprey 2006)

Websites

http://historyonthenet.com/Normans/normansmain.htm
http://www.britannia.com/history/monarchs/mon22.html
Note to parents and teachers: Every effort has been made by the publishers to ensure that these websites are suitable for children. However, because of the nature of the Internet, it is impossible to guarantee that the contents of these sites will not be altered. We strongly advise that Internet access is supervised by a responsible adult.

Places to visit

The Tower of London, Tower Hill, London EC3N 4AB
Durham Cathedral, The College, Durham DH1 3EQ
Battle Abbey, Battle, near Hastings, East Sussex TN33 0AD

Index

Numbers in **bold** refer to pictures and captions